the
PURPLE PIG
and other miracles

DICK EASTMAN

Charisma
HOUSE
A STRANG COMPANY

STRANG COMMUNICATIONS BOOK GROUP products are available at special quantity discounts for bulk purchase for sales promotions, premiums, fundraising, and educational needs. For details, write Strang Communications Book Group, 600 Rinehart Road, Lake Mary, Florida 32746, or telephone (407) 333-0600.

THE PURPLE PIG AND OTHER MIRACLES by Dick Eastman
Published by Charisma House
A Strang Company
600 Rinehart Road
Lake Mary, Florida 32746
www.strangbookgroup.com

Cover design by Justin Evans
Design Director: Bill Johnson

Library of Congress Cataloging-in-Publication Data
Eastman, Dick.
   The purple pig and other miracles / Dick Eastman.
       p. cm.
   Includes bibliographical references (p.   ).
   ISBN 978-1-61638-237-7
   1. Eastman, Dick. 2. Church work with youth. 3. Youth in missionary
work. 4. Intercessory prayer--Christianity. I. Title.
   BV4447.E3275 2011
   266.0092--dc22
   [B]
                                        2010030506

Portions of this book were previously published by Whitaker House as
The Purple Pig and Other Miracles, ISBN 0883680319, copyright © 1974.

10 11 12 13 14 — 9 8 7 6 5 4 3 2 1
Printed in the United States of America

Dedication

CONTENTS

Part Five
The Other Miracles

Part Six
Beyond the Pig

FOREWORD

O VER ONE HUNDRED YEARS ago God raised up the Student Volunteer Movement for Foreign Missions out of North America and Europe that touched the ends of the earth with the gospel of Jesus Christ. The Student Volunteer Movement mobilized twenty thousand students and young adults in less than fifty years (1886–ca. 1930) to preach the gospel in foreign lands. In 1910 twelve hundred of these missionary leaders gathered together in Scotland for the World Missionary Conference as they set their hearts together to "evangelize the world in one generation."

Now, one hundred years later, it is our conviction that the Lord is again raising up a young adult movement committed to unrelenting prayer and aggressive missions so that the Lamb who was slain may receive the reward of His suffering. In this "Antioch hour" of human history, we believe that the body of Christ is entering into a new season of convergence as the Lord brings together three movements—the missions, prayer, and church-planting movements—to finish the task of world evangelization and to pray back the King (Matt. 24:14; Luke 18:7–8; Rev. 22:17). God is bringing together the strength of these three movements so that the sum becomes greater than the parts.

In 1982 I believe the Lord spoke to me of this coming convergence while I was in Cairo, Egypt. He said that He would "change the expression and understanding of Christianity in this generation." I believe that at the heart of this convergence is night-and-day prayer for justice that emerges from thousands of Great Commission "prayer watches" operating in the spirit of the tabernacle of David. These prayer watches will be dynamically connected to finishing the task of world evangelization and the "blessed hope" of Christ's return. Undoubtedly, they will operate in the same spiritual culture and devotion that marked the tabernacle of David and the culture of prayer and missions that was in the church of Antioch in Acts 13:1–3.

The catalyst for this convergence will be spiritual fathers and mothers calling forth a global young adult movement that will plant hundreds of thousands of prayer watches even in the hardest and darkest places of the earth (Isa. 24:16; Lam. 2:19). These spiritual fathers and mothers will declare this convergence to young people throughout the nations, proclaiming to them that it is not just doable and not only biblical, but it is also essential to fulfilling the destiny of this generation.

I know of no spiritual father on the earth who has been more consistent and bolder than Dick Eastman in calling forth these prayer watches in the spirit of the tabernacle of David that are connected to the Great Commission. When I was just in my early twenties, new to my devotion and faith in Jesus, Dick greatly impacted me (and my friend Lou Engle) in my life of prayer and obedience to Jesus. The Lord used Dick to impart this spiritual DNA of a culture of prayer inside of me. And he hasn't stopped casting his "golden seed" of prayer and evangelism into the hearts and minds of thousands around the world over many years.

For those unfamiliar with Dick Eastman and the ministry he leads, Every Home for Christ (EHC), Dick is a most remarkable man of God, and his ministry has had unimaginable impact in the nations. Since 1946, Every Home for Christ has had evangelistic initiatives in 205 nations with more than 75 million decisions for Christ. These new converts have been discipled in 150,000 Christ Groups (house churches) that have been started by EHC with over 80 million discipleship courses taken by these precious saints. In their sixty-four-year history, they have given out 2.8 billion gospel booklets and are currently averaging 35,000 decisions for Jesus Christ every single day. Over the past five years, they have received reports of approximately 40 million decisions for Christ with an estimated 12 million in 2009 alone. On average, they are sharing the gospel with 900,000 individuals in 180,000 homes every single day. In addition to this incredible evangelistic thrust, they have started thousands upon thousands of Walls of Prayer (mostly in Asia), with many more thousands being started every single year.

I believe that the fruit of this ministry is directly connected to Dick's heart for prayer and the nations. The same spirit that gripped King David as a young man to contend for the fullness of God in his generation (Ps. 132; Acts 13:36) has obviously gripped Dick Eastman since he was a young man. Psalm 132 tells us that David made a vow in his youth to not rest until God possessed His inheritance on Earth. The result of his commitment to the Lord resulted in a great movement of prayer and worship in his generation that served as the foreshadowing of the End-

Time prayer and missions movement that God is raising up across the earth today.

Now, it is with great enthusiasm that I am writing the foreword to *The Purple Pig and Other Miracles*. This book tells the story of Dick as a younger man and his early ministry, known as the Prayer Corps. This ministry was a young adult movement rooted in 24/7 prayer and bold evangelism. The vision that he shares in chapter 10, titled "We Start Fires," is a clear representation of the convergence of prayer and missions that I believe the Lord is again raising up in this generation. What is remarkable is that Dick had this vision of 24/7 prayer in 1971, long before it would become normal in the evangelical world to talk about night-and-day prayer!

One young man, Brian Kim, who is part of the senior leadership team at the International House of Prayer, was deeply inspired by the "Fire House" vision of *The Purple Pig*. Though Brian is only twenty-seven years old, he has a tremendous vision for the prayer movement to fill the earth to accelerate the evangelization of the nations and the work of the Great Commission. To that end he established a new prayer and missions movement called the Luke18 Project. Dick's Fire House vision has served as a key model and an inspiration to this young and growing prayer movement. Since 2008, they have planted prayer furnaces on hundreds of college campuses with a vision to plant prayer furnaces on all twenty-six hundred college campuses in America. Ultimately they envision a global movement of young adults who will plant prayer furnaces in the hardest and darkest places of the earth.

Dick, my prayer is that this book, republished in this critical hour of history, would ignite the hearts of many more young men and women like Brian Kim to multiply your vision by planting tens of thousands of "fire houses" all over the earth so that the Lamb who was slain may receive the reward of His sufferings.

—MIKE BICKLE

FOREWORD

Engraved on a tablet facing the main entrance of Finney Chapel at Oberlin College, Ohio, are the words of Charles Finney's son: "That the youth of this foundation of learning may daily meet to worship God and that a son may honor the memory of his father. This chapel is built as a monument to Charles Grandison Finney by his youngest son, Frederick Norton Finney."

When I visited this chapel, my heart was deeply moved as I pondered how far Oberlin College has wandered and turned from its godly roots and its revival foundations. But, as I stood there praying, remembering Finney's revivals in America, it was as if I could see a young man in an Oberlin College dormitory at this moment praying and fasting for revival late at night, not knowing that the bones of Charles Finney lie buried a few hundred yards away. Suddenly I could see the God of remembrance being so moved by the young man's tears that He cannot contain Himself, and once again He pours out the throne gift of the Holy Spirit. A new prophet is born, and Oberlin College will now experience the flaming tongue of the gospel.

God's great work is always an act of generational transfer. When a generation honors the root, a nation will again experience the fruit. "There is hope for a tree even when it has been cut down...for at the scent of water it will bud and new shoots will spring forth" (Job 14:7–9, paraphrased).

In the 1960s and 1970s there was a root of prayer established in California, and as a young man in my twenties, I became a shoot of that root. I was radically converted to Jesus Christ at the tail end of the Jesus movement. A friend of mine said of that movement in California, "All you had to say is 'Boo!' and people would have gotten saved." In fact, that friend of mine walked up to two young men and asked, "What time is it?" and they said, "It's time for you to get saved." And right then and there he did.

What was that root of prayer that brought forth these shoots? Among many, one stands out to me in blazing Technicolor. It was a youth prayer movement born from the praying womb of Dick and Dee Eastman, who, among other things, established a house of prayer in Sacramento where young people would give a year of their lives to stand in the gap 24/7 and pray for souls to be saved. Those prayers, I believe, were instrumental in bringing forth the hundreds of thousands of souls being saved at that time.

Early on in the honeymoon days of my Christian experience I sat under the teachings of Dick Eastman. My whole soul would be lit on fire as the supernatural stories of God's divine movements were told from his weeping heart and explosive faith. Oh, how I was moved by the vision of prayer! I would weep under this great man's stories. I didn't know then that my tears were pointing me to my destiny. I didn't know then that he was a spiritual father producing through impartation a spiritual son. I am convinced today that TheCall and other prayer movements that I've been privileged to carry under God's initiation sprang from Dick Eastman's spiritual living room.

In Colorado Springs, in 2004, while leading fifty days and fifty nights of continuous worship and intercession with young adults, I was given a life-defining dream.

I was sitting, along with the visionary woman who financed TheCall, in Dick Eastman's living room. The whole room was filled with the glory of God, and Dick was my father and was radiating the splendor of Christ. In the dream he asked me to take a walk with him and said, "My wife was a strong woman. She gave birth to sixteen children." Suddenly I am no longer walking with Dick, but I am walking with a spiritual son, Brian Kim, on the same path. I walk a little further and fall on my knees, and I begin to pour out my heart with groaning and tears for revival. I awoke with the powerful presence of the Holy Spirit resting upon me.

I believe the dream speaks that TheCall and the houses of prayer movement that I have been privileged to give leadership to are really the children born from Dick and Dee Eastman's prayer rooms. Many other sons and daughters (prayer movements) sprang from that prayer root. Mike Bickle, my friend and founder of the International House of Prayer in Kansas City, traces much of his spiritual roots and inspiration to the teachings of Dick Eastman as well.

Recently my spiritual son, Brian Kim, has been enflamed with the vision of launching "fire houses" of prayer in a movement called the

Luke18 Project. His vision has been ignited by the early testimony of Dick Eastman's "Fire House" prayer movement described in this book you are about to read.

We are thrilled that for such a time as this, *The Purple Pig and Other Miracles* is being published again because we know that when other young men and women read this book, great waves of prayer for the harvest will once again be launched and maybe will bring forth the fulfillment of the great scriptural dream of heaven in Matthew 24:14: "And this gospel of the kingdom will be preached in all the world as a witness to all nations, and then the end shall come" (NKJV).

I write this foreword to *The Purple Pig and Other Miracles* so that the young people and older folks like me who read it may fulfill Dick Eastman's vision that the whole earth would be filled with houses of prayer that lead to evangelism and that every home would have a witness of Christ. I also write this foreword so that "a son may honor his father." Thank you, Dick Eastman, for what you have given to me over the last thirty years from your living room of prayer experience. I pray that men and women like Brian Kim will multiply your seed and that tens of thousands of "fire houses" would be released all over the earth and your children will be like the stars of the sky and the sands of the seashore.

—LOU ENGLE

Prologue
STAYING SMALL, BELIEVING BIG

I'VE NEVER FELT COMFORTABLE writing either an introduction or preface to any of my books. I've learned over the years that too many readers skip over these and head straight for chapter 1. So I'll just call this a prologue and personally plead with you to read these vital remarks before going any farther.

A good deal of what follows might easily be misunderstood unless you hear my heart before joining my wife and me on our amazing journey of answered prayer since a purple pig showed up on our doorstep four decades ago.

What I share in this brief prologue concerns a profound "defining moment" that happened a decade after our story begins in chapter 1. It was an encounter that puts everything I relate on the pages that follow in proper perspective. It came to me in the form of a vision.

I realize not all evangelical Christians are comfortable with someone suggesting he or she has had a vision. I can understand their concerns. In fact, as our ministry expanded to scores of evangelical denominations through our Change the World Schools of Prayer in the late 1970s and 1980s, I found myself having to adjust some of my usual terminology. Soon, instead of saying I had a vision, I would smile and casually say, "I had a dynamic mental impression!"

But no matter how one might describe it, what happened to me during that prayer encounter spoke to my heart so profoundly that it has impacted me all these years since. I share this vision here (or, if you prefer, "a dynamic mental impression") because a good deal of what follows is so highly personal that understandably it could draw undue attention to myself. This concerns me. My vision encounter hopefully will convey my true feelings in this regard.

I was in prayer in our backyard prayer chapel that over the years I've referred to as "the Gap" (something I'll explain later) where I would retreat daily for personal prayer. I had been quietly waiting on God for almost an hour. Suddenly I sensed God's presence in a most unusual manner. As had been the case on other similar occasions, I asked the Lord if He had something specific to speak to my heart that day.

What followed came in the form of a mental picture (or vision) that was as vivid as the words you read on this page. I saw two mountains far in the distance. They seemed to be connected. But the closer I looked, the more I realized there was a passage leading between the two peaks. It provided an entry into what lay beyond.

I further sensed I was on a journey, not unlike Pilgrim in the classic novel *The Pilgrim's Progress* by John Bunyan. As I journeyed, I was holding a continuing conversation with God.

Beyond the two ranges connected by that narrow passage shone an array of lights radiating a glow of unspeakable beauty. These extraordinary lights were most unusual and even seemed to give off an extraordinary fragrance, even at so great a distance.

"What is it that I see?" I asked the Lord.

"You are seeing My manifest presence—the essence of My glory and the place of My splendor and majesty."

"O Lord, can I go there and experience it for myself?" I queried.

"Yes, My son," was the reply. "Please come. Come closer!"

I began my journey toward God's manifest presence with great excitement. I could sense the joy of the Lord as never before. But as I journeyed toward God's glory, I noticed something peculiar. The closer I came to these towering mountains, the smaller the passage between the two became. Yet the mountains were growing larger with my every step. It was odd.

"There's something not right," I told the Lord. "The entry between the mountains should be getting larger as I draw closer. Yet it seems to be getting smaller."

"Oh, My child," the Lord replied. "You do not understand. The entry will become even smaller still the closer you come to the passage to My glory. And only if you are small enough when you reach that point of entry will you make it through."

Hearing those words I wept. I understood immediately what the Lord was saying. True humility is the key to staying small in our walk with God. Further, staying small in our own eyes is essential to experiencing God's manifest presence. We may *think big* in Jesus when it comes to our faith-expectations of what He can do, but we must *stay small* in Jesus if we are to see these faith-expectations become a reality.

Tears were flowing that day in prayer. I knew the Lord was calling me to a life of staying small in Him. I soon learned that the smaller we become in our own eyes, the bigger God becomes in what we see of Him and what He ultimately does in and through us. I thought of one of the most memorable quotes I've ever read regarding obedience and faithfulness. It was Mother Teresa who said, "God didn't call me to be successful; He called me to be faithful."

As I began writing this expanded follow-up to the original publication of *The Purple Pig and Other Miracles*, first written four decades ago, and adding thirteen new chapters telling the rest of the story, my wife and I were in Cape Town, South Africa, for the tenth anniversary of the Global Day of Prayer (GDOP). That day was Pentecost Sunday, May 23, 2010. It had been in Cape Town, South Africa, where the GDOP first began ten years earlier. An estimated 300 million Christians worldwide participated in this historic tenth anniversary event (broadcast globally by The God Channel TV network). Every nation on the earth had a prayer event this year (even North Korea), a first for the GDOP. Some nations had hundreds of events.

While Dee and I were in South Africa, a small group of eight evangelical leaders met to discuss how the expanding prayer movements might better interface more directly with growing evangelism movements. Dee and I were a part of that meeting. One of the brothers present, Doug Birdsall, the executive chairman of the Lausanne movement, shared a personal testimony. He described how he recently came across a small booklet written years ago in southern China that had deeply impacted his life. The title, Doug suggested, said it all when it comes to effective leadership—*Live to Be Forgotten in Order That Christ May Be Remembered!*

My prayer is that you will read these pages in the spirit of that title. The deeply personal encounters described in this book are not to draw attention to my unusual experiences with the Lord or the ways in which He has responded to my prayers, but rather to create in your heart a hunger for more of God and a consuming passion for those who are lost. May this prayer be answered as you turn the pages that follow!

—DICK EASTMAN
SUMMER 2010
COLORADO SPRINGS, COLORADO

Part One
THE GREEN BOMB

Chapter 1
PARDON ME, GOD

IT WAS A BRISK Minnesota March afternoon as the four of us rode along in my shiny, green 1959 Plymouth. (I suppose "shiny" would be a slight exaggeration.) The car had been in my possession a mere five weeks, and I was proud and ready to delight anyone willing to risk a ride in the aging relic. Little wonder it was nicknamed "the Green Bomb" by a classmate.

Our college choir was scheduled to sing that evening in a distant city south of Minneapolis. And as was occasionally our custom, a friend and I had convinced two girls, also in the choir, to accompany us. At the time I didn't realize the importance of this particular night. It was the beginning of a miracle I call the Purple Pig. It would be a miracle that today would involve thousands of 24/7 "prayer walls," "prayer furnaces," and day-and-night prayer centers globally (all of which I'll explain later) and the gathering in of a harvest of more than thirty thousand people responding every day to a global home to-home evangelism strategy. This is how it all began.

Much was on my mind as we left the campus for the concert. Dee, my date, sat quietly beside me as I drove the newly acquired automobile. Only two months earlier we had begun dating. And though we enjoyed each other's company, nothing had developed beyond a friendly relationship.

It seemed, however, that this might be changing.

Inside, my heart seemed romantically erratic. I was thinking to myself how lucky I was to have found such fortune in the girl beside me. Other thoughts as well occupied my mind. Events that had led to Bible school, my family at home, and God's plan for my life seemed paramount. It was one of my rare moments of silence as we drove along.

The Early Years

Life had been a real struggle for me as a teenager. Those early years were especially rough. A complexion problem earned the nickname "sandpaper face," and with it came the added stigma of being broke. We were on welfare. Even poor people brought us groceries. The whole town knew of our poverty. They found out just after a citywide track meet in which I participated in a relay. I had just turned twelve and was the only runner in the race without sneakers. We couldn't afford tennis shoes, so I ran in my socks, which was only slightly better than running barefoot. (The socks desperately needed darning.) Why the photographer for the *Daily News* showed up just in time for the relay I never could figure out. But he did, much to my chagrin.

Late that afternoon, after making the rounds of my paper route, I decided to glance through the afternoon edition of the news. Anxious to read of some last-minute baseball trade or see a picture on the sports page of my idol, Henry Aaron, I was completely stunned at what I saw. The picture was huge. And it wasn't Henry Aaron. There I was, for the whole city to see—crouched in a set position ready to run. I was in stocking feet, and one of the socks was so low it appeared to be falling from my foot. The whole town knew. We were broke.

And then there was our 1952 white Hudson. Off white. Way off!

"No kid should be faced with riding to school in a white Hudson," I used to say. (Now that Hudson would be a classic car worth a fortune!)

But I had to face the facts. We didn't have money. For quite some time Dad was out of work, totally disabled with advanced arthritis. It was during these days that real poverty set in. Finally, every penny was gone. Then a call came that seemed to save us from disaster, at least momentarily. It was the local radio station calling for their morning quiz time. Six dollars waited in the jackpot, plus a bag of potato chips, if someone in our household could answer the question. My brother Don took the call and amazingly had the answer. In several days the much-anticipated check for six dollars arrived, plus a coupon for the potato chips. Mom used half the money to pay a bill and kept the remaining three dollars for groceries. Things were much cheaper then, and three dollars could buy some of the basics.

The next day I stayed after school for a drama rehearsal, and when it was over, I waited for Mom to pick me up. I stood at a side entrance to the school hoping no one would see our off-white Hudson. When Mom and the Hudson arrived, I quickly crossed the schoolyard and jumped in. The car went notoriously slow, always providing people with an excellent opportunity to watch. This time it was worse. Just up the street the car stalled. We tried desperately to get it started but failed. I walked to a nearby gas station seeking help and returned moments later with the garage owner, who used a set of jumper cables to start the car. I'll never forget the look on Mom's face as the man stuck his head through the window and said, "That'll be three dollars, please." It was our grocery money. There was no more. (I remember thinking how much the guy reminded me of Hitler.)

Mother didn't say much. She just smiled at the attendant and handed him the money. He said, "Thanks," and climbed into his jeep. As he drove away, Mom put her head on the steering wheel and cried. It was a long trip home that night. Mother was really discouraged. And I kept questioning God under my breath.

"Why don't we have any money? Why are we always defeated by the enemy? And why doesn't God heal Dad?"

But most of all I found myself asking, "Is it possible, at all, that God has a plan for my life? If so, this night can't possibly be part of it. This is utter confusion. It's just a mess."

"Maybe Never"

I looked over at Dee as we neared our destination. She was beginning to mean much to me. In fact, love had happened to Dick Eastman. It happened in a moment, just outside of that rural Minnesota town heading for a concert in the Green Bomb.

That evening the concert was presented as usual. The powerful worship service took my thoughts momentarily from my earlier feelings of romance. It didn't take long following the rally, though, for my mind to pick up where earlier thoughts had left off. I kept saying to myself, "This is the night." But I had to do some quick planning before our return trip late that night to the college. I could hardly explain my feelings to Dee if I had to drive.

Just then the friend who accompanied us with his date on the trip came around the corner of the choir room.

"Would you mind driving back to Minneapolis?" I asked. "I mean, if you drive, it would give me a chance to talk to Dee about some things."

"Sure, man, I know what you mean," he answered with a sly smile. Several minutes later we were back on the road heading for the distant campus. Dee and I were comfortably seated in the backseat, getting along very well.

As I carefully calculated the situation in my mind, all indications pointed to one course of action. "This is the night. Tell Dee you love her!" But I wanted to wait for the perfect moment, which seemed to be arriving rapidly. In fact, two people couldn't get closer together. My right arm was wrapped tightly around her shoulder. And her eyes—I can remember well the unusual sparkle.

Nothing much was being said, but there was a lot of romance going on. Dee gently squeezed my hand, and I returned the gesture. She smiled, and I smiled.

"Should I propose too or just say, 'I love you'?" I mentally questioned. I didn't want to mess up the moment.

"What if she doesn't love me?" I wondered. But I knew I had to take the risk.

Then, very suddenly, courage came. Prefacing my remarks with a gentle kiss, I looked at Dee and smiled. "I have something to tell you," I said. "I love you."

The next sixty seconds are somewhat of a blur. Dee jerked away. I went numb.

The closeness had instantly evaporated. Dee had moved a foot away, but it seemed like ten. The warmth was gone, and I wanted to jump from the car.

There is no "quiet" to describe the quiet in the car at that moment. Dee looked at me. I looked at her. It was like an old black-and-white Dracula movie. I was the first to speak.

"Well," I asked, "don't you have anything to say?"

"What am I supposed to say?"

She moved another foot. Stammering slightly, I spoke again. "Well, sometimes when a guy says he loves a girl, she says 'I love you' in return."

"But I can't say that."

It was an icy moment to say the least. The front-seat occupants pretended to ignore us. I felt sick. There was no place to hide.

"Do you think you could ever say you love me?" I asked.

She thought a moment. It seemed like an hour. Very diplomatically yet tersely Dee answered, "Maybe in six months, but then again, maybe never."

It was a dark and misty Monday morning, well after midnight, when we arrived back at campus.

I was in love, but those earlier feelings of excitement had all but evaporated. Two words raced through my mind: "Maybe never." I said them repeatedly as I lay in bed: "Maybe never, maybe never."

It was during the following three days, however, that I saw the first real indication of God's plan for my future—and Dee's. Though I had seen Dee each of these subsequent days, we didn't discuss the events of Sunday night. By Wednesday, I was broken and discouraged. But God intended this. I was ready to hear His plan for my life. I was about to experience one of the most important days in my young Christian experience.

"I'm Taking Care of That Now"

It had been a long night stocking groceries at a nearby supermarket where I worked. I arrived at the college just in time for morning classes. By afternoon I was exhausted, though my discouragement kept me from resting. I decided to go into our large walk-in dorm closet to pray. It not only housed the clothes of room 308's three occupants, but it also served as the launching pad for hours of intercessory prayer, especially including considerable pleadings before exams!

That afternoon I especially needed time alone with God in the closet.

I didn't get to do much talking to God that afternoon. Instead, God immediately began dealing with me. Detailed impressions captured my mind. These thoughts were as clear as the words on this page. It was God's still, small voice. He was speaking to me personally. His presence literally poured into the room. There, below slacks and sweaters, I listened while God outlined an amazing plan of a harvest ministry that was to come in the future. I saw a powerful river of God's Spirit as it flowed into this ministry that would lead to millions of souls finding Jesus. But it would be a prayer ministry as much as an evangelism ministry. Then I saw the year that it would begin. The promise would commence seven years later on Thanksgiving Day, when I would be twenty-seven. Why seven years? God knew it would take that long for much-needed preparation.

I started to weep as I listened. I cannot remember feeling a greater sense of God's presence since I surrendered my life to Christ as a seventeen-year-old.

Suddenly He added something most interesting, especially considering the events three days earlier on that dismal Sunday night. I could not believe my spiritual ears.

"Dee will be your wife, just as you have desired."

I was overcome with joy. I don't remember exactly what I did, though I'm sure I shouted a little in that oversized closet. I couldn't contain myself.

"Yup," I thought. "It's settled. Dee will be marrying me. After all, God says so, and He's in charge of the universe. Good-bye, 'maybe never'! What God says goes."

Just then a perplexing thought occurred. The praise subsided, and my joy momentarily vanished. I looked toward heaven for help. I remember my somber prayer: "Pardon me, God, but would it be too much trouble for You to explain all this to Dee, before I tell her? She might take it a little easier from You."

I have often supposed God's first reaction must have been a divine chuckle, though He quickly answered my petition in that same still, small voice. It was a voice of calm assurance: "I am taking care of that now."

Wow! The excitement returned. God was taking care of it now. Three nights earlier I couldn't sleep. A hundred "maybe nevers" kept rushing through my mind. But now God said He was taking care of it. Of course, I wondered what "now" actually meant. The "nows" of God may not always be the "nows" of man. Did He mean this week, this year, when? The answer, I joyously discovered, came much sooner than expected. It was a "right now"!

It was almost five o'clock that same afternoon when I left campus to pick up Dee from the bank where she worked. I had just finished my prayer time in the closet. When she climbed into the car, I detected something different.

Dee sparkled as she spoke.

"Why don't we go out for dinner tonight?"

I was surprised though delighted. Up until then I had initiated every date. Now she was asking me out.

We left campus for Becky's Cafeteria (our spot) at six that evening. Though going through a cafeteria line may lack the romance of dining at an elegant restaurant, there was still an unusual feeling in the air. We found a table as far from humanity as possible and enjoyed the roast beef. A heavenly glow seemed to settle on the girl sitting opposite me. Her smile silently signaled that God was indeed taking care of it now. The "maybe never" was out of the question. I knew now it was merely a matter of time until I'd hear Dee reveal her feelings.

As we were leaving the restaurant, Dee casually asked, "Why don't we go down by the lake?" (Our second spot.) Since it was an ordinary weeknight, this was an unusual request. I knew something was on her mind. After all, couples seldom went down to park by the lake on a chilly March evening to discuss politics.

The warmth that had settled seemed to dance in her eyes as we drove along. Pulling up beside the moonlit waters I thought again of God's assurance earlier that afternoon: "I am taking care of it now."

We had parked beside this lake before during previous dates. Our dates had been far from normal, even from the start. We had agreed to pray together at some point on every date. This usually came after reading a Bible passage. Dee, with her beautiful alto voice, would sometimes sing. I was the congregation. I suppose people in cars parked adjacent to us—those not praying and reading their Bibles—probably wondered what we were doing.

As we sat there quietly, I thought again of the amazing events during the previous three days. Just then Dee asked if she could sing. Though she had sung on prior dates, I was startled at the request. On every other occasion I had asked her to sing.

I answered, "Sure," assuming she would sing a verse of a hymn or some contemporary Christian song and then we would pray. But something else happened. It was romantic yet spiritual. God's glory actually filled the Green Bomb!

Dee started singing, and with the melody came tears. She struggled for each word and never did finish the song; in fact, she kept her composure only long enough to sing four words clearly. She was singing "I Love You Truly," a popular wedding song of the day. It was exactly three days and one powerful prayer encounter after Dee's "maybe never."

And that's how it all began, the story of the purple pig. (The pig came seven years later and would forever paint a picture of God's presence and provision.) Since that week I've learned to cherish and remember my experience in the closet of room 308—not only for the promise of a perfect mate but also for that of a coming ministry, one that would find its focal point in prayer. It was clear that it would begin seven years later. The *why* of seven years only God could answer. I realized one thing, however: I was not ready for the ministry at that time. It would be essential to undergo seven years of much-needed preparation. They would not always be easy years, but I would have help in an extraordinary young lady. God had taken care of it that afternoon.

Chapter 2
APRIL TEARS

EIGHT MONTHS PASSED FOLLOWING my unusual prayer encounter in the dorm closet of room 308. We were in the middle of a rough Minnesota winter. It was December 1, 1964. The wedding was nineteen days away, and I was getting rather anxious.

For one thing, I lived in an apartment several miles across town from Dee's residence. My stay left unique memories, not the least of which was those last nineteen days of the coldest winter I can remember.

That week the small, already incapable oil heater in the center of my room stopped working. Unable to afford an electric blanket or the cost of repairing the heater, I borrowed Dee's electric heating pad. I would be awakened five or six times during the night by the unbearable cold and would move the heating pad to whichever part of my anatomy was most frozen. During these subarctic days the only place of warm refuge was the Green Bomb. But that only lasted several days before the car's radiator failed. Everything seemed to be going wrong. My only consolation was the coming wedding, just a week away.

Lying awake at night, moving the heating pad and thinking, I recalled the encounter I'd had eight months earlier in the closet. The wedding scheduled that next week testified to the validity of God's promise that He was "taking care of that now."

"If God promised me Dee, and I have her," I reasoned, "then the rest of the promise must be true—the part about the special miracle ministry involving prayer and a vast harvest of millions coming to Christ."

Half frozen but still thinking, I thought about the previous summer. God had spoken in a special way then, also confirming the promise given in the closet. I was traveling with a trumpet trio, representing the college in public relations. Following a weeknight rally in a small town north of Denver, Colorado, something compelled me to get alone. So I slipped out a side door of the church into the warm summer night. God had something important to show me. (Colorado would mean much to us in later years, as our international headquarters for the ministry I lead,

Every Home for Christ [EHC], would build its permanent facility, called The Jericho Center, in Colorado Springs.)

I felt a strong impression to lift my face heavenward, and as I did, my eyes caught a glimpse of a huge tree, its branches blowing gently in the soft summer breeze. I looked closely. The leaves became lost men and women around the world, hundreds of millions of them, waiting for a redeemer. They desperately needed prayer. In fact, they would be "prayed into the kingdom" even before they had any knowledge of the kingdom. True, they would need to first hear the gospel in order to believe, but prior to their hearing the Good News, the scales would be prayed away from their eyes so they *could* believe when they finally did hear.

God was speaking once again in confirmation of the promise given several months earlier. I didn't know all the details, only that it would involve a harvest initiated through prayer. And I knew that the beginning of the fulfillment of this promise would begin several years later. Then it would take a lifetime to see it all unfold. Of course, I didn't fully understand all this as I stood beneath those blowing branches, but I knew God could see it all, and I trusted God. Much later, in reflecting back on this moment, I would read how someone once asked Mrs. Albert Einstein if she understood the theory of relativity. She answered, "No, not at all. But I understand Albert, and he can be trusted." I also understood there was much to learn and experience.

The wedding was just days away, and I felt the sting of cold as my recollections of the previous summer faded. They were interrupted by the frigid winter conditions in that icy room. Outside it was 29 degrees below zero. I moved the heating pad once more and drifted to sleep.

Our wedding day finally arrived, accompanied by a storm front from the west. Amid blowing snow Dee and I were married in Toledo, Ohio, where Dee, her mother, and her sister had lived for eighteen years on the Wilkerson farm near the city. (Dee's father, a highly successful Ohio youth leader, was killed in a car accident when Dee was just three years old.) Dee, her mom, and sister spent seventeen years with her grandmother and granddad Wilkerson on the farm. Dee enjoyed those years and still has many stories about the unique Wilkerson household. She was only fourteen and living on the farm when David Wilkerson, a young preacher God was dealing deeply with, came from Pennsylvania to visit Granddad. He brought with him an amazing story of his call to New York and his burden for young people bound in drug addiction and hate. David would later chronicle his story in the remarkable best-selling book *The Cross and the Switchblade*. Granddad gave David the encouragement that day to ignore the criticism and simply carry out the vision God had given. That visit to Granddad's farm (described in chapter 13 of David's book) was one more part of the heritage Dee grew up with in an extended family of ministers (more than twenty-five of whom, including aunts, uncles, and cousins, would become preachers or marry preachers) who readily responded to the call of God no matter how unusual that call might be. All this would help prepare her for the direction God was to lead us in future years.

Dee and I celebrated our first Christmas on the farm. Gifts were out of the question until relatives came to our rescue. With their financial help we were able to buy a gift each, thus salvaging a gift-less Christmas. These seemingly insignificant gifts, however, became still another testimony of God's faithfulness. He cared about little things. He hadn't forgotten us.

Heading back to the college—following the wedding and Christmas festivities—we stopped at the parsonage of a pastor in southern Wisconsin who had earlier invited us to join his staff to work with their young people after we finished the current school semester, which ended just thirty days away. Having heard of the position two months before, we were already praying about it. So we decided to accept the offer, drop out of school, and begin our ministry as soon as the semester ended.

Both Dee and I were excited about this first ministry assignment, though we had little idea of the price to be paid. "Phase one" of the price was especially hard because it involved uncertainty. It hinged mostly on people and their advice.

"You're making a huge mistake," a respected college administrator advised. "Young men just don't succeed in the ministry by taking shortcuts."

It was true that I had had only two years of college, but I knew God was leading, in spite of much adverse criticism from friends and acquaintances on campus. Wanting to please God rather than man, I decided to stay near the prayer closet and move ahead precisely as led of God. It was soon apparent God wanted us at that church in southeastern Wisconsin.

Later, as I completed my education while ministering, including two memorable years attending Moody Bible Institute in Chicago, I saw the wisdom of God.

Thus our Bible college days in Minneapolis ended during a freezing

January. It was well below zero as we packed our sometimes trusty Green Bomb. We were finally on our way to Wisconsin.

God Doesn't Miss a Thing

It was a whole new adventure for the both of us. Nothing is more fulfilling, or challenging, than working with young people. With us, however, the challenging part was most apparent in those early months. It seemed we immediately locked horns with typical teen rebellion and disrespect. I soon became confused and even wondered if perhaps that college administrator hadn't been partially right in telling us not to leave school. This time, however, God had led me to a crucial crossroads in my ministry. The advice I heard from my senior pastor at our first church would set the tone of my entire ministry.

"It's not easy to work with young people," he cautioned. "You'll run into problems of rebellion almost impossible to handle," he added.

Then came the real advice.

"Prayer is the answer, Dick. If you get young people on their knees, your problems will disappear."

I started immediately to develop a prayer emphasis among our teens. They became the "prayingest" young people I knew. And the pastor was right. It made all the difference in the world.

Beyond the everyday problems of learning youth work, however, were the trials of establishing a new home. Both Dee and I worked full-time at the church for a total of sixty-five dollars a week. By April, just three months after our ministry began, we were having serious financial difficulty. Tears were common. And I remember how much it hurt me to see Dee cry.

"It just isn't fair, God," I would repeat often as I prayed. But humanly speaking little could be done. With groceries desperately needed—and bills to pay—we had only four dollars left to last that entire month. Adding to the chaos, our somewhat new Volkswagen (a "bug" that today also would be a classic like our old Hudson) encountered a brake problem, and the cost was an impossible twenty-five dollars. We lacked even a single dollar. I remember asking the garage manager for thirty days' credit. He said it wasn't a common practice, but he consented when I told him we would have to leave the car at the shop because we had no money.

It was, indeed, a discouraging April. But through these April tears God again taught us His ability to provide—a lesson that took seven years to comprehend fully. By mid-month relatives arrived from several hundred miles away. God had put us on their hearts, and they came for a visit. Opening the door of our small house trailer, we discovered arms filled with groceries, just enough to take us through the entire month.

But there was more. Just before leaving, Dee's uncle reached into his pocket. "I almost forgot," he said. "Someone told us your car was on the blink and you were unable to cover the cost. So we stopped by the garage to pay the bill."

That night as I quietly rested beside Dee, the April tears momentarily returned. But this time they were tears of thanksgiving. "You don't miss a thing, do You, God?" I prayed. "You just don't miss a thing."

Chapter 3
SEEING THE INVISIBLE

IT WAS LATE APRIL 1966. Our senior pastor called Dee and me into his office to share with us a special opportunity. He explained that our denomination wanted to begin a program to mobilize young people during the summers for short-term missions. Their pilot project was planned for Central America that summer, scheduled for the end of June and all of July. He was recommending that Dee and I be chosen to lead a team.

A young brother named Loren Cunningham had just begun such a program involving numerous denominations, and he had visited our church several weeks earlier. I had been invited over to our pastor's home after the service for pie and coffee and ended up spending the entire night listening to Loren share his vision of what he called Youth With A Mission (YWAM). Today, of course, YWAM is a household word in the evangelical community worldwide.

I vividly recall Loren describing his vision of tens of thousands of young people sweeping up on shores of distant nations like ocean waves. As a twenty-one-year-old, I told Loren, "If that happens, brother, it will change the world." (Which is exactly what is happening today.)

So naturally when our pastor brought up the opportunity to help begin something like this in our denomination, I was excited. It was to be the experience of a lifetime that also would indirectly teach me a new aspect of waiting on God that I have come to describe as creative prayer.

We spent the entire month of May and the first three weeks of June raising funds for the trip. Only a handful would be going, as this was a test case for our denomination's mission program. Our team would be going to the Central American country of British Honduras.

A seemingly unrelated event occurred in early May that was to become significantly related several months later. I received a letter from the editor of our denomination's youth magazine with a request for a series of articles. At the time, our denomination conducted a youth emphasis week annually, usually in the spring, when churches would focus on their young people. Because our youth program was growing and had a strong prayer emphasis, I was asked if I would consider writing the materials for the following year's weeklong program. It would involve a series of articles to be published in a fall edition of the magazine. The letter was quite detailed in outlining what was needed, which included a series of brief articles for the edition.

The editor described, for example, an already-chosen theme and asked me to compile various ways that this theme might be implemented over several nights of the week. Further, he asked for a message outline based on the week's theme for the youth leader or senior pastor to use for a Sunday morning sermon at the conclusion of the week. He also asked for a description of how a Friday night banquet might be decorated to fit the theme of the week and to develop an additional message outline for the youth speaker to use at the banquet. Also included was a request to describe at least two creative offering ideas, including a skit (complete with a script) that young people might use on a Sunday morning when a special offering could be received for the church's ongoing youth program.

It was quite a detailed letter with a comprehensive list of assignments. Because I had a full six weeks before leaving for Central America, and because the deadline for all the related articles wasn't until August 1, I agreed to accept it, my first such writing assignment. (My toes, however, had just touched hot water!)

Soon many things were happening in preparation for the mission trip. Shots for cholera and yellow fever were needed, confirmation letters had to be sent to missionaries on the field, and significant funds had to be raised for the trip. It was a busy time. Somehow that letter with those myriad assignments for next year's youth week became buried on my desk. (The hot water I was in was about to get much hotter.)

In a rush, in more ways than one, we finally boarded a plane for Miami with a connection to British Honduras. It was the last week of June as we began five weeks of ministry in the then remote Central American country that today has become a popular tourist destination known as Belize.

Upon arrival in British Honduras we discussed with a veteran missionary how to spend our time most effectively in his area of the world. We were a small team and wanted to make the best impact possible. The missionary suggested that because many British Hondurans were now learning to read and would devour any literature given them, we might want to consider going door to door with literature. It was agreed that we would employ this strategy.

We were quickly amazed at the response. Over the following five weeks some four hundred fifty people prayed to receive Christ as we met with them in their homes. It seemed that all we had to do was explain the gospel in the simplest of terms and give them evangelistic literature to help them understand more of what they had just experienced.

On the final night of the mission I was lying beside Dee in the sweltering heat with mosquitoes buzzing about everywhere. Unable to sleep and reflecting on the five weeks that had just passed, I imagined a vast army of Christian workers taking the gospel to every home in the world and sharing the Good News of Jesus face-to-face with them through the printed page. I envisioned that the printed salvation messages in many languages would have a decision card so interested people could request follow-up materials and understand more of what it meant to accept Christ as Savior.

Little could I have known that thirteen years earlier a young Canadian minister, my same age when he started out, had already begun such a work. He had launched it in Japan and referred to it as an Every Home Crusade. Nor could I have imagined that just a decade later I would become the international director of prayer mobilization for that same ministry, and a decade after that become their international president, a role I continue to serve to the present.

We arrived home from the fruitful trip to Central America the evening of July 30. The following morning, about nine o'clock, I went into the office to catch up on five weeks of missed mail (e-mails and text messaging were a distant dream) and anything else that might be pressing. I was stunned to discover several letters atop each other, all from the same person—the editor of the youth magazine. I opened the first and read, "We haven't heard from you lately and just wanted to remind you of your deadline of August 1 for the materials you promised. We're sure you haven't forgotten." He was wrong!

Two subsequent letters had followed, about two weeks apart. The message of each grew a little more desperate. In the most recent of the letters the editor mentioned he had tried to reach me by phone and had learned that I was out of the country. He was concerned. There was a measure of panic in his letter as he asked if I would be able to complete the project.

My panic, of course, was even greater as I read his last letter. I thumbed through many other letters on my desk looking for his original request.

When I finally found it, I couldn't believe how much material they wanted, something that hadn't seemed to register when I first saw the assignments.

My first reaction was that he and his team had selected a poor theme that would be difficult to develop into a weeklong emphasis. Of course, I hadn't thought of this twelve weeks earlier when I accepted the assignment. It was only now that I had such serious questions about the entire task. For more than fifteen minutes, I stared at each of the required assignments, and my panic grew with each passing minute. How could I have slipped up on this? By now it was past 9:30 a.m., and the deadline was the following day.

Suddenly a thought occurred that was to become profoundly significant to my future praying. It concerned God's omniscience. As 1 John 3:20 says, "God is greater than our hearts, and he knows everything." I realized that God could see into the future. What if I were to ask God what He saw about that week of youth emphasis the following spring? I quickly grabbed a couple of sheets of blank paper and a clipboard and headed for the furnace room in the basement. It was a place I had gone often to get alone with God in prayer. No one ever thought of looking for me there.

I grabbed a folding chair from a nearby Sunday school room and carried it in my other hand into the furnace room. I flicked on the light and sat quietly for a further moment, looking one last time at the items needed. By now I had memorized the list. I flicked the light back off and moved cautiously in the dark the few feet back to the chair. I didn't want anything to distract me.

The clipboard was resting in my lap, and I held the pencil in my hand. Two blank sheets of paper were attached to the clipboard. If anyone could have seen me in that moment it would have been an odd sight.

I prayed very simply, "God, because You know everything, I believe this means You can look into the future. And if that's the case, then it also means You can see every detail of what will happen during next year's youth week. Lord, all I ask is that You show me what You see." I recalled something Jonathan Swift, author of *Gulliver's Travels*, had said generations ago in defining the word *vision*: "Vision is the art of seeing things invisible."

Suddenly and inexplicably a divine creativity began flowing. I was indeed seeing the invisible. I thought of Romans 4:17: "God, who quickeneth the dead, and calleth those things which be not as though they were" (KJV). I saw the young people in my mind gathering in a church each of the nights of that week. I saw the various activities that would carry the assigned theme for those nights. In my mind, I could even see the theme-related decorations on each of the tables at the Friday night banquet. It was a breathtaking moment for my prayer life.

In pitch darkness I was writing with a pencil on paper I couldn't see. And I was writing as fast as I could. At one point I actually said, "Please, God, slow down. You're giving me too many ideas too fast."

I had no idea that I was writing some things on top of others. However, when I finished about thirty minutes later and turned on the lights, it didn't matter. Those pencil notations were merely reminders of what God had just shown me. Now all I had to do was go to my office and write out in detail what I had just seen. The scribbles would be enough to give me the direction I needed to write the several articles. I was filled with excitement. Nothing like this had ever happened to me before.

I rushed to my office, stopping by Dee's office first (she was the senior pastor's secretary) to tell her that I needed her to block out the rest of the day to type out some things as I wrote them. I had never learned typing in school, so it all had to be handwritten first. I hoped to have it all complete by midafternoon. Actually, Dee was well aware of the deadline and was feeling a bit sorry for me. For the next three and a half hours I wrote as fast as I could, outlining each of the things God had shown me. There were several pages required for each assignment.

As I finished each of the various segments, I would rush to Dee's office, where she was typing feverishly. I realized there might be a mistake or two in the final copy, but I also understood that a good editor would be able to take care of those typos easily.

By 5:00 p.m. it was all finished. Our local post office was less than half a mile from the church and closed at 5:30 p.m. Stuffing the finished copy into a large envelope, we rushed to the post office, arriving at 5:20. There were no UPS trucks or FedEx companies those days, but the post office did have something called "special delivery." For an added fee a letter could be sent to many locations overnight. We were able to send the articles special delivery and later learned they had arrived the following day by late afternoon. The deadline had been met. God, indeed, knows everything! And He was teaching us many new lessons about the uniqueness of prayer. But perhaps the greatest lesson of all is that prayer is the great problem solver because prayer touches God, and God can solve any problem.

Chapter 4

THE WHIP

NOTHING AFFECTED MY EARLY years of ministry more than the succinct challenge from our first senior pastor: "If you get young people on their knees, your problems will disappear." I watched it work. The focus on prayer had now become the most important aspect of my life and ministry.

Dee and I spent several years watching this prayer ministry develop in southern Wisconsin before God opened the door for ministry in California. Here in a climate of the emerging "hippie culture" of free sex and drugs, we saw the obvious need for a new prayer revolution.

Upon arrival in California, we employed the prayer emphasis with full force. Besides regular prayer meetings for our youth, weekend "prayer explosions" (prayer retreats) began. These were trips into the mountains where young people would spend whole days and nights in intercessory prayer, something I refer to in the next chapter and in more detail in chapter 9, "Tabletop Travail."

Prayer, however, was not limited to mountain trips alone. Back at the church, it was not uncommon for these young people to plan their own prayer meetings. I especially recall a Thursday night in the summer of 1969. I'd just returned from a youth choir tour and was excited about relaxing for a few days. Dee was about to give birth to our first child, Dena. Dan, a teenager from the church, approached me outside my office just as the choir returned from our tour. He was anxious for a prayer meeting. Though exhausted from the efforts of the trip, I decided to call a spur-of-the-moment prayer meeting for that Thursday night.

Forty young people attended. Those expecting something out of the ordinary were disappointed—at least initially. It was dry, empty prayer. So I asked the participants to cease their prayer efforts and sit quietly for a moment. Those kneeling returned to their chairs while I spoke for several minutes on the need to really care about prayer. Perhaps I was overly frank.

"We act like a bunch of high school students sitting through a class on Shakespeare," I chided. "Bored stiff!

"Prayer can't be treated like the biggest bore in the world. Real prayer is 'gutsy.' It costs, it hurts, it builds, and it does a multitude of other things that lead to revival. And that's why Satan will come at us if we have a spirit of boredom."

I asked how many cared enough for the needs of humanity to get back on their knees and give Satan the fight of his life. Many actually cheered as their hands shot up everywhere. Then the prayer meeting continued.

This time I watched the participants pray with zeal and concern evident on every face. Earlier they had prayed a mere matter of minutes and were ready to quit. This time they prayed ninety minutes without a trace of boredom. In a word, "attitude" had made the difference.

I had to stop them and call their attention to what was happening. It would be a learning experience. It took a moment for them to return to their chairs. I asked how they felt, and the response was one of excitement. When I informed them they had prayed ninety minutes, they were shocked. It wasn't long before they were back on their knees, this time for two additional hours of uninterrupted intercession.

The powerful night of prayer continued in a secluded prayer room in the back of the church. My wife was at home with no idea where I was. I had forgotten to tell her of the last-minute prayer meeting. And even if she had known, she could not have reached me since I was far from a telephone.

As the young people went to their knees for a third time, the Holy Spirit began a special stirring. Their brokenness is hard to describe. I started listening to some of their prayers. I was amazed to hear how many of them were praying specifically for Dee.

"Why Dee?" I thought, as I walked to the opposite side of the chapel. There, out of the listening range of the others, a lone teenager hidden away in a corner prayed almost identically to what the others had been praying. It seemed strange. They were all praying for the unborn child we were expecting in a couple weeks.

For several minutes their powerful prayers continued. Then, just as suddenly as it all had begun, the Holy Spirit seemed to stop them. None of our prayer meetings ended like this—not so abruptly in the middle of such intensive prayer.

No matter how I analyzed it, God was ending the meeting. So we sang a chorus, and I dismissed the group. Several minutes later I locked the doors behind me and headed home. It was 11:30 when I arrived. I was surprised to find Dee up and dressed. She was, in fact, getting ready to call the church in hopes of locating me. The baby was coming at any moment. I couldn't believe it. That very night a room full of young prayer warriors had prayed for this very event. We left immediately for the hospital, where our little girl, Dena, was born several hours later.

Three weeks after Dena's birth, I sat alone reflecting on the events of that unusual night. Why had God led Dan to call that prayer meeting in the first place?

"Perhaps there was a need I knew nothing about, a complication involving serious implications regarding Dena's birth," I thought. "Who knows, the child may have been healed just prior to being born, or Dee was spared some serious life-threatening problem.

"Whatever happened," I reasoned, "God has been faithful again. Once again, He has answered our prayers."

Pray! Pray! Pray!

As my concern for teaching our teens the power of fervent prayer increased, it wasn't long before they learned my true feelings on the subjects of both discipleship and prayer. Often I would stand at the door of our prayer meetings and question those who were leaving early. The investigation was sometimes frank, especially for those who had no worthwhile reason for leaving.

"What's the matter? Can't you hack it?" and "Don't tell me we have another prayer pansy in the group" were remarks one might overhear. Of course, I only made such remarks in jest, but the recipient usually got the message. And it wasn't uncommon for teens to turn around and go back to their knees rather than leave. In retrospect, I was probably a little too much of a drill sergeant.

It's not hard to imagine that I took considerable kidding from our teens because of my firmness. I especially remember the nickname given me on one of our choir tours. It came during their traditional morning cheer-time on the bus as we headed toward another town. Usually one of the teens would stand at the front of the bus and lead the others in the cheer especially written for the day, generally based on something humorous that happened at a previous concert or on the bus the day before. This particular day it was "Make Fun of Director Day," and a teen named Kirk was given the task of leading the cheer over the bus's loud-speaker. Several chuckled even before he began, and I knew a conspiracy of sorts had developed.

"Give me a D," Kirk intoned with vigor. Forty teens bellowed back, "D!" "Give me an I," Kirk continued. The choir responded loudly. When he asked for a C and a K, I knew they were out to get me.

Kirk continued, "Give me a W." (Loud response.) "Give me an H." (Even louder.) "Give me an I." (Minor screaming.) "Give me a P." (Intolerable.)

The giggling among the choir members made it clear they had a special joke to play on their leader.

Just then Kirk boisterously queried, "And what does it spell?"

In unison they responded, "Dick the Whip, the Whip, the Whip!" "And what does it mean?" Kirk shouted. Choir members screamed their response, "Pray! Pray! Pray!"

Thus began the days of "Dick the Whip" (as I became known to our youth group). It was part of an all-out, concerted effort to get teenagers on their knees. I believed prayer, much prayer, was needed to help build strong spiritual bodies and advance Christ's kingdom. Later I would hear how Billy Graham was once asked if there were any specific keys to the success of his crusades. He responded by explaining there were three: "First," he said, "pray! Second," he added, "is equally critical—pray. And the third," he concluded, "is the most important of all—pray!"

Prayer, indeed, initiates the plans of God, then sustains those plans in the developing stages, and finally brings about the ultimate purpose God has intended for those plans. Prayer starts it, sustains it, and finalizes it. Billy Graham was right—pray, pray, pray!

We were thus learning more and more about the critical necessity of prayer for all effective ministry. And it was exciting. For one thing, you never knew what to expect. And for another, it wasn't all just despera-tion and weeping. We also enjoyed the times God allowed for laughter in addition to those times of tears. Both played a vital part in the learning experience of the ministry of prayer.

As our prayer ministry among young people developed, I often recalled those powerful moments in a dormitory prayer closet several years earlier when God said, "I'm taking care of that now," regarding my future with Dee. The rest of the promise given in that closet, including multitudes coming to Christ one day as the result of prayer, was closer now than ever, though I still lacked complete details of the coming ministry. I only knew that God had promised to give me a fuller understanding of it in our seventh year of marriage at Thanksgiving time, when both Dee and I would be twenty-seven. What I could never have imagined is what would be taking place four decades later (today) in fulfillment of this promise. But first, there was a price to be paid. Everything of value comes with a price.

Part Two
THE BAKER HOTEL

Chapter 5
THE PRICE

I FASTENED MY SEAT BELT, awaiting momentary departure from San Francisco International Airport for Dallas, Texas, and an important spiritual life convention. I had little idea how important this trip was to be in God's calendar of events for my life.

As the plane lifted its giant frame from the runway, I glanced across the aisle. There, a middle-aged man intently studied a book. It had a catchy title, one that readily caught my eye: *God Can Do It Again*. A lady was pictured on the cover, and from the large byline I noted it was written by Kathryn Kuhlman, a healing evangelist. I knew little of her ministry, only that it somehow involved faith and miracles. Leaning over for a closer look, I was tempted to borrow the book for a time but decided, instead, to secure it for myself when convenient. Typically, I soon forgot this initial urge.

The following morning I attended several convention sessions. At noon, while walking back to the hotel, my journey led through a secular bookstore. Suddenly I noticed a book that didn't seem to belong. In fact, it rested beside another best seller at the time titled *Naked Came the Stranger*, with a half-nude woman on the cover. But it was the other book that caught my eye. The first word of the title jumped thirty feet across the room—*God*!

I looked more carefully. It was the book *God Can Do It Again*. I bought the book immediately, tucked it under my arm, and headed for the hotel.

Once in my room I found it difficult to do anything but read this newly purchased adventure in miracles. Incurable diseases cured, divided homes reunited, broken minds healed—all amazing victories of childlike faith.

I needed every word of it. Some four years had now elapsed since the promise of a miracle prayer ministry and a miracle harvest, the beginnings of which God had promised would be revealed in my twenty-seventh year, and I was actually secretly questioning if miracles like those of the early church could happen today. I needed this fresh account of "faith power."

I had read only minutes when it became impossible to see the pages for the tears. A spiritual hunger settled on me such as I had never experienced. I wanted God, all of God. It was a desperate groping, one that reached out for the very fullness of God's presence and His promises.

Laying the opened book on my bed, I began to weep over its pages. "Look at that title, God," I prayed. "It says You can do it again. I believe that, God. I really believe that."

I looked toward heaven. The light of a Texas summer sun set the room aglow. Inside my heart was even brighter, set aflame by the presence of a very close heavenly Father.

I feared being selfish with my prayer, though God knew my deepest motive. "God, do it again," I prayed. "Show me these miracles too. If possible, let me live to see these very things. The Bible says You are the same yesterday, today, and forever."

It was then that I heard God's voice as distinctly as four years earlier in that dormitory prayer closet. "Will you pay the price?"

"The price?" I thought to myself, kneeling broken beside the rumpled bed. I should have realized there would be a price. I'd heard it preached in a hundred sermons: "Revival will cost you something." And let's face it; such rhetoric is valid. Doesn't the oft-quoted revival passage of 2 Chronicles 7:14 demand the price of absolute repentance if we wish true revival? "If my people, who are called by my name, will humble themselves and pray and seek my face and turn from their wicked ways, then will I hear from heaven and will forgive their sin and will heal their land."

I continued weeping beside the bed. "What could God want?" I wondered. Standing to my feet I walked to the window. "Thousands must pass below this window daily," I thought.

I looked at the sidewalk filled with bruised and captive people like the ones Jesus spoke of in Luke 4:18—"The Spirit of the Lord is on me, because he has anointed me to preach good news to the poor. He has sent me to proclaim freedom for the prisoners and recovery of sight for the blind, to release the oppressed, to proclaim the year of the Lord's favor."

"They need help," I prayerfully mused as I gazed at the sidewalk below. "They need a miracle."

Boldly I lifted my face heavenward. I questioned God aloud, "What is the price?"

God answered as quickly as I had asked, but again with the question: "Will you pay the price?"

I was caught off guard. Wondering if I had heard wrong, I asked again, "What is the price?" And again I heard only this response: "Will you pay the price?"

It was now obvious that God did not intend to define the price, a fact that involved the supreme wisdom of God. Had I known on that sunny August afternoon what waited ahead, I might have walked out on the promise of God given four years earlier.

The tears continued to flow as I once again glanced out the window. "I really don't need to know the price," I thought. "It doesn't matter anyway. Those people are desperate for a miracle."

I lifted my face toward heaven a second time. "Anything," I pleaded. "God, I don't care what the price is. Let me see Your power reach those desperate people."

Three days later the convention was over, and events at the Baker Hotel belonged to a fast-fading memory. I dreaded a scheduled series of meetings the following week in the Midwest because of heavy sinus congestion and a painful condition in my throat.

Sitting in the doctor's office in Fort Worth, Texas, I never dreamed that the pain I was experiencing in my throat might be related to the price God was talking about at the Baker Hotel. I suppose I was too busy worrying about the pain. The doctor finally prescribed a typical sore throat cure-all, and I was on my way. Leaving the clinic I thought, "I certainly don't need a lingering throat problem."

"Lingering," however, soon became the proper expression to describe my condition. I knew something had to be done and determined to see another doctor when I arrived back home in California. Meanwhile, I tried in vain to communicate with those who attended the conference in the Midwest. My speaking just made my throat worse.

It was an unusually hot September when I returned home. The 100-plus degrees outside, typical of a Sacramento September, contrasting with the much cooler temperature of indoor air conditioning played havoc with my throat.

During the next sixty days I visited several doctors. The condition seemed irreparable. More than anything I worried about not preaching again.

Sitting alone and discouraged in my office on a rainy November day,

I answered the telephone. It was a college student from our church who was attending Bible school in Southern California. He had heard me mention Miss Kuhlman's book *God Can Do It Again* and called to say she would be speaking the following Monday in their college chapel. He thought I might want to fly down from Sacramento and be in the meeting. He knew I had been ill and that it might be serious.

"Why not," I reasoned. "Nothing else has helped my throat. I might even end up being healed." I realized, of course, that criticism would come if I told people I was traveling five hundred miles to have a lady pray for me. After all, hadn't I preached in the past that God doesn't need famous evangelists to do His work? But I had come to learn a very important truth since preaching those words. God does use certain people. He very often singles out individuals for no explicable reason and uses them. And, I believed, such was the case with this humble lady.

The following Monday I was on my way. Flying across a clear California sky I felt my faith increase with each mile flown. I found myself whispering repeatedly, "I'm going to be healed. I will be healed." Frankly, I expected total healing.

Looking back to these moments, however, I see that I had forgotten to ask two important questions. Was God finished teaching all that I needed to learn in preparation for my coming ministry? And was it really God's time to heal me?

During the service, Miss Kuhlman's tall figure stepped from behind the pulpit and began praying for people. They would fall as she touched them. I had never seen a manifestation like this. I was convinced something was going to happen to me. I waited patiently in line for God's power to touch me.

Slowly and silently, God's servant made her way toward me. She had already prayed for numerous people, and miracles were happening. A girl near me had a cast on her leg, and after falling to the floor, she broke the cast and began leaping for joy with absolutely no pain. My faith was obviously building.

By now the evangelist was coming toward me, but she quickly passed by me and prayed for the person next to me. I wasn't even prayed for. I had flown all that way and nothing happened. It was as if God told her, "He's not ready yet. I'm still working on him."

I was initially upset and hurt. I could easily have become bitter had God not provided a prompt and crucial lesson. This evangelist, like others with similar God-given gifts, was a mere tool in the hands of God. He uses them when and how He pleases. The evangelist was not responsible for passing me by; that act was God-ordained. There was something I had yet to learn.

Surprisingly I left the auditorium encouraged. Though my throat suffered as much as ever, I felt my healing was assured. Months later I would point to that moment as my actual healing, for it was in that chapel rally that God provided the needed faith, even though I retained the symptoms, which actually became worse, for six additional months.

Chapter 6

REMEMBER BENNY

A PREACHER WITHOUT A VOICE is like a desert without sand," I thought as my throat condition worsened. The promise given several years earlier in that college closet was hidden deep in my subconscious, along with the events of the Baker Hotel and that November burst of faith. I was too busy worrying about never preaching again to think of this unusual chain of events as pieces to some God-ordained puzzle for my life.

Through my distress I tried to keep busy. It was impossible to preach, though I could lead prayer meetings if I talked softly. So I decided to organize our first prayer retreat for our youth group in California's Sierra Nevada Mountains. We brought along nothing but bedrolls and Bibles. Volleyballs, horseshoes, badminton, and other recreational items were left behind. This was the dawning of a new era for me, something I document in more detail in chapter 9. I was learning what real prayer can do.

It was a special thrill that Saturday morning following our first full night of intercession in the mountains to sit on the sidelines and watch those young people pray. They were actually enjoying themselves. I knew then that a prayer revolution was indeed heading our way.

Since that first mountain prayer vigil, many subsequent prayer explosions have been conducted. And each has had its own fascinating highlight. None that I can remember lacked something of the supernatural. Teens often left such a weekend describing face-to-face encounters with Jesus.

Watching young people surrender to Christ in persistent prayer taught me many things. I especially came to realize that God's promise of power is not set aside for a select few, but it is available for any and all who will pay the price of commitment.

During the most painful days of my throat condition, God took me to an unusual prayer conference to learn this very lesson firsthand. It was one of the last meetings I would conduct for many months, as the throat trouble was about to take me from the pulpit. The lesson came through a mentally impaired teen named Benny. Benny was fifteen, but he had the mind of a six-year-old.

Several nights of the midweek conference were concluded, and the senior pastor of the church hosting the conference decided to devote an entire meeting that Sunday, open to adults as well as the teens, to allow young people to share what God had done in their lives that week. The teens themselves would do the preaching instead of a preacher. I was simply asked to serve as the moderator. It was actually little more than an old camp meeting "testimony rally" like those conducted years ago. Of course, this was a little risky, because no one knew what the young people might say.

As the Sunday service drew to its conclusion, four young people remained on the platform. In my heart I was thankful that our spontaneous time had been free of any out-of-the-ordinary incidents or spiritual know-it-alls using the opportunity to expound. The glory was all going to Jesus, for which I was pleased.

Not wanting anything to go wrong in the final moments of the meeting, I informed the congregation, "Now, if you haven't already stood to testify, please keep your seats. I feel these four young people are to conclude our time of sharing tonight."

I began calling on the four remaining youth one at a time. Finally, there was just only one left. Stepping to the pulpit, Carol began sharing her experiences of encountering Jesus as never before that week. Her testimony was deeply moving, and I was glad she was last. "This will be a perfect ending to the entire week," I thought to myself.

Then it happened. I saw movement out of the corner of my eye. Someone was walking down the aisle. I swallowed quickly, uncertain as to the course of action required. It was Benny. He was heading for the platform.

Several rows back two teenagers giggled. Others, near the front, quietly smirked. I had been told about Benny earlier in the week. He wasn't "all there," a teen told me, "so don't be surprised if he interrupts a meeting and does something odd." That was acceptable to me in the youth meetings, but this was a meeting for the entire congregation, and I was obviously concerned.

Benny was clearly on his way to the platform. It was impossible to alter the situation. Any unfavorable action would have added more confusion and embarrassment. I remember my thoughts distinctly. "Oh boy, Benny's going to ruin this entire meeting. He'll wreck it by saying something crazy, and the whole place will be in an uproar."

Benny had now reached the platform. With his slightly slouched posture, he climbed the several steps to the pulpit. His usual childlike smile was replaced by a quivering lip, and his face was wet with tears. I didn't know what to do, so I did nothing. I just let him speak.

"I know what you're thinking," the husky fifteen-year-old mumbled. "'Benny is going to ruin everything. He's gonna wreck this whole meeting. He can't even give a good testimony.'"

Every word spoken coincided with my exact thoughts. Somehow Benny knew. His tears were seasoned with both hurt and compassion as he continued.

"I know I'm not normal. I'm not like all of you. I was born different."

Benny wept like an orphaned child. Without realizing it, he had touched the hearts of the entire congregation. Some tried to keep from displaying emotion but couldn't. Most began weeping openly.

"I love you," Benny continued as he looked out over the congregation. "I love you all very much. It's true that I can't get a job like other boys my age. I can't even go to a real school like all of you. At my school we just make baskets. But I can love you."

Wiping away tears, Benny added, "And I can pray for you. Just remember; if you get discouraged, Benny is praying for you. It's not much, but it's all I can do. I'll be praying. Anybody can pray."

Benny's interruption was a turning point in my ministry, throat condition and all. (It would not be the last such interruption while leading a public meeting that would transform my life, as you'll soon learn in the pages that follow.)

Standing beside Benny, I felt the sting of tears upon my face. I had been humbled by the humility of someone who was radiating the humility of Christ. Something vital was learned in those moments concerning our future prayer ministry. The promised prayer army God would help us recruit (and all the prayer movements that might follow as the result) would consist of all kinds of people. Some would be uneducated, and some brilliant. Many would be unassuming in appearance. Some would lack the ability of others, but all would be choice servants of the Lord. Benny was right: "Anybody can pray."

Chapter 7
THE CARE BUCKET

NOVEMBER EVOLVED INTO A typical California December. It was cold and rainy. A once slight throat irritation caused by a simple virus was now a major concern. Seldom did a day slip by without fearful thoughts of the future. I found myself questioning God. Never once did I link the difficult situation to the commitment made in the sunlit Baker Hotel room three months earlier. God was getting ready to reveal the master plan for an exciting prayer ministry, but first, important lessons had to be learned in the schools of suffering and prayer.

December inaugurated the most intensive struggle yet in those early years of ministry. It is hard to forget those lonely nights spent sitting in the living room of our south Sacramento home as the December winds howled and the rains clattered against the back window. Unable to preach, I began researching the theme of prayer. I read every book I could find on the subject. Careful notes were taken and filed for future reference. Soon I found myself writing what I felt inside. I quickly learned there are other ministries besides preaching and promptly refused to be deprived of a ministry, even if it meant never preaching again.

A month before Christmas, my fears that something serious was causing my throat problem seemed momentarily justified as I consulted another throat specialist. Upon careful examination, he reported a slanting of a vocal cord, possibly indicating a foreign object pushing against it.

Tumor! That was all I could think of as the doctor revealed his finding. What once was casual concern had now become real fear. I was just twenty-six years of age. I expected the worst.

I couldn't help but wonder if I might lose my capacity to speak permanently. During these days it was often difficult to sleep. Night after night I would wait until I knew Dee was sound asleep and would carefully climb out of bed, close the bedroom door as quietly as possible, and go into our living room. We had recently purchased a new stereo FM record player, state-of-the-art for the time. I learned that if I turned on the stereo without turning up the volume, the display would light up enough so I could put a favorite long-play record on the turntable. The album featured the singing of a popular Christian bass singer of the day named Big John Hall. The third song on his long-play album was titled "They That Sow in Tears." It was a song based on Psalm 126:5–6: "They that sow in tears shall reap in joy. He that goeth forth and weepeth, bearing precious seed, shall doubtless come again with rejoicing, bringing his sheaves with him" (KJV).

I would place one of my ears as close to a speaker as possible, turn up the volume very slightly so I could hear it but Dee couldn't, and listen to the same song repeatedly. When the song came to the end, I'd place the needle again on the third song and listen once more.

Soon I would find myself weeping as I listened. I knew Jesus was enrolling me in His school of prayer and teaching me that prayer alone was the primary key to effective ministry.

One night, well past midnight, I told the Lord that even if I never preached vocally again, Dee and I would purchase a printing press and go to some faraway place like Africa or Asia and proclaim the Good News through the printed page. And, of course, we would pray. There were more ways to spread the gospel than by traditional preaching, I reasoned.

Little could I have known that someday I would do just that and lead a prayer and evangelism ministry reaching literally millions of people every month through the printed page, right where they live, while following up with twenty to thirty thousand people or more responding to the gospel and receiving Christ through this home-to-home evangelism strategy *every day!*

But that was for the distant future. For now I only knew I faced a very serious challenge. Three weeks later I was back at the clinic for a major tumor test. It was scheduled for the day before Christmas, and the results would not be available until seven days later. Circumstances would have appeared much more miserable, however, had it not been for heaven-sent comfort the day I took the tumor test. As I sat in the clinic waiting room, I sought help and assurance. Clutching my small New Testament and Psalms, I prayed softly, "I'm afraid, God, so afraid. I have no place to turn but Your Word."

I let my Bible fall open. From the page jumped these words, "Cast thy burden upon the LORD ... he shall never suffer the righteous to be moved" (Ps. 55:22, KJV). A warmth came over me. I knew God had spoken. No matter the dilemma, I would not be moved from that promise.

Typically, I desired an added confirmation. I asked God to speak a second time, just as Gideon had come twice to God with his fleece (Judg. 6:36–40). I closed my Bible, ignoring what others in the waiting room might have thought as they observed me. Placing the binding of my small Bible in the palm of my hand, I gently let it fall open again. My eyes were closed as I followed this unorthodox procedure. I placed my fingers on the random page, pointing toward a verse I couldn't see because my eyes were closed. When I opened my eyes I read with amazement the exact same verse: "Cast thy burden upon the LORD…he shall never suffer the righteous to be moved."

God had provided the same promise twice. It was all I really needed. That next morning the examination was given as scheduled.

Seven tense days slowly passed, and the final results came in: I was probably born with that slant in my vocal cord; at least there was no tumor. God had truly lifted the cares of the moment. He had not suffered the righteous to be moved.

My Christmas experience soon became a source of strength to those who visited me. One such occasion involved a thirty-year-old accountant, a man contemplating suicide. To him, everything seemed to be going wrong.

"Oh, I once believed in God," he affirmed, "but now I'm not certain He exists. And my home used to be happy, but I really don't love my wife anymore. She still loves me, but I feel so dead inside. Everything's just going sour. What's wrong with me?"

In my heart, I prayerfully searched for an answer. I didn't know what to say. My area of work was youth, and I certainly knew little of dealing with a potential suicide victim. Suddenly help came from heaven. The Holy Spirit impressed on my heart the ultimate problem solver: the care bucket. Frankly, it was something I'd never heard of before and sincerely wondered what it might be.

Sitting in my office, I had a powerful burst of faith. "Sir," I assured the accountant, "you've made the right decision in coming here today. You'll never be the same. The whole world outside will be different. The grass will be greener, the sky bluer, and you're going to be praising the Lord!" I had no idea why I said those words.

The accountant was not impressed. "But you just don't understand," he quietly advised.

"You haven't tried the care bucket yet, have you?" I asked.

"What's the care bucket?" he abruptly answered.

In my heart I asked God the same question, *"What's the care bucket?"* God immediately led me to the next step. I answered the man, "It's a bucket I keep under my desk for emergencies." Actually, this was the first time I'd even heard of it.

I quickly reached under my desk and pulled out an imaginary bucket. Here I was, playing charades with a well-educated accountant who was contemplating suicide.

"Here it is," I said, holding up the invisible object.

He saw little humor in my antics. Instead, he looked confused. "But I don't see anything," he responded. "What are you talking about?"

"I'm talking about this bucket in my hand," I answered firmly. "You've got to see it to make it work."

"But I don't see anything," he reaffirmed.

I couldn't believe I was doing this. "If you want release from your problems, you've got to see the bucket," I explained. "You've got to see it from your heart, with spiritual eyes."

Suddenly there was a spark of faith. The accountant, still quite solemn, answered, "Oh, I think I understand. We're just imagining." He paused for a second's thought and then said with a wry smile, "OK...I see your bucket!"

Quickly I offered an explanation concerning the use of the care bucket. Meanwhile, I was still holding the imaginary bucket at a very tired arm's length.

"You take all your cares," I explained, "and one at a time you stuff them into the bucket. Then you give God the bucket and walk out burden free."

With that I reached toward the somewhat bewildered businessman, my two hands clutching an imaginary bucket. "Here, take the bucket and try it," I entreated. Again there was a blank stare.

"Look," I added, "you've got nothing to lose. Go ahead and try it. Take the bucket."

The accountant looked cautiously toward an open window and then my half-opened office door to make sure no one was watching. He had little idea I was equally embarrassed. Here we were, two grown men playing mind games.

He took the imaginary bucket tentatively in his hands. Faith was indeed on our side.

"Now what do I do?" he asked, holding the bucket.

"You put your cares into the bucket."

"How do I do that?"

"Well, you hold the bucket in one hand and reach out and grab each care that comes to your mind and put it in the bucket."

I still couldn't believe I was sharing this with a man considering suicide. I demonstrated by reaching into midair and grabbing an imaginary care. I leaned over and dropped it in the invisible bucket, held tightly in his hand.

His eyes quickly shifted again from side to side, seemingly afraid someone might be watching through the open window or the crack in the door. Then, with a jabbing motion, he grabbed at the air several times, dropping cares into the bucket.

"Did you get them all?" I asked sharply.

"What do you mean?"

"I mean, did you overlook any cares? You've got to include them all," I added, "otherwise the bucket doesn't work effectively."

There was another momentary smile. He looked up slightly—carefully pondering the cares that had brought him to my office. As swiftly as before, he grabbed at the air a final time. "I forgot one," he said, and dropped it in the bucket.

"Now what?" the man asked.

Again I inwardly said, "Now what?" to God, not certain of what to do next. The impression came immediately. "We give the bucket to God," I answered, "and He cleans it out for us. Then He gives the empty bucket back for future use."

"But how do I give it to God?"

"It's simple. You just hold it up to God with both hands and let Him take it," I explained, motioning toward the ceiling as I spoke.

Quietly the man lifted his imaginary bucket high with both hands. To be sure, he looked rather foolish, though a powerful object lesson in faith was gaining impact.

Holding his tired arms in a position above his head for several seconds, the man asked, "What do I do now with the bucket?"

I grinned and answered, "What bucket?"

He replied, "This bucket," nodding his head toward the upraised imaginary bucket.

I said, "Do you see a bucket?"

The accountant seemed dumbfounded.

I said, "You can take your hands down. God has the bucket now. He has taken away all your cares."

There was an unusual presence of God in my office in that moment. The man seemed helped, though he had yet to display any obvious joy. For all practical purposes, the counseling session was over. I reminded the man that these events in my office must be taken by faith.

"It will probably hit you when you get outside," I said. "Remember what I said earlier. The whole world will seem different when you leave today. The sky will be bluer, the grass will be greener, and you'll be praising the Lord. God can do that, you know?"

We stood together and walked to the door. I asked the man to lay his hands on my little New Testament and Psalms, the same one I had opened at random at the doctor's office some months earlier, and we prayed hurriedly. The accountant then departed. I might have forgotten the entire incident had it not been for the strange sight I witnessed about thirty minutes later when I left the office for the day. I locked my office door behind me and walked to my car. As I drove out of our parking lot onto a busy street, I noticed something strange out of the corner of my eye. It was a lone figure standing in the grassy courtyard in front of our church. It was the accountant. He was easily visible to the thousands of motorists who pass that busy corner daily.

I couldn't believe what I saw. His face sparkling, the accountant was walking back and forth on the grassy courtyard, his hands raised toward heaven, rejoicing. There was no comparison to the man I had seen in my office. He would quickly look toward the blue sky and laugh. Then he would bend over, gazing at the grass—laughing even more. It was a sight to behold. The sky, indeed, *was* bluer, the grass greener, and he *was* praising the Lord—just as God had promised in our time of prayer together. He had discovered the power of the care bucket, and I had too.

"Cast thy burden upon the LORD…he shall never suffer the righteous to be moved." The accountant wasn't the only one ministered to that sunny afternoon. I knew now God was working out His plan in my life. My throat *would* be healed. In God's perfect timing, my testing would be complete.

Part Three
THE PRAYER CORPS

Chapter 8
THIS IS THE YEAR

THE THROAT SPECIALIST HAD revealed the negative results of the test and, as a last resort, recommended two weeks of total voice rest. Even my physician was playing a part in God's plan. The two weeks of total rest in Palm Springs provided opportunity to sketch an initial draft of my first book, *No Easy Road*, on the subject of prayer. And now, final victory waited just days ahead.

Events several years earlier in my dorm closet were much more on my mind these days. And I had plenty of extra time to think, being removed from the pulpit. It was much clearer now that real preparation is vital to a ministry—any ministry. Prayer preparation is one of the highest forms of such training. And I still had much to learn in this regard as the Christmas season passed into the new year. I was turning twenty-six (as was Dee, who is but a day younger than me). We were only a year away from the fulfillment of the seven-year promise God had given us when we were married.

March is beautiful in Northern California, and, as usual, it arrived like a lamb. We were in the middle of our annual stewardship emphasis at the church I served, and a special guest preacher had arrived for the conference. Having no service scheduled for the first Friday of the emphasis, I suggested we attend a special luncheon in neighboring San Francisco. Kathryn Kuhlman was the scheduled speaker. Earlier that week, a friend had sent two luncheon tickets for my wife and me, but Dee was unable to attend. I remember telling our visitor how much he would enjoy it, since I had attended the meeting she conducted the previous fall in Southern California.

It never entered my mind as we traveled Interstate 80 from Sacramento to San Francisco that a miracle might happen to me. The previous November I had visited Southern California where Miss Kuhlman was speaking with nothing on my mind but healing. And I returned in my same condition. This time healing didn't cross my mind. I had grown accustomed to my throat problem and was merely biding time to see what God might want Dee and me to do regarding our future.

Arriving at the San Francisco hotel where the event was scheduled, we were stunned at the size of the crowd attending the banquet. More than three thousand were crammed together at hundreds of tables in the hotel's largest ballroom. After the meal, I had my second look at this unusual lady evangelist. Beside me, my friend seemed a little puzzled. He watched the evangelist's unusual gestures and listened to her dramatic pronunciation of words.

Then it happened. An extraordinary flow of God's anointing settled. "A tumor is dissolving in the back of the auditorium, at that far table," the speaker declared, as a man jumped up shouting, "It's gone! The cancer's gone! It's gone!"

Both my friend and I wondered if this could really be happening.

But the gifts of the Holy Spirit seemed to be in full operation. The rally truly belonged to God's agent from heaven, His Spirit. Skeptics sat silently amazed, my friend included. Those who came to see God work rejoiced.

My friend had never witnessed anything like it, nor had I, even though I had been in one of Miss Kuhlman's meetings the previous fall. And what amazed my friend most, as it did so many others, was the nonemotional approach to it all. Nothing had been worked up. It wasn't shallow psychology. God was doing something, and doing it in a uniquely sovereign way. I was soon to be personal living proof of exactly that.

Suddenly the evangelist was pointing at our very table. There were hundreds of tables in the hall, and she was pointing directly at ours. We were left of the stage facing from the crowd, perhaps ten or twelve tables back. Not only that, but Miss Kuhlman seemed to be pointing directly at me. I swallowed hard. Initially the pain of my throat condition was still there. But then it happened.

"Right over there," she declared as she pointed at me, "someone is being healed of a lingering throat condition. God is touching you now."

In that instant a heavenly power saturated both my soul and body. I must admit my initial response was fear.

"How on Earth did she know?" I reasoned. No one except my guest even knew I would be there. But even as I questioned what was happening, I felt a strange warmth come over me. It was, in fact, literal heat. It was as if someone had poured warm oil on me.

Much more than mere physical healing happened in that moment.

My spirit was touched. I felt God. And within ten days I was back in the pulpit. In a moment the months of initial testing were over. The price, it seemed, had been paid. Never again would this same throat problem keep me from the pulpit. In fact, the condition left as quickly as it had come. It has never returned. In the years that followed, I would teach prayer seminars equivalent to preaching as many as sixteen thirty-minute sermons in any given week and never suffer the same problem again.

The following summer my first book was scheduled for publication. By now the prayer emphasis was spreading. Youth leaders were planning church-sponsored prayer retreats everywhere. The Jesus movement was being discussed openly by the press. Unexplained healings began taking place. Demonstrations of God's power and glory not previously seen at our prayer retreats and crusades were now frequent. Those unusual experiences in the college prayer closet and the Baker Hotel suddenly made sense. A powerful thought repeatedly came: "A massive revival and harvest of souls is soon coming to Planet Earth. All we have to do is contend for it with prayer and fasting."

Eleven exciting months passed after my healing. I heard of revival fires burning everywhere. I was so overjoyed when the New Year arrived that I almost forgot the date. It was January 1, 1971. Seven years earlier God had made a promise in a cluttered walk-in closet of a college dormitory. The year 1971 would be a year of birthing the ministry that would consume Dee and me for the rest of our lives.

Climbing into bed following an all-night church-sponsored New Year's Eve gathering, I wondered about the promise I had received seven years earlier in the college dorm closet. What would it involve? Would it be necessary for me to leave my post working with the youth of our church? Where would we live? Who would help us? What part would this prayer ministry play in global evangelism and world revival?

Though many questions needed answers, one fact was clear. I whispered it to myself as I drifted to sleep. "This is the year! The promise takes place Thanksgiving Day this year!"

Chapter 9
TABLETOP TRAVAIL

Ir was a cool, misty October weekend in 1971. It was the year of promise for Dee and me. One hundred seventy-five young people from at least twenty churches throughout Northern California had gathered for a weekend prayer retreat amid the towering redwoods of the region.

These prayer retreats had begun two years earlier when God put on my heart that we had many great fun activities for young people in our church, including a ski club, a full-size gymnasium, a coffee shop, and winter and summer retreats that were always fun-filled. We even had an annual trip to Disneyland in Southern California as well as exciting choir tours. However, we had nothing like a weekend getaway exclusively to seek the Lord.

I vividly recall the first such retreat, which I mentioned briefly in chapter 4. The Lord had put on my heart during a Wednesday night youth meeting that I should take as many young people as were willing into the nearby mountains for a weekend of nothing but prayer. The first of such prayer retreats (which we soon called Prayer Explosions) followed a few weeks later. It became an awesome weekend of seeking God. Only twenty-two young people participated, but it was truly life changing. It would lead to numbers of churches getting involved in these weekend vigils over the following twenty-four months, including the retreat in the California redwoods mentioned above when one hundred seventy-five passionate, God-seeking teens gathered.

We had learned much from these retreats, and they clearly prepared us for the vision of starting a 24/7 prayer ministry with resident youth that was soon to come.

It was that first Prayer Explosion that set the tone for all the retreats that were to follow. We arrived in the Sierra Nevada Mountains at about 7:00 p.m. The teens had driven in several cars with some young adult helpers, having left Sacramento immediately after school was out. By the time we arrived at the retreat center, the teens were noticeably weary. After all, they had been to school all day and then had the long drive into the mountains.

We gathered in the lodge, where a beautiful fire was burning in the fireplace. I formed a half-circle of chairs so the twenty-two teens could sit. I encouraged them with a few appropriate passages of Scripture and then suggested they get on their knees and begin praying. For perhaps thirty to forty-five minutes each young person prayed aloud as others agreed. Some prayed more quietly than others, but all participated.

Then, suddenly, one by one they began sitting up in their chairs. They had prayed for everything they could think of. So they just returned to their chairs. In a matter of moments all the teens were sitting with blank looks on their faces. It was a look that conveyed, "This isn't very exciting." I could tell they were weary. We had come with the intention of praying all night and all the following day. We had actually prayed less than an hour.

I knew we were in trouble as I looked at their faces. So I graciously said, "I know we came to pray all night, but God also knows we are human and have human bodies. We are all weary."

I paused and added, "Now, we could all go to the nearby cabins with our sleeping bags and sleep until about six in the morning and start again, or we could get back on our knees and fight the devil."

I cannot recall why I made that specific concluding statement—"or we could get back on our knees and fight the devil." Suddenly, a thirteen-year-old in the group named Peter, the youngest of the twenty-two, who was sitting at the other end of the half circle of chairs from me, lifted his fist and began shaking it. Boldly he declared, "I say we fight the devil."

I was stunned by Peter's youthful determination. All the rest of the group began weeping. They agreed with a corporate shout. I then encouraged each of them to move their chairs from the half circle to any place in the large room they chose.

The main lights in the lodge were turned out, and the fire from the fireplace cast a pleasant glow across the room. I felt it was a great atmosphere for quiet prayer. However, in a matter of moments, the prayer would not be quiet. There soon came a move of tears across the lodge as the teens began praying. Imagine one of the past great revivals in history, and you would have some idea of how they were praying. It stunned even me. This was no longer a typical corporate prayer meeting where everyone was casually agreeing with one in the group who happened to be praying aloud. They were all praying aloud. It was simultaneous audible prayer as happened in every great past revival. And it continued for hours.

I especially recall how at about three thirty that morning one of the "elders" in the group, Carolyn (a seventeen-year-old straight-A student and cheerleader for a local high school), was flat on her face just a few feet from the logs burning in the fireplace. She was sobbing uncontrollably. I went over and stood behind listening to her groanings. Amid those groanings there were passionate pleas that the young people of California who were bound by drugs would come to know Jesus.

All this was happening at the height of the so-called hippie movement of the 1960s and early 1970s in California. Drugs were rampant. Teens from everywhere across America and throughout the world were flocking to California. Teens of the era were called "flower children." A popular rock song of the era encouraged youth, "If you're coming to San Francisco, make sure you wear a flower in your hair!" A humorist added, "America is slanted toward the West Coast, and everything that is loose, rolls." And the misfits and counterculture people were coming. We were getting every sort of searching young person migrating to California to get "high." And high they would get. Hundreds of thousands had no idea they were coming to meet Jesus!

In front of that fireplace, I heard Carolyn pleading for an awakening among these misguided youth who were coming in droves to California. She claimed thousands of them for Christ—tens of thousands, in fact. Carolyn was praying in a harvest.

Amazingly, within six months of that first Prayer Explosion, another explosion took place in California. It became known as the Jesus movement, which leaders like Billy Graham would later describe as a great awakening of our generation among youth. Of the thousands of young people who would come to Christ, most had been living a hippie lifestyle.

I will forever believe that the intense travail of seventeen-year-old Carolyn and the twenty-one others at that first prayer retreat was somehow involved in a birthing process of the Jesus movement. I had already become convinced that great awakenings always are born in prayer. Now I had watched that birthing process occur before my very eyes.

The following morning, after most of the young people had prayed the entire night, we had a light breakfast. God put on my heart the thought of sending these youths into the nearby hills near the retreat center to wait quietly in the presence of the Lord. They were to hear from God, and God alone!

I dubbed this season "Quiet Dialogue With God." I told the teens that for the next several hours no one would be permitted to speak to anyone but God. It had to be a time of total silence. They were to take their Bibles and go find a place to be alone with God. God's Word was to become His voice to them, and they were to seek only Him. I told them we would all gather back with the ringing of the retreat center's bell and share what God had shown each of us.

The young people followed my instructions to the letter. I had never seen even a small group of youth this size remain absolutely silent for several hours. Even as they were walking from the lodge, not a word was spoken to each other. It was amazing. Off they went. When we rang the retreat center's bell three hours later, they promptly gathered. I could tell immediately something remarkable had happened. Almost every teen had eyes moistened by tears.

When we gathered in the main lodge, I asked the young people to share their experiences. One after another they opened their hearts. We heard amazing testimonies of encounters with the Lord unlike any of us had heard before. I knew God was doing something remarkable. And it had happened simply because we had taken the time to get alone and be quiet before the Lord.

I particularly recall the testimony of a sixteen-year-old high school girl who during quiet dialogue went for a walk through the towering California pines. She suddenly sensed a strange closeness of the Lord and began singing "I Walked Today Where Jesus Walked." Though very much alone, she heard the crackling of footsteps on the pathway behind her. Frightened, she interrupted her song and turned to see who was there. A careful glance revealed no one, though the footsteps continued until they stopped beside her. She was amazed and confused. She turned and walked forward a second time, singing another line from the same song. Again she heard the footsteps. Stopping in the path she waited and listened. They came beside her again, and stopped.

"I was frightened at first," she said, "but then I knew what was happening. Jesus was there, right beside me. I never knew He could be so close."

Two years and numerous such retreats had passed. It was now early fall of 1971. The number of young people participating in these Prayer Explosions had grown from twenty-two to one hundred seventy-five.

We had gathered at a YMCA camp in the redwoods near the coast of Northern California. There, nestled among trees hundreds of feet tall, we had gathered for what would become the last of these prayer retreats before my receiving the vision of starting the Prayer Corps as described in the pages that follow. Little could I have known that it was at this gathering that I was going to experience an encounter equally as intense, and perhaps more so, as that of Carolyn two years earlier.

At these prayer retreats, I had learned quickly that it was important to have organized corporate prayer at the start of the meetings to keep the attention of the participating young people. So, upon arrival, we had several hours of what might be referred to as a Concert of Prayer. This is generally an organized time of directed prayer where there are different prayer activities that involve participants in a flow of corporate prayer.

I would have teens pray in groups of two or three for certain objectives, and then there would be a time of singing and worship. This might be followed by a season of different young people praying out prayers based on certain Scripture passages that I might assign. This would be followed by even more corporate worship. I would then ask various teens to come and share any burdens they had for their family, church, or school. Then we would have corporate prayer over each of these focuses.

My goal was to keep their attention in a corporate setting until at least midnight. I would then challenge each young person to find a quiet place in the main lodge to simply seek the Lord in his or her own way. I always was certain a fire was burning in the fireplace for an atmosphere of warmth. I also challenged young people always to pray with an open Bible. Read the Word and then pray it, I would suggest.

We tried to plan these prayer events in a setting where somewhere near the main lodge, even attached to it, was a cafeteria or a hall where we could offer doughnuts, coffee, and hot chocolate throughout the night. I would tell the teens there was nothing wrong with slipping into that room anytime they felt like it to have a doughnut, coffee, or hot chocolate. If others might be in that room at the time, I encouraged them to share with each other what God was revealing to them. However, I reminded them that we had really come to seek God. In our preplanning I also encouraged teens to bring a sleeping bag in case they simply couldn't last an entire night in prayer. They would have assigned cabins where they could go and rest for a few hours if they so desired. We also would always be sure to have several adult chaperones with us to help manage all this. The fact was, however, that most of the young people did pray the entire night at each of these prayer retreats.

It was in this context at the Prayer Explosion in the California redwoods in the fall of 1971 that an experience would occur that would profoundly impact my life. It was to become the setting for a life-changing experience of travailing in prayer that was to birth a 24/7 live-in prayer ministry for young people that would follow in the immediate months to come.

"Please, God, Help Me Care!"

It was about three o'clock in the morning. There was a typical standard-size "library table" on one side of the large lodge where the young people were praying. It was sturdy enough to hold my weight, and I was sitting on the table with my legs dangling. I was watching the young people pray in the lodge, which was highlighted by the glow of the large fireplace in the center of the room. It was a wonderful sight. Some of the youth were quietly weeping. Others were just talking to God in an almost casual manner with open Bibles. In several instances I saw two or three young people praying together. It was beautiful.

Suddenly I realized that even though the setting was beautiful, and the teens were obviously being deeply impacted, I personally hadn't sensed any special prayer burden myself. I was more of an observer—a desert amid an oasis of prayer.

Only a few moments passed when I asked myself a simple question: "Why do I feel absolutely no emotion when so many people are dying and going into eternity this very moment without knowing Christ?" It was such a simple thought.

I quietly added, "Why don't I care more for the lost?"

In that moment I casually prayed, "Please, God, help me care!"

I could never have imagined how such a simple prayer would be answered so suddenly. A few tears began welling up in my eyes and flowing down my cheeks.

I sensed something was about to happen but didn't know what. I prayerfully added, "Yes, Lord, I really mean it. Help me care."

Soon, tears were flowing freely down my face. A burden for the lost was settling, unlike any I could ever remember. Before long I was sobbing. This was no ordinary, quiet moment of a tenderhearted experience. I was sobbing in ways I could never remember. At one point I had to clutch my side because the weeping was becoming uncontrollable and even painful.

In a matter of moments I was bending over the table and beginning to fall toward the floor. I was conscious of this fact but could do nothing to stop myself. I was truly agonizing in the Spirit.

As this was happening, the passage in Romans chapter 8 that speaks of the Holy Spirit groaning in and through us with utterances of prayer came to my mind. I knew I was experiencing this very manifestation.

By now I was clearly falling from the table as my head fell between my legs. I didn't know what to do. I could not stop what was happening.

A few of the nearby teens wondered what was happening to their youth pastor and jumped up to help me. I quickly sensed several had gathered around me. In some ways what was happening was humorous. One of the teens said, "I think he's falling off the table." I thought, "I'm glad you figured that out." Yet, still I could say nothing. My groanings continued.

Another asked his peers, "Do you think we should catch him and put him on the floor?"

I couldn't speak a word, but I found myself thinking, "Please, please catch me, or I will fall on my head."

Several held me and began to lower me to the floor. It would have been hilarious had it not been happening to me.

One of the youths suggested they place me on my side. Still, I was groaning in prayer and couldn't speak a word, but I was grateful for that further suggestion.

In moments I was lying on my side in a fetal position. Frankly, I was embarrassed. Yet I couldn't stop what was happening. This was no ordinary encounter. I hadn't planned it, nor had I sought it. I continued sobbing uncontrollably. I felt like someone who was giving birth to a baby.

Obviously men can't understand the full significance of the true birthing process, but because my wife, Dee, had only recently had our first child, I understood more of what was involved in that process. What the Bible calls *travail*, I understood, is like the contractions of a woman in labor. Without that labor, there is no birth. I knew I was giving birth to something. I wasn't quite sure what all this meant in those moments, but I knew something beyond my control was happening. By now I was completely surrounded with young people, many of whom had laid their hands on my head and shoulders and were praying for me.

This "birthing" went on for several hours. Suddenly, the most wonderful peace came over me, and I knew that something profound had happened. In those moments I heard the still, small voice of the Holy Spirit speak, "Your ministry for the future has been born tonight."

I didn't fully understand what all this meant until several weeks later (at Thanksgiving time of 1971) when God would set in motion that which was soon to take full form. I could never have imagined that in the decade following there would be many thousands of Schools of Prayer conducted all over the world in more than 120 denominations. Nor could I have known that in several more decades (at the time of this writing) we would be involved in a ministry taking the gospel to the homes of nearly a million new people *every day* (living in about two hundred thousand homes) and gathering in a harvest of as many as thirty thousand souls daily who would respond to the home-to-home evangelism and be followed up with Bible courses in their own language.

I only know my tabletop travail at that YMCA camp led to incredible victories and blessings in the months and years that followed. That simple prayer, "Help me to care," was answered in a most profound way. Over the months that followed that prayer would lead to a multitude of other experiences, including the launching of a prayer ministry that would birth many other movements of prayer globally and led to an accelerating harvest I describe in the pages that follow.

Chapter 10
WE START FIRES

WHILE RESEARCHING THE SUBJECT of prayer, I had read the challenging account of David Livingstone, one of the great forerunners of modern missions. Livingstone wrote a special prayer each year on his birthday for the coming year. I soon acquired the same habit, writing out a prayer on January 25 of each year, my birthday. I would write that prayer on the back of each new wallet-sized ordination card I received from my denomination. It meant especially much to me this particular January—seven years after God had promised an unusual ministry of prayer that would "pray in" a vast harvest of millions of souls. I realize this was a bold thought, but it was something God had given me in prayer seven years earlier.

The written prayer that year (1971) even involved a rather unusual number of souls I felt God wanted me to claim for the kingdom. The prayer began:

> *Lord, I claim this year [1971]! It will be the start of winning one hundred million souls to You. I don't know how, but You will help me.*

I realize this was a rather ambitious prayer for someone who had seen, at the very most, twenty-nine young people receive Christ in a single meeting. And that was our all-time record. To this day, I have no idea exactly why I wrote out the number one hundred million. But I still have the original copy of that ordination card in my prayer closet at home as a reminder of the God-given faith to write that number in 1971.

In chapter 30, "An Accelerating Harvest," I describe where that prayer has taken Dee and me since those days and why I believe the massive acceleration of prayer movements globally is responsible for this ever-increasing harvest we are witnessing today.

But as I wrote that prayer in 1971, I sensed there was something more, something very specific I was to do. God's promise of seven years earlier involved a missing link for our involvement in the coming harvest.

It would include a massive movement of intercessors. Many would be young people, and it was to begin soon.

Summer arrived and slipped by quickly, with both victories and defeats. On the one hand, an exciting revival had continued in our local church for three months, affecting the whole community. On the other, our senior pastor succumbed to cancer, which left a cloud of questions over the church about the future ministries of several associate pastors, including mine.

Fall finally arrived. A new pastor was elected and the associate pastors were retained. During this busy chain of events I had forgotten my written prayer at the beginning of the year. The words "this is the year" were buried in my subconscious.

It was November now, almost three weeks before Thanksgiving. Plans for our usual Wednesday night youth rally were made, and I came ninety minutes early to my favorite place of prayer behind the baptismal tank in a storage area of the church.

"Human plans are vanity," I thought as I climbed the stairs to the secluded place where I would often retreat to for quiet prayer. This particular night I felt the futility of human planning more than usual. I just wanted to be alone with God.

Entering the room, I was met with something unexpected. It was the full reality of what God had promised seven years earlier. I remembered the 1971 ordination card in my wallet and fumbled for it and the written prayer on the back. With trembling fingers, I once again read its contents. As I did I started to weep. (Interestingly, I would later misplace that written prayer and not discover it until some thirty-seven years later when I would see how powerfully God had kept that promise.)

"I claim this year," it read. Ten months previously I had tearfully penned this prayer. And now, in a whisper, I was asking God an important question—"Do You remember that promise seven years ago? O God, was it real or just an emotional pipe dream?"

I found a folding chair in the corner of the storage room and sat down. Again the still, small voice of God returned. But this time it wasn't so still, nor was it small. God spoke powerfully: "I do not forget My promises."

As I sat quietly, I was almost afraid to speak. But I had two important questions to ask: When will this promise commence? and What will it involve?

God answered immediately, each word penetrating my heart: "Because you have asked tonight, I will show you tonight."

A detailed vision of the promise given seven years earlier followed. I saw a powerful prayer army involving a people—many young, some very old—who walked with God. Their power was found in answered prayer. Holiness was their joy. Hundreds were joining the ranks as they marched. And revival involving an unprecedented harvest of lost souls followed in the wake of their marching. In fact, wherever this army marched, it was like the wake of a huge battleship cutting its way through the ocean following behind them.

Suddenly the vision became specific—so specific I had to grab a page of scratch paper and write what I saw.

Before me I saw a large wood-frame structure. It was a house, a very large house. One might describe it as a mansion. Christian young people were coming and going. Entering the house, I learned two things immediately. Those residing at this center were here to pray and minister to the Lord continuously. I saw a catchy title written on the outside of the center. It read "The Fire House." An occupant explained to me the reason for the unusual name.

"Every town has a fire house to put out fires. We want to see a godly fire house in each community to start fires—fires of revival. That's our ministry," the youth added. "*We start fires.*"

I looked closely at the young people involved. They were high school graduates, talented and committed—the finest young people I had ever seen. They reminded me of "the holy people" described in Isaiah 62:12. Isaiah labels them as "sought out," or in our language, "the cream of the crop." The second thing I learned was that these young people were a part of a new movement called the Prayer Corps. During those years the Peace Corps, started by President John F. Kennedy in the 1960s, was having considerable impact globally. Young volunteers were going out to the nations in the name of peace to help those in need. Now there would be a Prayer Corps of radical young intercessors going forth in the name of Jesus to impact the nations through prayer.

Once inside the center, I discovered the key to the whole program. Glancing to my right, I noted a special room marked by a sign attached to the door. Large letters across the top declared it to be "the Gap." It looked as if a young person had hand-lettered the sign. Below, in smaller letters, was printed the scripture, "I sought for a man among them, that should make up the hedge, and stand in the gap before me for the land..." (Ezek. 22:30, KJV). I knew that verse very well, and whoever painted the sign had left off the final words: "...that I should not destroy it; but I found none." I asked the Lord why these words were missing, and He answered, "I'll show you why."

The door opened before me. There a young lady stood near the middle of the room, looking down on a globe. So vivid was the vision that I recall specific details. She had brown flowing hair and silver-rimmed glasses. She was praying for different countries of the world. Hers were prayers marked with deep concern, not just an idle passing of time. When she finished, another young person took her place. Following that person, another came, then another, and still another. They were all young people. It continued day and night without ceasing.

I could see immediately that the Gap was the focal point of the ministry. And it wasn't to be a place where paid help or even volunteers sat waiting to counsel people who call a hotline seeking guidance. Prayer, actual intercessory prayer, never ceased in this most extraordinary room. Truly, God would never see the Gap empty or the hedge unattended.

As the Spirit of God continued my unusual mental tour, I watched the participating young people more carefully. They were truly committed young people who loved the local church and were willing to support it while giving themselves to continuous prayer.

As the vision continued, I jotted down my every observation. A definite key to the ministry, I noted, centered in a spiritually mature couple who would direct the program. They served as resident directors under the executive leader of the project—the local pastor. It was clear they were all submitted to local pastoral leadership.

"But what about financing the project?" I asked myself while watching these young warriors in action. I soon had my answer.

Each young participant had come with the understanding of giving a year of his or her life to prayer and evangelism. Participants had promised to work at least half the year for the ministry's support and the remaining six months full-time for the Lord in projects of evangelism and local church activities. These young people, in return, received a small weekly allowance for personal needs, plus food, lodging, and other expenses while ministering.

In my "heart-vision" I could readily see that none went without the basic necessities of life, nor was there displayed any unhappiness over the plan. They were too busy rejoicing in the opportunity afforded to minister unto the Lord continually and to reach the lost with the Good News of Jesus. And the local church was rejoicing too. It cost them little, if anything, to maintain this ministry, though it provided an abundance of helpers for various phases of church activity.

I sat quietly in that storage area thinking. Mental pictures of the center had disappeared as suddenly as they began. I was now studying the numerous details I had jotted down on paper. I had complete assurance the ideas given in the vision would work, even though many questions remained to be answered. Timing, of course, was all important. When would we do it, and how? The promise of seven years was slowly becoming a reality. At least I now had the plan. And I knew God wanted more than just a single center, though we had to start with one. What I didn't understand at the time was how all this would lead to a vast harvest of souls. That was to come later.

David Wilkerson came to town the following week for a two-night crusade in our large civic auditorium. After one of the evening rallies, Dee and I shared the vision with him over a late dinner. His encouragement was greatly needed. I had not mentally prepared myself for the subtle attacks of the enemy, including those from people who would initially see little need for such a prayer center.

And there would be others who would not understand my motives or the vision itself. I recall David Wilkerson's advice: "Don't listen to people who criticize. You've got to learn that now. They'll call you crazy. You should have heard what they called me when I started in New York. But I had to listen to God. I received my mandate from God and acted. Once you get that mandate, you can't afford to stop for anything."

Thanksgiving morning 1971 was sunny in Sacramento. I was lying in bed half asleep and yet meditating on the significance of the day. Today was actually the day of promise, according to the promise given me in that dormitory walk-in prayer closet seven years earlier. In my mind, the Prayer Corps officially was to begin this day.

Beside the bed our phone rang, momentarily startling me. It was Gene Browning, an African-American brother from the inner city of Sacramento who was known for his powerful praying and dynamic preaching. He was not aware of my thoughts when he called or of the detailed promise God had given seven years before.

"Brother Dick," Gene declared, "I just phoned to tell you I've got a house full of brothers praying for you right now. We started at six o'clock this morning when God gave us a powerful burden for you. I saw Satan attacking you with full force, but God just gave you the victory. I called to tell you the promise is yours."

Gene was almost shouting on the other end of the line as he repeated, "It's yours, Brother Dick. It's yours! And it starts today!"

I sat up in bed and felt a tear coming. My heart was pounding. "It's mine," I said to myself. "It's mine, and it starts today."

Chapter 11
CALL THE WORLD TO PRAYER

EVERYTHING WAS HAPPENING SO fast. Christmas was only days away, and we were caught amid the hectic holiday activities. I came home from a busy day at the office looking forward to a quiet, restful night.

It was late as I entered my study. I left the light off, blindly feeling around in the dark for my brown leather chair. I slumped down for a few moments' rest, though the doubts and questions of the week kept me wide awake. I was thinking about the Prayer Corps. Could it really develop as I'd pictured? And where would we find young people willing to give a year of their lives for such a ministry? What about a prayer center? How would we go about starting one—and when? The whole task momentarily appeared impossible. Then, as it had happened so often before, the room was filled with the presence of God. The voice spoke plainly, the words ringing clearly in my heart: "Call the world to prayer."

It startled me. I sat up and looked around. Before I could think it over, the voice echoed a second time, "Call the world to prayer." It was the same plain challenge.

But I wanted to be sure. My prayer was very simple as I quietly asked God to speak again. There seemed to be an even greater presence of God flooding the room. This time there was no doubt: "Call the world to prayer."

God had made Himself clear.

From that moment I knew God wanted me in a full-time prayer ministry birthing 24/7 prayer ministries and challenging believers to start prayer gaps in their homes, churches, and even campuses. This wasn't the first prayer movement in history, and it certainly would not be the last. But for now, it had to be on the front lines of spiritual warfare. The Prayer Corps would not only pray for the scores of evangelical organizations claiming souls but would also get right in the battle with them. And through it all, Christians everywhere would be challenged to pray for revival and the advancement of Christ's kingdom.

Call the world to prayer! By all standards it was unrealistic. You don't get up on Monday morning and say to yourself, "Wow, this week we will get the world praying."

In the first place, a majority of Christians would rather do anything *than* pray. In the second place, Satan would rather have Christians do anything *but* pray. Thus we were unfortunately fighting ourselves as well as Satan. I did understand one thing: prayer was foundational to completing the Great Commission (Matt. 9:37–38; 28:19). Andrew Murray, author of the classic *With Christ in the School of Prayer*, summed this up well: "The man who mobilizes the Christian Church to pray will make the greatest contribution in history to world evangelization."[1] I knew I wouldn't be the only one to accept this challenge, but I wanted to be the one to join the others who would.

David Wilkerson had been all too right. Some were using words like *crazy*. A pastor heard of the Fire House concept and bluntly asserted, "I don't see a need for it." He added, "My church is growing, and I don't pray."

I couldn't believe any Christian leader would make such a statement. But it didn't stop the ball from rolling. The Prayer Corps, complete with its first Fire House, was well on its way.

Everywhere I went I shared the concept. Some were excited; others had questions. A close friend even called in hopes of salvaging my spiritual life. "I'm concerned, Dick, and disappointed. I hear you've gone off the deep end." (I wanted to say that when I started my walk with Jesus, I dove into the deep end and had been there since!)

"What do you mean?" I asked, trying to sound calm as I spoke.

He tried to be a little more cautious as he answered, "It's those fire houses you want to start everywhere. I've heard about the problems you're having with the young people in your center there in Sacramento."

The brother was shocked and embarrassed to hear we hadn't even opened our first center yet. I had only shared the idea with a few ministers, and already the worst seemed to be happening. A tongue-plague was spreading.

By now I was justifiably discouraged. Initially I had thought everyone would be elated about a new prayer movement. I assumed people would rejoice over a ministry involving clean-cut young people rather than the constant, sometimes overdone emphasis on the dropouts and misfits.

I might have quit the entire new adventure were it not for the memory of God's distinct mandate: "Call the world to prayer." And I constantly reminded myself that the original idea for the project had come from heaven anyway. The details of the Fire House were born in prayer, as well as details for my personal ministry. The laying on of hands at altars of crusades, the format for all-night prayer meetings, and the plan of recruiting youth for the Prayer Corps all had originated in prayer. God had indeed set forth the entire plan, and it had to work.

But Satan doesn't go down to defeat easily. He decided to put an obstacle before me. A respected minister who invited me to his church for a series of meetings decided to cancel the meeting. He took this action *after* I had arrived in the city for ministry at his church.

I came home defeated and hurt. I was now closer to questioning whether I had heard the voice of God after all. "Could any of this be self? What if all of this is really me and not God?"

I began questioning both the details of the Prayer Corps vision and those of my personal crusade services. I stood alone in our family room, broken inside. "God," I pleaded, "what's happening to me? It seems like Satan is closing in for the kill. I've no place to turn. If You don't help, it's all over. God, I've got to hear exactly what You want me to do."

At no time do I recall being more desperate. I was in a wilderness of despair. The room was strangely quiet. This time no great voice thundered from heaven, and no angels were in sight to minister. But on the table lay my new copy of *The Living Bible*. I grabbed it quickly and asked aloud that God would provide guidance. I let the Bible fall open and immediately read, "You must obey all the commandments of the Lord your God, following his directions in every detail, going the whole way he has laid out for you" (Deut. 5:32, TLB).

I couldn't believe my eyes. It was a clear confirmation from God's Word. The plan I had been given for future Prayer Corps centers, as well as for my personal ministry, could not be altered. I had to follow God's direction "in every detail," going the whole way!

The next day I chatted with a young college graduate and his wife who had come to Sacramento for Prayer Corps training. They would eventually serve as the first resident directors of our center. (The wife, interestingly, had flowing brown hair and wore silver-rimmed glasses— exactly as I had seen months earlier in my vision.) The husband had prayed two hours that afternoon and felt God wanted him to share a message with me. I remember his words clearly: "Dick, God really spoke to me about the Prayer Corps ministry today. He said we're not to change the plan He's given, even slightly. No matter what anybody says, we've got to do just as God said from the start."

Unaware of my confirming experience the day before, the trainee added, "And just as I finished praying, I asked God to give me a word of Scripture for you."

He was holding the same translation I had, *The Living Bible,* as he spoke. Thumbing through the pages he finally reached the verse. "Here it is," he explained, and began reading from Deuteronomy chapter 5. "You must obey all the commandments of the Lord your God, following his direction in every detail, going the whole way he has laid out for you."

He saw me smiling as he read. I couldn't contain myself as I explained what had happened a day earlier. Excitedly we rejoiced together. The plan was of God. The details were His details, and He set them forth exactly as He did for a reason. We couldn't drop the plan and begin another. We had to go God's way, all the way.

In the immediate months following, we watched the Prayer Corps progress and develop. Our mistakes were many, but we had to correct them and go on. Quitting was out of the question, no matter how great the obstacles. It was all part of the new lesson, that of persistence and determination.

While visiting France sometime later, a deep impression of this important lesson was learned. It happened as we toured the Palace of Versailles just outside of Paris. One of the rooms we visited had once served as a bedroom for a famous French king who hired a noted artist to decorate the ceiling. Lying on his back hours each day, the artist gave six years of his life to create the painting. Upon completion, the scaffolding was removed, and as he stood on the floor below, carefully gazing upward, he saw an error that had been undetected when working so close to the ceiling. The artist's pride was shattered. He walked from the chamber and killed himself.

Two things were at once obvious as I applied this lesson to the work of the Lord. For one, we can't quit when we make a mistake. We admit it and go on. For another, any program or project looks better on paper than it does in reality. It is not possible to sketch the personalities of people on paper, and people make programs. Thus we learned to maintain the original plan God had given of the Fire House, though we accepted necessary adjustments in accordance with people's personalities. We were learning new things every day. And God was guiding and directing as we did.

Details of the Prayer Corps' plan were immediately put into a manual. The booklet was finished even before we organized our first actual center, which repeatedly brought an interesting question from would-be critics: "How do you know it will work?"

I would simply respond, "Because of Jericho." And when the inquirer would ask, "What does Jericho have to do with it?" I would remind him of Joshua's plan. This ancient Israeli leader announced the plan before the battle. He really believed in it. God had given him a plan, and in Joshua's mind it had to work. And work it did. The trumpets blew, the people shouted, and the walls of Jericho toppled. "Yes," I would casually respond, "I believe in the plan because of Jericho."

Part Four
THE PURPLE PIG

Chapter 12
THE MINNEAPOLIS MIRACLE

WILL YOUNG PEOPLE BE willing to give up a year of their lives, including salaries and other material things, to work solely for the Lord?" It was a question I faced repeatedly.

Working with young people for seven years had taught me one thing. Youth harbor many idols, from rock singers to unsaved friends. The bondage can often be severe. That's why I wondered about their willingness to relinquish this grip on worldly things. God decided it was time to answer this question once and for all. And it all happened in Minneapolis.

I was invited back to my alma mater for a week of spiritual emphasis. Here, seven years earlier, God had made a promise to me concerning the very ministry that I was now establishing.

Three days prior to my trip to Minneapolis, a minister of the city called to confirm my visit to his church. As a part of my visit, I would speak to his congregation the day before the activities began at the college. We also had agreed to conduct a prayer retreat that previous weekend for young people of his church, including any students from the college who desired to participate. Then, the following week I would speak at the scheduled spiritual emphasis week at the college. The pastor voiced anticipation that a powerful visitation of God would settle on both his congregation and the students.

Hanging up the phone, however, I found myself faced with the same empty feeling I had felt at times before. It was that dreadful "unanointed" and "unqualified" sensation. Not a single message burned on my heart for the coming meetings.

Looking up, I saw my reflection in our bedroom mirror. I appeared unusually tired and felt very much alone. I even thought of returning the call and canceling the trip. But instead I prayed a rather confused prayer. "I can't go, God. I've nothing worthwhile to preach or share. I'm really not qualified to lead an entire week of meetings for college students. O God, if You want me there, You've got to provide a miracle anointing." I stood at the mirror thinking, "I really am nothing!"

Almost immediately a powerful sense of God's presence came over me. I was weeping as I heard a still, small voice from within: "Now that you're nothing, you're ready to go!" Until this moment, I wasn't prepared for the trip. Now I knew I had to go. I was excited about what might happen.

Before leaving the room, I sought additional direction from God concerning the coming meetings. And though much was impressed on my heart during these moments, I remember one thing in particular.

"You will see something new you have never witnessed before. It will involve a new element of worship and commitment."

Several weeks later I was in Minneapolis. The weekend prayer retreat at a camp outside the city was attended by almost two hundred young people, more than half of whom were students from the college. Monday arrived, and the spiritual emphasis week was to begin that morning at 10:00 a.m. I had been staying at the home of the pastor who had scheduled the prayer retreat. His son was a student at the college and planned to drive me to the campus that morning.

Upon arriving in the city several days earlier, I had little idea what God had meant when He had told me weeks earlier that I would see something during this week that I had never seen before. Whatever it was would involve new elements of worship and commitment. Now the first morning of the conference had arrived, and as I awakened, I still didn't know what it meant. Having yet to determine what I would speak on that first morning, I prayed rather frantically. Suddenly God impressed on my mind a series of things that He was going to do that week. So definitive were these things that I decided to write each of the items down. The list included ten specific occurrences. One thing He showed me was that on the first night of the emphasis there would be more people jammed into the campus chapel after midnight than at the start of the mandatory meeting for students. I couldn't imagine how that could happen. He also spoke of a "supernatural, spontaneous song" continuing throughout the night, beginning after midnight on the opening evening.

Another thing He showed me was that His presence would be so strong by the third day that students would be prostrate and weeping even throughout the halls of the campus as well as in the school's library, which was just adjacent to the chapel. That too seemed baffling.

But it was item number two on the list that stood out above the others: "On Tuesday night there will be a wave of sacrifice and a demonstration of discipleship on this campus unlike anything you or the students have ever witnessed. It will be the beginning of a life of total surrender for many."

I was stunned as I tucked the list randomly into my Bible. I knew that nothing I had written was anything I could make happen on my own. I was understandably anxious.

As the pastor's son drove me to the campus, he described the desperate need for a revival among the students. Years later he told me he even questioned his own faith at the time. As we drove along Lake Avenue, the student spoke, "I sure hope God shows up, because we really need it. We have students preparing for ministry that I don't think are even saved." He added a question: "What do you think God will do this week?"

I answered, "I have no idea," and almost choked on my words. I realized I did know what God was planning to do. At least, if I believed my list. But in that moment I lacked the courage to share this with the young student.

The student kept talking, while I became strangely silent. A battle of faith was raging within.

"Do you really believe I will do these things this week?" was the voice I heard within. God was again speaking. Boldly but silently I said, "Yes." I thought the matter was resolved until the voice spoke again. "Then are you willing to read the list to all the students this morning before any of this happens?"

Now I was more than anxious; I was terrified.

I was still sitting beside the talkative student in dead silence as we drove along, but my heart cried out to God.

"Are You serious? The students will think I'm crazy. And what if I read these things and nothing happens?"

"Then you really don't believe I spoke," came the reply. The wrestling continued in my spirit for a few long moments until I finally inwardly made a deal with God. I told Him I would read the list only if He spoke directly to me at the end of the morning meeting and that it had to be in a supernatural manner so that I had no doubt whatsoever that He was directing me. I really didn't know what I meant by "a supernatural manner." Maybe a parrot would fly into the chapel, land on the pulpit, and squawk, "Read it now!" (A good sense of humor sometimes kept me going.)

As I began speaking that morning, I was so caught up in sharing what had happened during the weekend prayer retreat that I totally forgot the list. Then, toward the end of my message as I tried to inspire students to believe God for great things that week, I declared, "Although none of us knows all that God intends to do this week, we do know it will be good because God is good!"

As I spoke the words "none of us know all that God intends to do this week," a strange thing happened. To this day I cannot explain it. When I placed my Bible on the pulpit near the end of my message, it randomly opened to the exact spot where I had tucked the list of things God revealed earlier that morning. But stranger still, I had picked up the folded list and without realizing it was waving it in my hand. No sooner had I said, "None of us knows," when the Lord chided me, "Somebody knows!"

I stopped everything, took a deep breath, and told the students what had just happened. I then read the list to an equally stunned student body. The first night came and went. Everything God had spoken happened. None had left the chapel before midnight. Amazingly, there were more people in the chapel after midnight than during the actual service. I had no idea how that could be. I later learned students had slipped out of the meetings at different times to call friends from other campuses and churches to tell them what was happening. Incredible waves of spontaneous worship in song continued late into the early morning hours, something also on the list. God had spoken saying, "There will be a supernatural song that will continue all through the first night." Students were still singing spontaneously when the sun came up the next morning.

God was fulfilling everything I had read from the list.

By the following evening there was an obvious sense of anticipation as students gathered for the meeting. Some, in fact, had never left the auditorium from the night before except to use the restrooms. The auditorium seemed to be aflame with God's glory. It was the night God had promised "a wave of sacrifice" and "a demonstration of discipleship."

But a strange thing happened as I began preaching. Satan himself seemed to stand directly before me in opposition. He was challenging my faith. A strange spirit of apathy suddenly filled the auditorium. The anticipation of God truly working that evening had all but evaporated.

The opposition didn't lessen as the evening progressed. At times my mind would go momentarily blank, and I would start a thought again. I had not attempted to speak on the themes of "a wave of sacrifice" and "a demonstration of discipleship" because I didn't know what the Lord meant when He showed me these were to happen that second night. Now it was unlikely that anything of significance would occur that night. I clearly was not getting through with my message. These were the days early in my ministry when if I thought I wasn't getting through to a crowd, I would preach louder and louder. Thankfully it's a habit long ago broken. Within thirty minutes I was almost hoarse. Finally I decided to bring my "attempted sermon" to a close. I was really putting the crowd out of their misery.

And that's when it happened. Just before an opportunity came to end the meeting, a lone student stood to her feet and quickly left the packed auditorium.

"That's it," I thought. "They're now so angry they're walking out. My list had said we would see a demonstration of discipleship and a wave of sacrifice. But this is pathetic. I'll probably have an empty auditorium before I can even say the benediction.""

A Wave of Sacrifice and a Demonstration of Discipleship

I was still wrapping up my message when something startling occurred. The lone student who had left the chapel a few minutes earlier had returned, but not to her seat. She was heading straight up the aisle toward the platform. Because every seat in the auditorium had been taken, I wondered where she was going. In her hand she gripped a black object. It was her wallet.

Standing before a crowded auditorium of classmates, the student walked boldly up the platform steps and headed straight toward the microphone and me. Students everywhere inched forward in their seats, wondering what was about to happen.

"Brother Dick, please forgive me, but I have something to say."

There was little I could do. I had to let her speak. Tearfully she addressed the crowd.

"God told me to go to my dorm room and get this. It's my wallet, and in it is all the money I have in the world."

She then turned and spoke directly to me. "Brother Dick, I'm so very, very sorry. I really didn't hear any of your sermon."

As she paused momentarily, I inwardly chuckled. "Thank God at least one student was spared the pain. That's the worst message I've ever preached."

The student continued, "All through the meeting, I just kept hearing Jesus ask me, 'How much do you love Me?' I finally told Him I loved Him more than anything on the earth. He then asked if I loved Him enough to go to my dorm room, get my wallet and all the money I had hidden in my dresser, and give it publicly in the meeting tonight." Tearfully she concluded, "I said yes, and here it is!"

She handed me her wallet and stepped awkwardly from the platform. Then, as quickly as she had come forward, she returned to her seat.

I stood before the students momentarily stunned. In my heart the melody of a Scripture song began. It was Numbers 23:19. I felt impressed to hold the wallet above my head and lead the students in the chorus that I had taught those of the student body who had attended the prayer retreat held the previous weekend.

> God is not a man, that he should lie; neither the son of man, that he should repent: hath he said, and shall he not do it? or hath he spoken, and shall he not make it good? (KJV)

Those who had learned the chorus at the prayer retreat joined me in singing. Eyes closed, I continued to hold the wallet with an upraised hand. It was my confirmation of the promise given early the previous morning that there would be a "demonstration of discipleship" that night. To me, this lone act accomplished just this. It was both an act of discipleship and of sacrifice. And something else was clear. Nothing I had said from the pulpit prompted this public act of dedication. It was merely the spontaneous response of someone who had heard the voice of the Lord and responded obediently. But the night was far from over.

We sang the chorus a second time: "God is not a man, that he should lie, neither the son of man, that he should repent…" My eyes remained closed as the singing continued. Still I held the wallet above my head, not knowing exactly why.

Suddenly an unusual wind of conviction seemed to settle upon the hundreds of students and other guests present. I could hear unusual sounds, like that of a crowd moving about on a busy street. I opened my eyes slightly, though continuing to sing. Students were coming from everywhere toward the platform. They were emptying their wallets, the majority giving everything they had. It was truly a miracle, a miracle of commitment such as I had never witnessed.

Thousands of dollars were given during the next thirty minutes. The ultimate total reached in excess of $27,000, a huge amount for that time and the number present. Later I looked in the wallet given earlier by the student who interrupted me, and it contained $260. It was the girl's entire savings. It was her "widow's mite."

Dollars, however, were not the only things sacrificed that night. Students began leaving the chapel moments after the Holy Spirit began moving. Within two hours the platform looked like a junkyard—televisions, musical instruments, rock records, radios, sports equipment, photographs, a rifle, plus a mink-trimmed coat, lay everywhere. I had never suggested at any time that anyone do anything like this. It just suddenly happened.

Soon other items lined the platform, including the keys of several automobiles given that night to the college. One student rushed down the aisle weeping, clutching in his hands a car stereo jerked from his car's dashboard just moments before. He put it on the altar and with it placed a box of rock and roll tapes.

Two days later I felt led to ask students or guests to share what had happened in their lives that night. Many responded.

One student claimed special deliverance over pride. She had placed a large trophy on the altar Tuesday night. She had received it the previous summer in a beauty contest. She not only kept it in a prominent place in her dorm room but also placed a picture of herself winning the pageant in front of it. "Tuesday night, as we worshiped," she said, "I saw it as a stench in God's eyes, and I ran to my room to get it and bring it to the altar."

A tall, lanky college student shared an especially memorable testimony. He was sitting near the back of the auditorium when the wave of conviction first settled. God spoke so directly he was startled.

"I was sitting there when God asked me if I was willing to give everything I had. I thought a minute about what I had on me and told Him I would. So I walked to the front and emptied my wallet. I even threw my change down, pennies and all. I was watching people respond around me when God asked me why I didn't give everything.

"He asked me about the hundred dollars I had hidden in my dresser drawer in the dorm. It took awhile to sink in, but finally I went and got it."

The student smiled as he explained what happened next.

"I returned to my seat shouting victory when God hit me right between the eyes. He said, 'I thought you said you loved Me?' I was sitting there shaking when God said, 'What about your new ten-speed bicycle hanging in your closet?'"

Some of the students laughed as he spoke. I chuckled too. After all, few college students keep a ten-speed bicycle in a dorm room closet.

"I started arguing with God. I wasn't about to give up my bicycle. Man, I wouldn't even take my bike out in the rain. I loved that bike so much I even told God He could have my car but not my bike. I loved it so much that every night I'd carry it up the stairs to hang it on a special hook in my closet, right by my clothes. I practically worshiped that bike."

The youth took a step backward and hung his head. Clearing his throat, he tearfully continued. "God asked me again if I loved Him with all my heart, and I told Him I did. But He hit me up again for my bike. So I finally gave in. In fact, I practically ran from the chapel to our dorm. I didn't want doubt to catch up with me. So I got the bike as fast as I could and carried it down the stairs. When I reached the street, guess what? It started raining. I probably looked like an idiot crying and pushing my ten-speed bike across the park in the rain. But I've never felt better. All the bondage is gone. I never felt so free."

As the student stepped from the platform, I remembered two nights earlier when he rolled his bicycle down the center aisle. It was the most unorthodox thing I'd ever seen in church. But knowing the whole story helped me understand why he had to take that step. It was part of what God spoke to me when He gave me that list early Monday morning— including item two on the list that a new "demonstration of discipleship" and "wave of sacrifice" were to come on Tuesday night.

An equally memorable blessing flowing out of Tuesday night's events happened to a young pastor visiting from a distant community. One of his young people was a student at the college.

Very late Monday night, while students worshiped God in spontaneous singing well past midnight, that student phoned her pastor explaining how powerfully God had touched her. She encouraged him and his wife to come the following evening. So convincing was her plea that her pastor and his wife drove into Minneapolis for the Tuesday night session.

At the end of the meeting, as the wave of sacrifice began settling on the gathering, the young pastor heard the same impression that so many others were hearing: "How much do you love Me?" It was something clearly orchestrated by the Holy Spirit, as I had never used that expression in my message that night.

What happened to that pastor might never have been known to me or the students had the pastor not returned to the campus two nights later when testimonies were given from those impacted the previous Tuesday evening.

He gave this account:

> On Tuesday night when students began tossing their wallets and possessions on the altar, I wept to see such commitment. Then

God began to deal with me about the two hundred dollars in cash I had in my pocket. It was money I had saved to purchase a new clothes dryer for my wife, which she desperately needed. But honestly, I was still far short of what it would cost. I had wanted to buy it for her for her next birthday, which happened to be the following day—Wednesday.

The more God dealt with me, the more I knew I had to give the two hundred dollars and trust God for my wife's need. So I told my wife, who was worshiping beside me, that I needed to go to the front of the auditorium to join the students. I didn't tell her I intended to give away her birthday money.

When I arrived at the altar, I turned sideways so my wife couldn't see what I was doing. While praying with my left hand raised, I reached into my right pocket and carefully removed the two hundred dollars. I let the bills fall to the floor in a way that no one could see what was happening.

Tearfully the young pastor continued:

I felt such relief as I walked from the front of the auditorium. I knew that God was supreme in my life, but I had no idea of the blessing waiting just ahead.

The following night, Wednesday, I had to be at our church for our midweek Bible study and prayer service. Otherwise, my wife and I would have come to the meeting here. I had never seen God move as I had Tuesday night, but God had a huge surprise for us Wednesday night.

Our church is not large, and the gathering on Wednesday night was small but still more than usual. I had no idea as to why. After the service, my wife waited on me as I turned off the heat and locked the doors of the church. We drove to our parsonage thanking God for His faithfulness and especially for what we had experienced the night before at the college. I still had not told her I gave away the money I would have used to buy her a birthday gift.

As we drove into our driveway, I stopped the car to open our garage door. As the headlights flooded our garage, we were shocked to see a garage full of our congregation. I didn't know how they conspired to do this without my wife or me knowing about it, but they did. They shouted an enthusiastic "surprise" and began singing "Happy Birthday" to my wife.

What followed can only be described as a special miracle. The gatherers parted like the Red Sea, and there before us was a brand-new clothes dryer. I'm certain it cost double or triple what I had given the night before. I had told no one of my desire to buy a dryer for my wife, and even she didn't know I was saving up money to buy her one. Only then did I tell my wife what had happened the night before. We wept as we thought of the amazing ways God blesses those of His people who are obedient to His voice.

By the third day of the meetings so many attended that the crowd spilled over into the halls and the library, which was across the hallway from the chapel. When God's presence came that day, many at those locations ended up prostrate before the Lord in prayer and worship, fulfilling His word about students being prostrate in the campus hallways and library.

As the week drew to a close, all the things on my list from the previous Monday morning had happened. I welcomed these unusual happenings at Minneapolis with an open mind and heart, though some felt it was overly emotional.[1] These unusual events, which since have been repeated in numerous settings elsewhere, answered my most frequent question concerning the next generation: Would young people really be willing to pay the price needed to see true revival sweep the earth? God began answering that question for me at that college campus in Minneapolis.

"There will indeed be a remnant ready for a ministry of total commitment," I thought as the crisp winter winds ripped at my face just prior to boarding the plane for a much warmer climate in California. "We might as well begin making plans," I mused. "God is going to have His army."

Back in Sacramento the foundation of the Prayer Corps ministry was rapidly taking shape. A friend stopped by one evening to discuss the Fire House concept with me. During the conversation he asked the obvious: "Where will all the money come from to start these prayer centers, and what about you and your family? You can't jump into something like you're talking about without careful thought. You've got to be practical about this."

I was ready for my next lesson. It would be the key to all that was happening as this new venture was unfolding. It was necessary to learn that God would always provide, even when everyone about us failed. And to teach me this, He used the purple pig.

Chapter 13

THE PURPLE PIG

IT WAS A TYPICAL northern California January—miserably foggy. And the weather seemed to be a perfect picture of the future. During December, details of the Prayer Corps had developed rapidly. Mid-January came and passed with no center in sight. We had encountered an obstacle every new ministry faces sooner or later. People everywhere seemed excited about the concept but wanted someone else to prove it first. Pastors would say, "Praise the Lord! It's gonna go...and I want to hear more when your first center is actually working." Others would say, "Well, if it's of God, it will prove itself. We'll have to wait and see."

Amid the discouragement of failing to meet our first deadline of a center by January, I faced still another decision. It concerned my position as an associate pastor at our church. The more I watched the Prayer Corps develop, the more I realized how much time it would involve. I sensed prayer was to be central to my life's work but didn't relish resigning my present position. The church I served was an ideal church with a congregation of thirteen hundred possessing a unity of purpose and the closeness of a much smaller congregation. Thus the very thought of leaving created inner turmoil, though I soon discovered much of my discontent was brought on by an unwillingness to relinquish that which meant so much to me. But I finally made the decision to resign.

My heart was distressed deeply the evening I chose to break the news to our senior pastor, but I knew God had given me a mandate to begin this new ministry. The time had definitely come to put all else aside and step out in faith for this new venture.

When I opened my mouth and quietly addressed my pastor, a strange thing happened. It seemed like liquid peace was pouring out upon me from heaven. All the turmoil was immediately gone. There was an unforgettable calm. My mind was made up, and God confirmed the decision with a river of peace.

That night I had one of the most vivid dreams I can ever remember. I was flying, actually soaring like an eagle above the Sierra Nevada

Mountains of northern California. The view was extraordinary and the peace beyond human understanding. I was soaring with God.

It was decided my official responsibilities at the church would terminate following a thirty-day period. The extra month would provide the church ample time to find my replacement. It would also allow me further opportunity to develop the Prayer Corps ministry before jumping in head over heels.

During those initial days several new questions arose concerning the new project. Dee and I talked most about finances. Maintaining a home and family in California was expensive. In addition to this, establishing and operating a center with fifteen or twenty resident prayer warriors would be costly. And there was no guarantee of outside support. Because the ministry was new, few churches realized the significant financial need. Thus our monthly budget had to depend on faith alone. And if our faith faltered, the ministry would fail.

February was especially difficult for both Dee and me. Several speaking engagements far from home cluttered an already rugged schedule. Dee remained home with our two-year-old daughter, Dena, who was doing her best to live up to the psychologists' descriptions of the "terrible twos." It was even more difficult for Dee since she was only three months from giving birth to our second daughter.

The week following my resignation a three-day crusade was scheduled for Detroit, Michigan. It would be there that God would teach me a lesson of a lifetime. It centered on His ability to provide everything needed, a lesson soon to become the most important Dee and I would learn in those formative years.

Tangible Worship

I arrived in Detroit expecting to minister to a small contingent of ministers at a leadership conference. Two hundred participants were anticipated. During the several weeks leading up to the gathering, however, the Holy Spirit began drawing leaders and youth. Now over a thousand were expected—not only youth leaders but also hundreds of young people as well. The entire venture had exploded into something far more involved than any of us had anticipated.

Two pastors met me at the airport. They were responsible for originally organizing the effort. We talked of the two-day meeting as we drove along Detroit's snow-covered streets. Both ministers voiced joy over the large crowd expected, but I was quick to sense an obvious feeling of concern expressed by both ministers. Quite simply, there was no money to cover the cost of all the additional people coming. Packets had to be prepared for the Saturday sessions at considerable expense. Already the added costs had reached a thousand dollars. And there was the problem of my personal expenses. My airfare added hundreds of dollars to that total. We agreed to make it a matter of prayer, thus placing the situation in God's hands.

It was early morning when I arrived at my hotel. I was looking forward to several hours of much needed rest when God began dealing with me in a now familiar manner. It started with a single thought that I knew originated from heaven: "Why must we depend on man's means and methods to accomplish God's purposes?"

Almost instantly God impressed on my heart that we were to receive no offering on Saturday night. Friday night, the first night, an offering could be received, but not the second night. Instead, what had happened in Minneapolis would happen again. The Spirit of God would take care of every need. He Himself would take up the offering.

Late that afternoon one of the conference directors picked me up at my hotel for the first evening rally. As we drove to the meeting, I explained that God had impressed me He would take care of the budget by His Holy Spirit and not by man. Thus no ushers would be needed Saturday night, which would be the most attended meeting. The offering baskets can be put away, I suggested.

The young pastor was startled. For a moment he said nothing. I could tell he was struggling. Then, trying to be kind to his guest, he responded, "Well, Dick, it's whatever you feel. But don't forget our budget lacks a thousand dollars for all the added packets, and we have nothing toward that, not a nickel."

It was quiet in the car as we drove to the first rally. For a moment I questioned the wisdom and timing of my words. What if God hadn't really spoken? What if through my foolishness, the conference ended deep in the red? Expenses would probably come out of my airfare and honorarium (which we desperately needed to help meet our Prayer Corps budget).

That first night, Friday, the rally was conducted as scheduled. A deep work of the Holy Spirit began as a visible flow of God's presence and power saturated the auditorium. But the final outcome of the rally wasn't all victorious. For a crowd well in excess of one thousand, the offering received for all the expenses was unusually low. When all was counted, a dismal $253.00 had been received. It was about 25 cents per person. We were short almost $750.00 just for the packets already prepared for the next day. How would they pay the printer, who had yet to be paid?

Saturday was a busy day. Morning and afternoon I was scheduled to share ideas with youth leaders who had registered. Fortunately, over seven hundred participants paid the single one-dollar registration fee. (Imagine such a fee today!) The planners of the conference were thrilled. After totaling all the income and adding up the expenses, the bills could be paid—that is, all bills except my plane fare, personal expenses, and any added honorarium. I was the fall guy. My heart sank. The test was no longer theirs. It was now mine alone.

It was a long day. And I faced the evening rally with a tossing sensation in my stomach. I wondered what God was planning for the concluding rally. It was important that I get alone and pray through the matter. I wasn't even certain what I should speak on. In a secluded room near the main auditorium I sought God's plan for the night. In minutes He put a theme and message on my heart. Then He showed me a mental picture of the evening rally, especially its conclusion. I saw young people coming from everywhere and worshiping God with their hamburger and soda money, something similar to what we had seen in Minneapolis. I also saw them giving a prayer offering—writing on slips of paper how much time they would pray each day for world revival and the global harvest of lost souls.

The picture of commitment was beautiful. I was seeing it in advance of it actually happening, but with spiritual eyes. What I saw was "tangible worship." But I wondered how it would happen. My mental questions were quickly answered as God quietly spoke, "I am going to ask everyone present to make a sacrifice, and as they listen and obey, you will see a miracle."

I was excited as I prayed. I knew God had intervened with His own personal plan. Something wonderful was going to happen that night.

But God was not finished speaking. I was momentarily caught off guard as He declared, "But I will not ask those present to sacrifice what they have, nor will I bless as I have promised, if you are not willing to give all you have."

All that I have? What could that possibly mean? I had little, if anything. I still lacked even my airfare.

Then it hit me. I'd never made a lengthy trip like this from home without purchasing our two-year-old daughter at least some kind of an inexpensive gift. Usually while waiting for a plane connection, I would buy some little trinket or small stuffed animal. And Dena had come to expect these gifts of love when Daddy returned. I just couldn't go back empty-handed. So that's why my prayer went something like this:

I'll give You all I have, Lord, if You'll just let me keep a dollar or two to buy Dena some small gift. It won't be much, maybe a little stuffed mouse or child's necklace—something small. I promise.

God's response penetrated my spirit. He wanted to know if I was truly willing to give all. And did I love Him more than even my daughter? (Much later I would learn that the more one loves God, the more that person will love others, including his spouse or children. To love God the most is to love others more!)

"God, that's a ridiculous question," I responded. "You know I love You more than anyone!" I fired back.

"If you love Me, then you will give all. And if you give all, I will bless you in return with, first, a miracle tonight, and second, new love for your daughter and others unlike anything you have previously imagined."

The passing seconds seemed like hours. It was difficult releasing the grip my heart held for our two-year-old daughter.

Suddenly God spoke again. "And if you will obey Me, then you can expect those present tonight to obey Me. Only then will I do for you what I said I would do."

As abruptly as the whole thing began, I made my decision. Everything in life had to be secondary to my heavenly Father. Everything! He meant more to me than anything in the world.

Holding all my money tight in hand, I lifted it heavenward and dedicated it to God. The inner battle that had lasted a mere five minutes was over. I knew immediately God would do a lasting work in that night's rally. So I sang Numbers 23:19 in that small church classroom and returned to the main auditorium in preparation for the service.

If the previous night was one to remember, this night could be labeled historic. The crowd exceeded fifteen hundred, with people sitting in every available space, even on the floor along the walls. Then, as the rally concluded, teens were standing everywhere worshiping the Lord. Almost immediately God was speaking by His Spirit, exactly as promised. I merely told the crowd we would wait to see what God would do. "If He instructs you to do something, simply obey Him," I suggested. But I never told them God was going to take up the offering.

Then it happened. It started with one teenager, perhaps thirteen years old, who came forward and dropped something on the carpeted area in front of the altar. I couldn't tell what it was. It might have been his hamburger money. Soon young people began coming forward from all parts of the auditorium, dropping their gifts as they passed. Hundreds came. Many adults present also joined in this unusual act of worship in giving.

During the course of the evening I too dropped my gift on the platform. It was all the money I had. I would go home penniless. I told no one I was doing this. I purposely waited until others had done so, not wanting to suggest they sacrifice just because the preacher did. Everything had to be done out of pure obedience to the Spirit's leading. As scores of teens began marching, I carefully explained that the proceeds were not for me. We made it clear that the committee of ministers who organized the event would pray over these gifts and determine what to do with them.

After the stage area was cleared that night, almost two thousand dollars had been accumulated. It was a miracle of obedience and commitment. And once again we had witnessed the unorthodox. The words declared in Luke's Gospel seemed so appropriate: "We have seen strange things to day" (Luke 5:26, KJV). And as in Luke's day, these strange occurrences brought glory to Jesus.

Many long-standing idols disappeared from the hearts of young people as they crossed the platform that night in obedience to God. Hundreds departed the auditorium ready to embark on a new life of exciting discipleship. And as for me, I was about to see the fulfillment of God's promise made during my private time of prayer earlier that day. I was soon to find that new love not only for my daughter but also for lost souls everywhere. That had been at the heart of God's promise that afternoon.

An Episode of Love

It was cold and blustery as I left Detroit. But I was excited. There was so much to tell everyone back home. Arriving in Sacramento, however, I discovered a rather sad state of affairs. I had expected to throw my arms around my daughter and explain all the wonderful things that had happened.

But it wasn't that way at all. Entering the house I found my wife standing by the kitchen sink in tears. Dena was seated at the dining room table fulfilling every description ascribed to her age group. She was two and was being terrible! She had poured cereal all over the table and the floor. Kool-Aid was splattered everywhere. And she was frantically beating on the table with her spoon.

By now I had forgotten the high points of the weekend meetings, including God's promise to me during that afternoon prayer time. My real concern was for Dee. Everything seemed to be pressuring us mercilessly as we ventured into our new calling. Dee was most distressed about finances, and I couldn't blame her. There was no indication where the money would come from. On top of all this, Dena was suddenly a bundle of nervous energy. And Satan was standing in the wings, taking advantage of every situation.

My immediate reaction was anger. I walked sharply over to Dena and spoke with a firmness just below a shout. To be honest, I yelled. The sixty-second verbal correction was uncalled for, but I was exhausted and deeply concerned for the emotional state of my pregnant wife. Dena was crushed—first, by the fact that her daddy hadn't brought her the usual gift, and second, by my reaction to all that was happening in our household.

Dena was now weeping uncontrollably. Behind me, in the kitchen, Dee was shaking her head disdainfully, also in tears. Then I remembered. Today was supposed to be a day of a new, fresh love for my daughter. But instead I had conveyed the opposite. So I too started to cry. It was quite a sight, a house of tears.

Embarrassed to have Dee see me crying, I took Dena into her bedroom, where we sat together under her pink-canopied bed. She continued to cry as I fought back the tears. There was a sudden, strange closeness between father and daughter. I held my daughter at arm's length, speaking softly. "Dena, Daddy is sorry. He is very sorry. You must know that I love you more than ever. You've got to know that."

I thought she might be too young to understand, but she responded immediately. Throwing both arms around my neck, she started patting me on the back with her right hand. It was an experience I could never forget. I sensed how it must be when depraved man reaches up and puts his spiritual arms around a holy God, loving Him as my child loved me in that memorable moment. Then, quietly but powerfully, God whispered in my heart, "Here is the love I promised you."

In the days following God elected to teach a final lesson surrounding this entire episode of love. He wanted us to learn He was indeed our provider, the source of all we would need and desire in the days ahead.

Abraham, His Ram—Dick, His Pig

Late one evening the following week, I decided to stop at our office and pick up the mail. Entering the darkened room, I was startled by the presence of a large box resting in the middle of the floor. It was addressed to me, with a return address indicating it was from Detroit. I quickly opened the huge box, discovering a large green garbage bag inside. Lifting the huge bag from the box, I reached for a pair of scissors on my desk and with a quick snip opened the bag.

I couldn't believe what I saw. Inside was a huge, stuffed purple pig. It was given by a teenager in Detroit who felt impressed of God to purchase a special gift for my daughter. Sometime during my speaking in Detroit, I had mentioned Dena. This teen remembered those remarks, and God used them to speak to her heart. And according to the note that accompanied the pig, this heavenly directive came to her the very night God had promised me a new love for my daughter—if I would but sacrifice a simple dollar-or-two trinket. Now God was returning a much more memorable gift that would forever hold a powerful prophetic significance.

Hurrying from my office to show Dee, I felt like a child with a new toy. I could think only of Abraham as he put Isaac on the altar (Gen. 22). Abraham held his sharpened blade in hand, ready to sacrifice his only son. But God saw the true heart of Abraham. It all had been a mere test. Suddenly, the angel spoke, "Now I know that you fear God" (Gen. 22:12). Abraham was abruptly halted in the act of sacrificing his only son. But a sacrifice was still needed. Turning from the altar, father and son discovered a ram caught in the bushes. So they named the place Jehovah Jireh, meaning "the Lord will provide."

I rushed home with the pig. It was sitting beside me in the front seat of the car as I drove along, thinking of Abraham's experience with Isaac. God had seen my need and knew my desires. Not only had He supplied every need, but He also threw in a special love gift besides—the purple pig.

I rounded the corner of our street, Elton Court, and pulled into the driveway. Dee was as thrilled as I was about the thoughtfulness of God and the obedience of a sincere Detroit teenager. I never learned her name, as the gift and note were anonymous. Though it was late, I couldn't resist waking Dena and showing her the purple pig. I was anxious to observe her reaction to a stuffed animal as big as she was.

"Dena, get up. Your pig is here!" I shouted.

Dena sat straight up in bed. Her eyes shot open wide. I had placed the purple pig at the edge of her bed on the floor. Dena rolled out from under the covers and onto the floor in one elaborately executed leap.

"My pig! My pig!" she shouted, dancing around her new purple friend as if she knew all along that it was coming. In moments she was on its back, bouncing up and down as if riding a pony. Grabbing both its ears, Dena declared, "I love my pig, Daddy. This is a nice pig."

I slept well that night—drifting to sleep with a beautiful thought. Abraham had his ram; we had our pig. This was important to our infant ministry. With a new and somewhat frightening faith venture only days away, we had learned something invaluable. Jehovah provides!

Chapter 14
THE GREEN FROG

O NLY SEVEN DAYS REMAINED before we embarked on the new prayer ministry full-time. To this point I was attempting two jobs: one as youth minister and the other as Prayer Corps director. But that was soon to change, as the time was rapidly approaching to begin our first 24/7 prayer center.

During this time I was scheduled for another spiritual emphasis week at a Bible college in southern California. Here the moving of God's Spirit duplicated both Minneapolis and Detroit. Six months earlier, in Minneapolis, God had promised a new wave of commitment and discipleship. It had happened again in Detroit. I was about to witness it for a third time.

The unusual "sacrifice rally" occurred on the fourth night of the college-sponsored gathering. As a somewhat shaky sermon neared its conclusion, I asked the congregation of students and visitors to stand with me for quiet praise. Then we waited for the Holy Spirit to take action. I knew He was dealing with personal idols in the lives of many. Several rather long minutes passed as we all stood in solemn worship. I thought that perhaps this time little would happen. It was an eerie silence.

Then, quite unnoticed, a student slipped from the rear of the auditorium. Almost immediately, another left. Soon several more departed. I knew what was happening. They were not upset and leaving because they were angry, but conviction had settled and action was resulting.

Five minutes later the first student to leave returned, walking hurriedly down the side aisle carrying an expensive blue surfboard balanced on his head. Reaching the platform, he threw the board down sharply. Then both hands shot up. "Praise God! I'm free!" he shouted, as he bounded from the platform.

A second student now returned. Having no idea what the student before him had sacrificed, he too brought a surfboard, also brightly colored but with wild, psychedelic stripes.

In less than thirty minutes the platform was filled with would-be idols. Baseball gloves. Trophies. Radios. Stereos. Assorted rock records. Pictures of movie stars. And even whiskey bottles and packs of cigarettes. (And this was at a Bible college!) There was even a new wedding gown, something I didn't understand. Yet I knew God works in mysterious ways. Perhaps He was stopping something that in the future could have brought untold heartache. And one young couple returned an hour later carrying a brand-new television set. Both wept as they placed it on the altar. They later confessed it was taking up too much of their time and hindering their personal relationships with each other and their spiritual walk with God.

A young minister visiting from a neighboring community sat quietly in the auditorium observing these strange events. But before long he too was lost in prayer. By midnight God was dealing deeply with his heart. He left the auditorium and headed home. The following morning he was back. Hitched to his car was a shiny sailboat. Inside the sailboat a motorcycle was carefully tied down. He handed both ownership titles to the college president. Then he explained what happened: "Last night God promised me a double portion of His Spirit. All I had to do was remove those idols of my life that were taking up so much of my time. I had no choice but to go straight home and get my boat and cycle."

As the powerful wave of sacrifice came to its conclusion, I had a strange feeling about several of the items placed on the platform. I saw some of them as "little Isaacs." As mentioned earlier, God asked Abraham to sacrifice Isaac as a test. He was allowed to have Isaac back only when he passed the test. I knew some of the items given were part of a God-sent test. I particularly wondered about the significance of a toolbox.

So, the following day I encouraged students to take back items if they felt the worship of that item no longer existed. In some cases students actually bought back such items for a price, the money eventually going for a campus project. One student had given his Bible merely because God asked him to put that which he loved most on the altar. Out of simple obedience he acted. Later, he retrieved his Bible from the platform, leaving a ninety-five-dollar check in its place. He had emptied his entire savings account for his own Bible. I, like others, questioned the incident—at least until I realized how much the young student would appreciate God's Word from that point on. How could this student ever forget the night he bought his own Bible back for ninety-five dollars?

And then there was that toolbox. An older student who looked to be in his thirties came to the platform and picked up the toolbox. He quickly explained to the crowd why he had placed this on the altar the night before. I had no idea why some of the student body recognized him. I could only tell that they must have known him from their reaction.

"Many of you know me," he said. "I'm the guy who fixes most of your cars when they break down. I was a mechanic before God called me to Bible school, so this was easy for me. You thought I was giving you a good deal for what I charged you compared to other mechanics. But I've charged you all way too much. This has become a profitable business for me."

He wiped away tears as he continued. "From now on I'm going to use these tools to fix your cars for free! And that includes any student here."

This clearly was an Isaac sacrifice. Some items, however, could not be considered "little Isaacs." They were more like "little Jerichos"! These are idols that must come down. And one such item—brought by a young coed—was a fluffy green frog. The girl remarked during testimony time that she could never take it back. It would forever be an idol to her even if she paid a price. It had stood too long between her and God.

I listened attentively as the student shared her testimony. Suddenly I felt an unusual impression. "Take the frog home to Dena. It will remind you of this unusual night of miracles. You can put it beside the pig."

"That's a great idea," I thought, reaching for the large stuffed frog. But it wasn't quite that easy.

Almost immediately God impressed me further, "That will be one hundred dollars, please."

"One hundred dollars? Why, that's ridiculous," I thought. "After all, the pig was free, and I could buy a stuffed frog like this for fifteen dollars at Toys 'R' Us."

For a moment I thought it might be "self" speaking. But a wise Bible teacher later corrected me on this account. She testified, "Neither self nor Satan ever asks anyone to give money to the work of the Lord." So, if I wanted the frog, I had to pay the price. I paid the one hundred dollars to the college and took the frog. It would serve as a reminder of the constant price that must be paid if we want to give our all to serve Jesus, something important for me to understand for what lay ahead.

I returned home with the hundred-dollar frog. As I had imagined, Dena loved it. The frog was almost as big as the pig and soon took its place beside the purple pig at the foot of Dena's bed.

The following day, Sunday, was my final day as an associate pastor at the church I had served for almost five years. On Monday our faith venture was to begin.

It was a different feeling Monday morning as I stood beside our relatively new automobile purchased just six months earlier. I wondered if we would be able to keep it. I thought the same about our home. Standing alone in the garage, I was mentally calculating what we would need to maintain our home and keep the Prayer Corps ministry going. Naïvely I remarked to myself, "If we can just pray in one thousand dollars a month, we'll make it."

Our first month's budget exceeded my early estimates considerably—by five thousand dollars. But God gloriously supplied, though looking back still brings chills. In fact, I have often jokingly told congregations, "Had I known on March 5 that our first month's budget would require five times as much money as I'd anticipated, I would've checked into a local hospital March 6 to have a nervous breakdown in advance, by faith."

During the next ninety days things happened fast. At least, looking in retrospect, they happened fast. At the time everything seemed terribly slow. A new date was set for opening our first prayer center. This time it was March 15. But this date—like our earlier deadline on January 15—passed without indication of a possible building. Word filtered back that even close friends questioned our new venture. At times I even wondered if the whole idea might be a mere pipe dream.

Three weeks later, a young couple arrived from Detroit. John and Cheryl Sterner came with three young children. The Sterners had packed their belongings by faith and moved all the way to California. John was, in his own words, a Presbyterian-turned-Methodist-turned-Charismatic. I didn't care what they were if they loved Jesus. He and his wife clearly radiated the love of Christ. Their children too seemed to have a special touch of God's Spirit upon them.

John was in town only a day when a local businessman who was helping us gave him the task of finding us a building. I was out of town, and this businessman from our church had an important business obligation. Knowing nothing about Sacramento, John had only one recourse—prayer. He asked God to lead him as he opened to the housing section of a Sacramento paper. He began turning pages, looking for the biggest real estate advertisement he could find. Suddenly, it lay before him. He reached for the phone and dialed. Answering the phone was a congenial realtor who listened attentively to John as he described our needs. Almost immediately the man interrupted, "This couldn't possibly be the Prayer Corps ministry you're talking about?"

"Why, uh, yes, as a matter of fact it is," John answered.

It was soon revealed that the realtor attended our church and was well aware of our new ministry, though he had no idea we needed a building. "I have exactly what you need," he answered. "I'll show it to you this afternoon."

Several days later, I stood before the large wood frame building on O Street near downtown Sacramento. It was only blocks from our state capitol. The house was strangely similar to what I had seen in my earlier vision of our coming Fire House. It had all we needed: four separate apartments, several baths, room for a large kitchen, plenty of dining space, and a very large backyard that could eventually become a "Garden of Gethsemane" where corps members and guests could read their Bibles and worship the Lord. Most importantly, the building was in an estate controlled by the State of California, and the asking price was only $22,000, though it was valued at almost double the price. (Today the property, because of its location, would be worth $500,000 or even more.)

The whole thing was an incredible miracle. Only two weeks earlier this business friend and I had left a one-thousand-dollar deposit with another realtor on a property three times as costly. An elderly couple wanted $68,000 for the building, and we offered $58,000. It was our first offer, and we were ready to increase it if necessary.

After making the deposit, I returned home to pray over the matter. God impressed me to open my Bible for further direction. I opened immediately to 2 Chronicles 25:9, where eleven powerful words leaped from the page: "The LORD is able to give you much more than this" (NKJV).

I, of course, thought this scripture meant God would give us the $68,000 house, and even more. One can imagine my dismay when the owners decided to keep the property. They decided not to sell for any price.

But now, looking at our new facility, it all made sense. The property I was gazing at would cost us only $125 in monthly payments, plus taxes. It was a full one-fourth less than the other property, though the house actually had more accommodating facilities. The location too was much better. And the zoning was commercial. It was ideal.

Looking back at the entire incident, the promise of 2 Chronicles 25:9 was remarkably true: "The LORD is able to give you much more than this." God had spoken, and the blessing was ours.

We began the tedious task of closing the deal. This took more than a month.

Meanwhile, another young couple, Larry and Dotty Krake, arrived from Santa Cruz, California, where they had been attending Bible college. They had agreed to help direct Fire House Number One for at least two years. Two additional couples helped begin that first center: the Sterners from Detroit, whom I mentioned earlier, and Dale and Beth Decker from Hawaii. The Deckers would later take the vision to Hawaii to establish a fire house on the island of Oahu.

By mid-May the couples and corps members began moving into the rambling house on O Street, which had to be renovated to serve the needs of the new ministry. This took several weeks.

More than once we had to sit down and redefine our reason for being. Our primary function was prayer. Thus the Gap had to be established at once. A careful look through the house revealed that no single room was suitable for the Gap. It was agreed that the best place for the prayer room was the basement. There was, however, no actual basement in the house—just a small area where a person could stand if stooped over.

Thus, step number one was to carve out a basement and build a "made to order" Gap. In the meantime, twenty-four-hour prayer would continue in a temporary Gap near an upstairs apartment.

Both spiritual and physical labor continued. Those not praying were digging. Those not digging were hauling. (It reminded me of the Book of Nehemiah.) And we rejoiced to learn that Dale Decker from Hawaii was a journeyman carpenter. He was, of course, unanimously elected to be our foreman. (I couldn't pound a nail without hurting myself!)

It took two weeks to lay the Gap foundation in the newly carved out basement. Several feet of hard clay had to be broken up with picks. The forms had to be laid for the pouring of cement. It was also necessary to cut a hole in the floor just inside the front door to build a stairway to the Gap.

A month later the room was completed. It was a masterpiece of design, considering it was built totally by the hands of us novices—plus Dale! Dale and Larry put in all the finishing touches: indirect lighting, special wood paneling, and attractive side benches for kneeling. Beautiful orange shag carpet (shag carpet was the "in thing" in those days) was installed by a friend. Two blackboards were attached to the walls. One had painted on it "Prayer Request Board" and the other, "Victory Board." Two telephone lines were installed for urgent prayer calls. And a special spotlight in the middle of the ceiling illuminated the globe on a round table just below it. I had seen all this in my initial vision. On the entry door was attached a sign, painted by one of the members, that read *The Gap*. Below were these words from Ezekiel 22:30: "And I sought for a man among them, that should make up the hedge, and stand in the gap before me for the land..." (KJV). The "but I found none" part of that verse was left off because there would always be someone "standing in the Gap" here at Fire House Number One!

That day twenty-four-hour prayer for worldwide revival and the harvest of millions of souls began in the new Gap. It continued year after year: 168 hours weekly, 672 hours monthly, 8,736 hours annually. Christmas Eve young intercessors were praying. Easter found them praying—holidays were no exception. Every hour, day and night, someone was "standing in the Gap, making up the hedge." Some believed it was the first such 24/7 youth prayer ministry ever. The vision of the previous November was now being fulfilled.

Fire House Number One was now more than a sketch on paper or a casual dream. The cream of the crop of young people had joined our fine resident couple, along with the two couples in training, for an entirely new adventure. Each had paid a price in coming. None knew completely what they were getting into; it was all so new. But the army was finally marching.

And the prayer soon began ushering in a variety of small miracles. Linoleum was needed for the kitchen floor. So our young intercessors prayed for linoleum. And a short time later, while several of the team had slipped out for hamburgers, someone slipped in with a large roll of linoleum. It was exactly what was required. And it was left in the kitchen, exactly where it was needed. We never knew who brought it.

Drinking glasses were needed to serve the twenty residents of the center, so the girls prayed, asking specifically for green and gold plastic glasses. I'm not sure why that specific color. It seemed a rather naïve prayer. But it was sincere. The following day a large box arrived with many items included. A big paper sack was pulled from the box containing a large supply of plastic glasses. They were colored green and gold. Go figure!

July is hot in Sacramento. And this year was no exception. I thought of the corps members across town in the sweltering prayer center on O Street. Dee, Dena, our two-month-old infant, Ginger, and I still lived on Elton Court. It was late as I tucked Dena into bed. It wasn't often that Daddy was home and able to share in Dena's prayers. Moments earlier

I had slipped into Ginger's room and breathed a quiet prayer at the side of her crib. "Baby Ginger" was now a vital part of our household. She arrived the same month our first center opened.

"God, You've been gracious," I prayed softly as I tiptoed carefully from Dena's darkened room. The night-light cast a shadowy glow across the foot of her bed. There they were—both of them—looking up at me and smiling—the purple pig and the green frog. Stuffed animals don't talk (except in *Toy Story*!), but these seemed to have a special message. They were saying, "Jesus never fails."

Chapter 15
TIMOTHY TIGER

FIRE HOUSE NUMBER ONE was celebrating its six-month birthday as Dee and I sat in the airplane preparing to take off for London. Plans to visit Europe and share the vision of the new prayer ministry excited me, though it was only a few days earlier that doors had opened to take Dee. Previously it had seemed out of the question for both of us to go, especially considering the tremendous cost involved. But as usual, God provided a miracle.

Here's how it all happened. Most of early fall was spent ministering away from home, and I was looking forward to a week off before embarking on the lengthy trip overseas. I came home on a Saturday afternoon, exhausted from a month-long series of meetings. I was greeted with a kiss and a message to call the president of a Midwest college. While in prayer, he had felt led to call me concerning a spiritual emphasis week scheduled at the college just two weeks later. It was during the very time I had planned to rest. My first reaction was a categorical no. However, a voice within reminded me I hadn't really prayed over the matter.

Alone in our bedroom, I prayerfully considered the situation. I rehearsed events of the extremely busy month just completed and the activities planned for the following month in Europe. I was exhausted as I thought it through. I quickly reasoned, "I've been away from my wife for too long already. It just isn't fair. But what if Dee could go with me to Europe?" I mused.

It was a nice thought, but it had to be erased from my mind—there simply wasn't enough money.

As I lay on the bed thinking, I couldn't dismiss the desire to visit another college campus. I had seen more lasting fruit among Bible college students than in any other personal ministry. Out of these students come our future ministers and missionaries. If they learn to pray with passion, anything can happen.

Visiting the college seemed the thing to do. Then, in lieu of my being home for that week, we would trust God to provide finances for Dee to travel with me to Europe.

I prayed quietly for a moment and called Dee into the room. I explained my idea. She was excited about the thought of going with me to Europe but reminded me of our lack of finances. We finally agreed we would trust God to provide, and I returned the call to the college president confirming that I would come for the weeklong series of meetings.

Little did I realize a lone prayer warrior had been praying for us at our prayer center that very day. For several hours she had only a single prayer on her heart—that Dee would be able to take the trip with me to Europe. It was a most unusual prayer, especially since no one knew we were both anticipating going—except the Holy Spirit.

Three days later a check arrived in the mail from a totally unexpected source, designated specifically for Dee and me personally. It totaled Dee's exact airfare, plus ten dollars. Both of us would be able to make the trip. But first I had to fulfill my speaking engagement at that college in the Midwest.

The Miracle School

In a matter of days, I was greeted with the freezing winds of an early North Dakota winter. Though it was only October, the temperature had already dipped to just ten degrees above zero.

On the college campus of Trinity Bible Institute in Ellendale, North Dakota, I was met with a modern-day miracle. Facilities there were valued well in excess of four million dollars, though the Bible school purchased the property for just one dollar from the state of North Dakota. It required a constitutional amendment by the legislature of North Dakota to release the property—which had once been a state teacher's college—to this Christian institute.

It was almost impossible to believe. Rising near the entrance to the forty-acre campus was the new men's dormitory. It is just one of twenty buildings on the campus and cost almost a half-million dollars to build. Amazingly, the state legislature of North Dakota had to allocate funds totaling $350,000 to pay off the original debt on that dormitory before they could sell the entire campus to Trinity for a dollar. God is amazing! The building was only a year old at the time of the miracle purchase.

Dr. Roy Wead, president of the college, shared some of the details of the miracle with me. At their previous campus, according to Dr. Wead, it was a rarity to secure funds for such things as a new IBM typewriter, which would cost six hundred dollars. In fact, their college administrative office owned just two typewriters at that time. (This was long before the age of computers.) When arriving at the new campus, however, the excited staff of Trinity's teachers discovered thirty brand-new IBM typewriters as part of the personal property.

Another extraordinary miracle involved the college library. Five years earlier the state added thirty thousand volumes to bring the Ellendale teacher's college library into alignment with those of other state schools. The increase actually made it the largest library in the state, thus giving Trinity Bible Institute one of the finest libraries of any Bible college in the Midwest. Originally Trinity had only a two-thousand-volume library. Now its library exceeds sixty thousand volumes.

Trinity was indeed a miracle. But God brought us to the campus to see a special "spiritual" miracle. We were to witness an extraordinary manifestation of God's power and glory.

Go Will Do it Again

By Wednesday afternoon, three days into the spiritual renewal emphasis, it was obvious God wished to move in a deeply stirring manner. My instructions received during personal prayer that afternoon were clear: "Take the students out of the crowded chapel at the conclusion of the service, and lead them to the large adjacent gymnasium. There organize them into small, standing circles of six to eight persons each. Then pray for them one at a time as the disciples did in Acts 6, with the laying on of hands."

Though the plan was highly unorthodox, I followed it to the letter. (By now I had noticed how often God uses unorthodox methods to affect both believers and unbelievers deeply. Doing things differently takes a "whack" at our pride, and our pride is something that desperately needs "whacking.")

That night following my simple message three hundred students were led through a freezing North Dakota wind from the chapel to the gymnasium, where they began organizing in small circles. Immediately God's Spirit came. Many fell prostrate on the floor, insensible to their surroundings. It was reminiscent of revivals of a hundred years ago—like an old Methodist camp meeting. I know some question these things happening in our day, but I saw it with my own eyes. An unusual presence of the Lord had descended. Many worshiped for hours—some the entire night.

Soon conviction of personal idols settled on the meeting. John's admonition, "Dear children, keep away from anything that might take God's place in your hearts" (1 John 5:21, TLB), seemed to penetrate the consciences of many students.

The following morning a powerful wave of sacrifice surged across the campus. What had happened in Minneapolis, Detroit, and Southern California was happening again in North Dakota. A night of power and blessing led into a day of silent heart searching. Conviction was now taking effect in outward tangibles. As morning chapel concluded, students quietly waited before the Lord. Many began weeping; several left the auditorium. Several minutes had passed when two students returned. One, a young man about twenty years old, carried an expensive, well-polished shotgun. His testimony affected the entire congregation deeply.

"It may sound funny to you guys, but I've worshiped this shotgun. This morning God showed me how bad it had gotten. Lately I've even stopped praying and reading the Bible. When studies or circumstances got me down, I'd take my gun into the woods and actually talk to it. Honestly, I would talk to this stupid gun."

Then the broken student publicly apologized to faculty members for his poor grades. Likewise, he apologized publicly to God for his neglect of spiritual matters.

But especially moving was this student's public apology to his wife for spending more time with his shotgun than with her. Standing before several hundred students, including his wife, who also was present, the young husband begged for her forgiveness. His wife leaped to her feet and rushed toward him at the front of the chapel. Both embraced as tears flowed freely.

If bringing a shotgun to the altar seems slightly unorthodox, one can imagine my feelings when a student brought an old shoe and a tie. It seemed so out of place among the fur coats, transistor radios, expensive jewelry, and other valued items already lining the altar. The old shoe and tie looked like a joke. And until I heard the whole story, I had little idea how deeply the student was moved to make this unusual sacrifice.

While standing at the conclusion of the rally, the young student felt a powerful conviction of humility. Directed by the Holy Spirit, he walked to his room. There God impressed him to bring an offering of humility. He was instructed to bring the least valued items he possessed and place them on the altar. It was a very difficult thing for him to do, knowing that fellow students would be watching, especially considering the two least valued items he owned: a single shoe, the mate to which had been long lost, and an old narrow tie of 1955 vintage. When the student acted, however, an unusual anointing settled upon him. It had been a test of humility. And the moment he acted, Christ seemed to come in person and touch him. He had passed the test. His deep brokenness was evident to all.

Towering above the many items placed on the altar that unusual morning was an impressive orange-and-black stuffed tiger. I was elated when the student giving the huge tiger asked if I would like to take it home for my daughter. I knew Dena would be overjoyed. When the tiger arrived a day later, Dena and I were sitting alone in the family room looking at the huge stuffed beast. It was twice the size of the purple pig. I explained to young Dena that some nice friends at a Bible school far away loved her very much and sent it especially for her.

Based on Daddy's suggestion that the tiger have a Bible name, Dena quickly named him "Timothy," and he took his rightful place alongside the pig and the frog.

Late that night I slipped into my daughter's room to say another quiet prayer beside her bed. It was getting to be a wonderful habit. There was much here to remind me of God's goodness.

Dena had tucked Timothy Tiger under the covers beside her. At the foot of her bed sat the purple pig and the green frog. The pig spoke of the goodness of God to provide for every need. And the frog reminded me of the price paid for the promises of God.

Now, there was Timothy Tiger. He too had a message: *God will do it again.* The beautiful waves of discipleship and commitment can indeed be expected repeatedly until Jesus returns. And other miracles should also be anticipated. Christians everywhere, I felt, would soon crave a much closer walk with God. This move of God's Spirit, though sometimes misunderstood by those taught so long against such manifestations, would soon find even greater evidences that God wants to visit His people in unusual ways.

I could literally feel these prophetic promises being answered as the prayer continued hour after hour and day after day in the Gap at our newly established prayer center. Already five thousand prayer hours had been logged. And the Prayer Corps' beginning wasn't the only miracle we had witnessed. Other things began happening. There was still a freshness and excitement about it all. I could sense it as never before. A new visitation of God was just around the corner.

Part Five
THE OTHER MIRACLES

Chapter 16
MOSES AND ME

IT WAS FOGGY WHEN Air France flight 926 landed in Brussels. My brother, Don, flew in from Chicago, and together we visited our cousin Sandi, who was then serving on the staff of Continental Bible College—a newly established European Bible institute in Belgium. After several days of planning, God put it on our hearts to take a trip behind the then iron curtain. There, opportunity would come to share the new Prayer Corps vision in an area of the world so desperately in need of prayer.

Before leaving Brussels for the lengthy automobile journey, I had several days to reflect on the first eleven months of our young prayer ministry. So many exciting miracles had already happened. And through it all, a most essential area had been learning to hear God speak, a subject generally referred to as "divine guidance."

God's individual dealings with fallible man are, of course, nothing new. Anyone with faint knowledge of Scripture realizes God spoke to people in ages past. There were the patriarchs, the prophets, and the apostles. But these people—as some of us were unfortunately taught in Sunday school—are thought of as unique human beings, selected as choice "spiritual giants" who achieved such a high plane of pious living that they actually earned the right to talk with God. And get replies.

Further (as some of us also remember being taught) these supernatural dealings are supposed to have disappeared with the canonization of Scripture—when the Holy Bible as we know it was completed. Therefore we don't need such personal communication. We only need to read our Bibles.

With this in mind, it is easy to see why I was shocked—though thrilled—to learn that God still talks to people today. Frankly, all the fundamental biblical principles of heavenly guidance are of little value if we cannot believe that God still communicates to His children today—in very specific ways—just as He did centuries ago.

A quick look at Scripture readily reveals numerous ways God has spoken to people in the past. We could briefly mention just a few.

For one, God has used angels to convey His messages. One of many examples is found in Daniel 10, when an angel brought Daniel a long-awaited answer to prayer.

Reading the Book of Daniel also points out the manner in which God has used dreams to speak to men. Consider also the use of visions. In Acts 16, Paul is guided to Macedonia by a heaven-sent vision he experienced in the night.

Scripture is also replete with instances of God's speaking directly to men using an audible voice. Saul of Tarsus, before his name was changed to Paul, heard an audible voice on the Damascus road (Acts 9:4).

And what about God's Word itself—the Bible? Every page has its special message from God. The Holy Bible is, in fact, our criterion for all that we discuss within these pages. After all, it is from Scripture that we first learn God has talked with men in the past. And Scripture is where we learn how He has spoken. The Bible, in its simplest definition, is God speaking to man. In this regard I wholly agree with those who say that Scripture is our primary means of divine guidance. (See chapter 19, "Romancing the Word.")

There is, however, another manner in which God speaks today. I refer to God's "still, small voice" spoken of in 1 Kings 19. Elijah had fled the insane queen, Jezebel, and was in hiding, hoping to die, when the angel of the Lord brought God's message with the accompanying phenomena of wind, fire, and even an earthquake. Scripture clearly states that God's message was in none of these manifestations, though His presence no doubt caused them. Moments later, however, God elected to speak softly. It was a peaceful "still small voice" (1 Kings 19:12, KJV), and though the Bible has always been and must always be our most important source of divine guidance, I have also come to appreciate God's still, small voice. Whether it is labeled a "heart impression" or just "heavenly thoughts," we still must acknowledge this to be the voice of God. Indeed God can—and does—speak to His children today.

Recognizing that God does speak today is only the first step in understanding divine guidance. It also becomes necessary to comprehend the second premise that God speaks from His dwelling place. Thus if we learn where God dwells, it will help us learn how to listen. In John's Gospel we read, "If you love me, you will obey what I command. And I will ask the Father, and he will give you another Counselor to be with you forever—the Spirit of truth. The world cannot accept him, because it neither sees him nor knows him. But you know him, for he lives with you and will be in you" (John 14:15–17).

Suddenly I saw it—a truth that would transform my understanding on the matter of hearing God's voice. It was simple though profound. The Holy Spirit had been with the disciples to this point in their experience. Soon, however, He would dwell within them. I pieced this together with such statements as, "The kingdom of God is within you" (Luke 17:21), and Paul's words, "Don't you know that you yourselves are God's temple and that God's Spirit lives in you?" (1 Cor. 3:16).

This, then, is the second basic principle in understanding divine guidance. *God lives within us.* Therefore we should expect to communicate with Him from where He lives—in our very hearts made possible by the work of the Holy Spirit. Some usually think of the voice of God merely in terms of audible sounds, when in reality hearing God speak can very often mean a quiet heart impression.

"But how do we listen?" some might ask. To many Christians, hearing the voice of God seems to be a mystical adventure—a rare encounter rather than an everyday experience. But listening to God's still, small voice is really not that difficult. Let me illustrate.

I could point to the sky and declare audibly, "The sky is blue." But I can also close my eyes and say quietly in my mind, "The sky is blue." The words said in my mind are as clear and distinct as those spoken audibly. I heard them. They were real words, though not audible. This is how the still, small voice of God very often comes. In a sense, it is a quiet thought or impression that flows out of one's heart and into his or her mind.

Going even deeper into Scripture, I discovered a third basic to understanding divine guidance.

We all have a right to hear God speak. Jesus Himself made this crystal clear. It is our privilege as well as our responsibility to hear His voice. Scripture declares, "And when he [referring to Jesus] brings out his own sheep, he goes before them; and the sheep follow him, for they know his voice" (John 10:4, nkjv). Christ later explains, "My sheep hear my voice, and I know them, and they follow Me" (v. 27, nkjv).

As I continued my search, I was reminded of Moses in his communication with God. (See Exodus 33.) The Bible says, "The Lord would speak to Moses face to face, as a man speaks with his friend. Then Moses would return to the camp, but his young aide Joshua son of Nun did not leave the tent" (Exod. 33:11). The two would talk conversationally. God would speak and Moses answered. Then Moses spoke and God answered.

As I studied this passage, a beautiful thought occurred. There was something I had in common with Moses. I too could talk to God conversationally as a friend. I had a right to hear God speak. It is the right, I concluded, of every believer.

There is, however, a final essential aspect concerning divine guidance. *When hearing God speak, we must act upon that which is spoken.*

"'Obey me,' says the Lord, 'so I can do for you the wonderful things I swore I would if you obeyed'" (Jer. 11:5, TLB). This was the powerful command of God given to Jeremiah. And we cannot reject it as mere Old Testament teaching. The message is as clear today.

It was at a prayer retreat in those early days that God taught me the importance of taking action when He speaks. Opening my Bible to a random chapter in Ecclesiastes, I began reading, "Dreaming instead of doing is foolishness" (Eccles. 5:7, TLB). The time had come, I realized, that Christians must act when God gives them direction. Dreaming alone has never accomplished a thing. Isaiah's words stress a similar truth: "Your ears shall hear a word behind you, saying, 'This is the way, walk in it,' whenever you turn to the right hand or whenever you turn to the left" (Isa. 30:21, NKJV). We must act when we receive a directive from the Lord.

So, as the Prayer Corps ministry increased in scope and vision, I found myself constantly learning new things about divine guidance and hearing God's voice. The four major aspects of guidance were now clear: (1) God does speak to people today. (2) He speaks from His dwelling place, the heart of His children. (3) Further, it is our right to experience divine guidance. (4) Finally, what God instructs us to do we must carry out.

But lessons on divine guidance are certainly not without potential problems or questions. The most frequent question is usually this: How can we be perfectly certain it is really God's voice we are hearing?

This is a valid question. Most students of the Word are aware of the three voices a Christian might encounter when seeking guidance. For one, there is *the voice of self.* In my experience, this voice seems to cause most of our problems in the matter of seeking divine guidance. A young man may ask God if it might be permissible to marry the prettiest girl in his church. At once he hears a clear yes in his mind. But it could well be "self" answering rather than God. And the lad might end up embarrassed and bewildered before the incident is over.

We must also be on guard against *the voice of Satan,* our enemy. If we are not careful, Satan may attempt to convince a Christian that it is actually God who is doing the speaking. We must watch carefully for this second voice, learning to discern it and refusing to listen when it comes.

Last, there is the voice the follower of Jesus wishes to hear: *the voice of God.* Believers sometimes find great difficulty in responding to this latter voice because God's will may sometimes differ from man's will.

Concerning these three possible sources from which direction may come, it is certainly necessary to determine when we may be receiving deceitful directions. Thus, even before we allow ourselves to listen mentally, we must rid ourselves of the two destructive voices that might possibly come—those of Satan and self.

The Bible gives us complete authority over Satan if we will only resist him. Scripture declares, "Resist the devil, and he will flee from you" (James 4:7). This, of course, can only be done after we meet the qualification stated just prior to these words recorded by James: "Submit yourselves, then, to God." Our prayer for guidance, then, begins first with total submission to God and His will, followed by a verbal resistance of Satan.

The second deadly voice—that of self—is equally deceitful. To rid ourselves of self in prayer, it is necessary to nail all personal wishes to the cross of commitment. Then, as we pray, our minds must shift to "neutral" concerning a given request. (The self voice is actually dealt with at the very beginning when we submit everything we have to God, as explained in the above verse in James.)

In the earlier illustration I spoke of a young man who might desire the prettiest girl at church and asked God if it were permissible to marry her. As you recall, the yes answer was probably more of self than God. The lad actually wanted to hear yes and therefore said yes to himself. This, of course, is clearly a dangerous way of seeking divine guidance. The youth's initial attitude should have been one of complete submission. He should have prayed until it didn't matter whether or not he married that attractive girl or not. Only then would he be truly ready to ask God for specific guidance in the matter. (Please note how God dealt with me regarding Dee, as I described much earlier in this book. When I felt God was saying, "I'm taking care of it now," I waited for it to happen. I didn't force it to happen.)

When the voices of Satan and self are disposed of, it means the next voice we hear is that of God's. After all, we have followed a biblical plan of resisting Satan and self, and we can expect God to keep His promise to direct us.

Gazing back at those early months of developing the Prayer Corps, my daily journal includes some twenty-five instances where specific guidance or encouragement came in answer to specific prayer. Several of these instances have already been shared. Hearing the voice of God—to us in the Prayer Corps—had truly become one of the "other miracles" in our new ministry. Those going into the Gap always found God close enough to converse with. Indeed, His will soon became more than just a vague generality. God would actually speak to those who would listen and willingly obey. And this fellowship with God, after all, is the height of spiritual intimacy and the key to discerning the voice of God.

Chapter 17

I SEE JESUS

THOUGH MANY EXCITING NEW spiritual delights came during the formative years of the Prayer Corps, one prayer miracle in particular concerned visions—specifically, visions of Jesus. For centuries God has promised such unusual visitations, as the prophet Joel bears out: "And afterward, I will pour out my Spirit on all people. Your sons and daughters will prophesy, your old men will dream dreams, your young men will see visions" (Joel 2:28).

While recording the first exciting months of our new prayer ministry on paper, I recalled the previous summer when I slipped away from the heavy schedule in Sacramento for a month's ministry in Texas. Here I observed yet another indication that we could expect the supernatural in answer to prayer, exactly as Joel had predicted.

A highlight of this busy month in Texas was a two-day Prayer Explosion (a weekend prayer retreat) attended by over two hundred Texas teenagers. They came for nothing but prayer and praise.

At two o'clock that Saturday morning an unusual flow of the Holy Spirit settled on the crowd of young people who were sitting expectantly on the floor. Suddenly they were standing in unison. Hands lifted quickly in praise. No earthly leader directed them. I had not suggested they do this. It was spontaneous. Then the crowd began singing softly the age-old anthem "All Hail the Power of Jesus' Name." As participants continued singing, the song increased in volume.

Soon the zealous young prayer warriors were clapping their hands in praise. It sounded like thunder as I watched in awe. Ten feet to my right, a sixteen-year-old crumpled to the floor—insensible to her surroundings. "Had she fainted?" I wondered. But I quickly learned she was simply overcome with God's presence. Soon the entire place was filled with the glory of God.

Later, after this amazing time, the young girl shared her testimony. She explained, "All of a sudden I was standing praising God with everyone else. We all were standing and praising God and singing about

Jesus. I opened my eyes—just for a moment—and couldn't believe what I saw. Jesus had walked right into the room. He was actually here. I couldn't even stand on my feet. I fell to the floor. His glory was just too beautiful."

I suppose psychiatrists might label such occurrences as religiously delusional. Others might respond, "Well, anything can happen when young people are driven to such high levels of emotionalism." But I was there, and I know this was not the case.

It is my opinion that this girl really saw Jesus. Too many instances have been recorded involving well-balanced young people of the highest caliber who testify to similar encounters. And often there has been little display of emotion at all prior to such visible demonstrations of God's glory, just a keen sense of God's presence.

Years later after becoming president of Every Home for Christ, I would hear a similar account from a veteran leader in our ministry, Fred Creighton of New Zealand. It happened while Fred was serving as senior pastor of Hamilton Central Baptist Church, one of the largest Baptist churches in his nation. During a time of prayer with another of our EHC leaders who was visiting him at the time, Fred had this unusual encounter:

> I do not recall any great emotion leading up to this event...it just happened suddenly and unexpectedly. I looked and saw Jesus bending over me as I bowed before Him. He was dressed as I have often seen Him in pictures as the Good Shepherd. There flowed from Him what I can only describe as love incomprehensible. As I bowed before Jesus, one word pulsated through my entire being. It was the word "Shepherd." Three times this "commissioning" word flowed through me. These were moments beyond description. In this encounter I was commissioned by the Lord Himself. So vivid was this experience that I had no option but to share it with the elders of Hamilton Central Baptist Church. They had no doubt that I had met the Lord and received a new commissioning. Their response was, "We cannot keep you here; we must release you."

Fred and his wife, Fran, were soon commissioned by the church as missionaries to the nations and under the continuing covering of their congregation have served twenty-seven years in a full-time capacity with EHC. True to his calling by Christ Himself to be a "shepherd," Fred, with his wife, Fran, continues to serve as an anointed shepherd to our global

EHC leadership team. And it all began with a vision of Christ Himself!

At a Midwest spiritual renewal campaign I conducted during our Prayer Corps days, another stirring account illustrated the power of a vision of Jesus. The vision came to a young mother who had tragically lost her three-year-old son earlier that year. God had touched her in the meeting, and for more than an hour she was deep in worship. The mother shared her stirring story.

> I was lost in the presence of the Holy Spirit when I heard a voice calling me. It was the most beautiful voice I'd ever heard. I opened my eyes and saw Jesus surrounded by little children. He asked, "What do you see, My child?" I answered, "I see You, Jesus, and many little children."
>
> I was surprised when Jesus spoke again. He said, "No, My child, you must come closer." So I came closer and stopped. Then He asked the same question again: "What do you see?" So I answered one more time, "I see You, Jesus, and many little children."
>
> I was startled when Jesus told me to come even closer. He motioned to me gently with His right hand. So I went as close as possible. By now I was just a few feet away. My eyes were glued to His face, and His eyes seemed to reach right out to me. Lifting His left arm slightly He asked, "Now what do you see?"
>
> I couldn't believe my eyes. Jesus was actually holding my little boy in His arm. It was real, not just my imagination. And my son was smiling; he looked so happy. That's when Jesus spoke again. "I am taking care of your child until you can join him."
>
> When Jesus said those words the vision ended. I was back in the auditorium where I'd started. I had been with Jesus and my little boy.

How this happened to the young mother I cannot fully explain. But I do believe she actually saw Jesus. She had been taken into Christ's presence as surely as Ezekiel had been carried by the Spirit to a valley of dry bones (Ezek. 37:1).

How does an atheist react to a vision of Jesus? I have heard of several instances where dramatic conversions of unbelievers, even atheists, resulted when someone experienced a vision of the glorified Christ. This happened to Tom, a young Hawaiian. Tom had little idea why he was even at the inter-island church camp except perhaps to cause a little trouble. He openly mocked me at the conclusion of one of the sessions, angry about something I had said. Then it happened. Tom was standing beneath a large palm tree outside the camp auditorium following the third night meeting. His experience closely parallels that of Saul of Tarsus traveling the Damascus road (Acts 9). Several campers stood beside him in a circle. Suddenly he fell to the ground—like Saul of Tarsus, who fell prior to his conversion. Tom, like Saul, also had a vision during his experience on the ground. It was a vision of Jesus on the cross. His testimony the following morning beautifully concluded with, "I can't tell you all that happened or how it happened. But I do know this, I went down on the ground an atheist, and I got up born again."

I understand how a skeptic (even a strong believer) might suggest Tom's experience happened because of the intensity of emotions during the meetings. However, one thing was clear. Tom's experience led to his conversion. The fruit of the encounter was a transformed life.

When our daughter Dena was three years old, she too had a vision of Jesus. It happened just as the Prayer Corps ministry was beginning. I remember the night it happened. I had returned home from a busy seven-day speaking tour, exhausted. To my dismay, Dena had developed a serious case of the flu. It was necessary to stay up with her the better part of the night. And her frequent crying out brought her father understandable concern that something far more serious might be occurring. Accompanying the stomach problem was an unusually high fever.

The following day we asked Prayer Corps members to remember Dena in prayer throughout the day and night. They did, and it worked. Dena slept without incident. Her healing was abrupt and certain.

By morning Dena was bouncing around the house in her typical kangaroo style. She stopped only long enough in the family room to offer her dad a smile and pronounce a childlike medical bulletin.

"Hey, Daddy," Dena declared. "Jesus came by me last night and took my fever off me." It was short and to the point. Dena had been healed.

I chuckled as my daughter hopped from the room—though I wondered if she actually understood what she said. Then, several months later, I received my answer. This time I was the one sick with the flu. Dena came beside the bed inquiring, "Do you have a fever too, Daddy?"

I explained I too was ill just as she had been several months earlier.

"Do you want me to pray for you, Daddy?" Dena calmly questioned in the slurred words of a three-year-old. I was frankly quite surprised by the offer.

"Yes, I'd like that very much," I answered, closing my eyes and waiting to hear her prayer.

Dena began mumbling. Nothing understandable was said, just a few under-the-breath mumbles. I tried not to laugh. It was humorous though touching. As her "prayer mumbles" ended with a poorly articulated "Amen," Dena leaned over to whisper in her daddy's ear. She wanted to ask an important question.

"Did He, Daddy? Did Jesus come by and take your fever off you, too? Did you see Him like I saw Him?"

It hadn't occurred to me three months earlier, on that bright May morning when I first heard my daughter's testimony, that Dena might have actually had a heavenly visitor during the night. But to my daughter, it was very real. And for months after the experience Dena spoke often of the night Jesus came by and took her fever off. That's why I've come to believe she actually saw Jesus. After all, even a child has a right to see visions of the Lord.

Indeed, this is the age of the unusual, and we should expect it to be filled with miracles. Scripture certainly promises an increase of the supernatural in mankind's final hour, and visions are definitely a part of this powerful move of His Spirit. They must not be taken lightly or shrugged off as "merely emotional." Quite often this is the very means God uses to place a burden on the heart of a prayer warrior. Soon after my daughter's experience this was illustrated by a vision given to a thirteen-year-old following an intense Bible study. The vision began with a voice repeating clearly, "Pray for Colombo." But due to a lack of understanding, the words were immediately thrust aside from the teen's mind.

"All I could think of was a television series called *Columbo*," related the teenager. (At the time *Columbo* was a popular television program about a crafty detective.)

"I thought it was ridiculous to pray for a TV show, so I just forgot about it and went home." Once home, the lad retired for the night. But he was abruptly awakened several hours later when a clear vision of lost multitudes came. This time he heard another name: "Ceylon!"

It echoed repeatedly in his mind. And as the young man heard the strange word repeated, faces of thousands passed by him in his vision, looking longingly for spiritual help.

"They were lost souls," related the adolescent. "But I had no idea where Ceylon was, so I flicked on a light beside my bed and reached for a small globe off the shelf. It took a while to find Ceylon. I couldn't remember ever hearing of such a country. But I found it. It's located near the southern tip of India. When I found it I couldn't believe what I saw. In bold letters was Ceylon's capital city with a star by it. It's Colombo!"

Today we see remarkable fruit from this teen's prayers. Those prayers coincided with the precise time the ministry I now direct, Every Home for Christ, began its home-to-home campaign in what is today known as Sri Lanka (formerly Ceylon). Recently our ministry celebrated its fortieth anniversary of evangelism and discipleship in the nation. Since that young man prayed four decades ago, more than 235,000 Sri Lankans have responded to our Every Home Campaign there, and more than 200,000 have graduated from our four-part Bible correspondence course. This has resulted in hundreds of churches being planted and even a Bible college and seminary to train rural pastors being established in a remote area of this island nation in the Indian Ocean.

Chapter 18
MANIFESTATIONS

E VERY MAJOR REVIVAL MOVEMENT in modern and biblical history has testified to outward manifestations of inward spiritual experiences. When it is God who is clearly manifesting Himself, we refer to it as "the manifest presence of God."

The word *manifest* means "readily perceived by the senses" or "to make evident or certain by showing or displaying." The word *manifestation* has several definitions that may be helpful for our understanding: (1) The act, process, or an instance of manifesting; (2) a perceptible, outward, or visible expression; and (3) a public demonstration of power and purpose.

While in college I especially enjoyed my studies in church history. Early revivals—complete with unusual demonstrations of God's power and conviction—made for exciting reading, though I never dreamed we could see similar occurrences today. Yet this is indeed the case.

In the early days of establishing the Prayer Corps ministry, we observed numerous supernatural incidents that reminded us of those early revivals. One phenomenon mentioned several times in this book is that of falling prostrate. Though not always easily explained and often open to criticism in today's religious climate, falling prostrate dates back as far as the Old Testament. It is also reported numerous times in the New Testament.[1]

True, this specific manifestation has been associated far more with the emergence of the charismatic movement in the mid-to-late 1970s, but interestingly the manifestation is what has attracted many believers of mainline denominations and even those of a Catholic tradition who have hungered for more of God.

I can understand how some evangelicals question such manifestations and why they may consider them to be the result of excessive emotionalism. Others feel (and sometimes justifiably so) that some of this is brought about by the manipulation of the evangelist or preacher. I wish I could say that such is not the case.

Yet I have personally witnessed those who have experienced such a phenomenon and were either dramatically converted, instantly delivered from years of addictions, or restored in personal relationships that seemed impossible to heal.

I have seen, for example, a grown man get up from the floor and rush to his wife to ask for forgiveness for abusing her and being unfaithful. I have seen a teenager stand up from such an encounter weeping and saying publicly into a microphone before hundreds, "Mom, I don't know if you're here tonight, but I'm so very, very sorry for my rebellion against you and Dad. Please forgive me. I promise I'll do anything you ask—I'll clean my room, do the dishes, come home on time from dates, anything. I just love you so much." And in that instant her weeping mom, who was indeed in the crowd, leaped to her feet and rushed to her daughter, where they embraced in a public display of forgiveness and repentance.

I have seen a man touched by God in this same manner rush out of the church to his car in the parking lot, retrieve his golf shoes from his trunk, and rush to speak to me at the front of the auditorium because he had something to say publicly to his wife. After calling his stunned wife forward (who clearly was in a state of shock), he confessed tearfully, "Honey, never again will I let golf take your place in my life. Here are my golf shoes. If my golf clubs had been in the trunk, I would have brought them too. I don't care if I ever golf again. I love you so much. Please forgive me." And with that, the young housewife fell into her husband's arms weeping.

These kinds of experiences erased all doubt in my mind that they might be superficial or excessively emotional. I have concluded that God was clearly at work in these instances. Allow me to explain.

Falling prostrate, to be sure, is not some new biblical doctrine. It is, indeed, not a doctrine at all but a manifestation. One cannot build a case for it being "the norm" in our Christian experience, nor can a case be built that such manifestations are unbiblical. Judging from the numerous times this manifestation is mentioned in Scripture, the experience is a mere aftereffect of God's presence, which very often produced either great fear or powerful awe in the hearts of those who experienced it.

In the latter part of Ezekiel 1, Ezekiel describes falling on his face while observing a strange vision of a wheel in the middle of a wheel. This wasn't particularly a voluntary prostration. He fell because of the awe connected with his vision. In Moses's case, however, he fell deliberately before the Lord as an act of humility. (See Numbers 16:4, 22.)

In John 18 we read of Christ's arrest in the Garden of Gethsemane.

Here, a "band" of soldiers (probably six hundred, according to commentators) arrived at the garden looking for Jesus. When they did, they collided with Christ's power. When Jesus merely spoke the words "I am He," the entire company fell backward to the ground.

In all, my personal trek through Scripture has revealed more than sixty instances of prostration. Sometimes it is involuntary, due primarily to the glory of God. In other instances it is voluntary, as a simple act of humility. Then in still other cases we see voluntary (and sometimes involuntary) prostration happen to those captivated by a powerful burden of prayer. (Appendix B lists numerous scriptures regarding this manifestation.) Though sometimes criticized in some religious circles, many other emotional responses fill Scripture—including dancing, leaping, shouting, lifting hands, weeping, and even groaning in prayer. As already suggested, I personally do not feel this should necessarily be the norm, but we shouldn't be surprised if such manifestations occur.

The question that justifiably comes, of course, is this: Is there value in such experiences today, and do we need this sort of emotional outflow? Some may wonder what practical effect experiences like these actually offer the believer. Particularly during the early days of the Prayer Corps ministry, I personally witnessed several such encounters that helped me realize there was practical value in such experiences.

In Northern California a serviceman named Felix visited a series of meetings I was conducting. As the meetings drew to a conclusion, I explained there would be an "after service" that included the laying on of hands for spiritual needs. Felix had long desired courage to witness and came forward for prayer. He was standing with approximately twenty-five others who also came for prayer. As prayer was individually offered, several fell to the floor. (This was a manifestation that continued only for a season of my ministry, and I did not question when some years later that manifestation ceased. I knew that my calling was to the nations.)

That night I repeatedly passed by the young serviceman, feeling that God was still preparing him inwardly. Little did I know he was fighting a battle about the emotional responses he was observing around him. Suddenly I felt impressed to pray for the soldier. Like the others, Felix fell to the floor. (Again, I can't explain exactly how or why this manifestation happened. It just did.) The remainder of this soldier's experience is best shared in his own words.

I came forward for something practical, not just some emotional
trip. So when I saw people fall over, I wanted to get out of here
as fast as I could. It was spooky. Yet something held me. I kept
asking God to give me practical power to get the gospel out to the
guys I knew at my barracks. And while I prayed, I watched what
was happening to others around me. Then, when God's power
came on me, I knew something happened—though I still questioned if it would be practical. So I sat up and asked God to speak
to me about all of this from Scripture. When I finished praying,
I let my Bible fall open. I looked down immediately to a passage.
It was Philippians chapter 1. The first verse I saw was verse 12.
I began reading, "And I want you to know this, dear brothers:
Everything that has happened to me here has been a great boost
in getting out the Good News concerning Christ [TLB]."

But Felix didn't stop with these words. He continued, "For everyone
around here, including all the soldiers over at the barracks..." (Phil.
1:13, TLB).

The congregation and I laughed and cried with Felix that night. Never
before had I seen a biblical confirmation with such accuracy. God had
indeed given Felix a practical experience. He couldn't wait to return
to the barracks that evening to share the Good News with his fellow
soldiers. When Felix finally finished his time in the army, he joined the
Prayer Corps and was one of our most faithful intercessors.

In subsequent days, when I would hear a few Christian leaders say
that such manifestations were at best "the flesh" and at worst "satanic," I
would ask, "When would Satan or the flesh try to draw a barrack full of
soldiers to a knowledge of Jesus Christ?" It simply made no sense.

Careful examination of John 16 reveals several interesting things
about the work of the Holy Spirit that are valuable to our discussion.
For one, Jesus explains that the presence of the Holy Spirit would bring
glory to Himself. Further, the Holy Spirit would provide the Christian
with comfort or help. Jesus also declared, "When he, the Spirit of truth,
comes, he will guide you into all truth" (John 16:13). Thus, from a truly
practical standpoint, a move of the Holy Spirit should guide people
into a much greater passion for God's Word. (See my following chapter,
"Romancing the Word.")

In Fort Worth, Texas, I saw an instance where bodily prostration was
actually the start of just such a love for God's Word. It happened on a
Wednesday night during a time after our service devoted to the laying

on of hands. An eighteen-year-old requested prayer for a lingering health problem. But prior to prayer, I felt God would do something far deeper when the Holy Spirit touched the young man. So I explained this to the youth.

"I know you desire healing, but I see something far more lasting happening to you tonight. You are about to fall in love with Scripture. You will love God's Word as never before."

The following night during an open-mic time of sharing, the youth related a most moving testimony. After Wednesday, he arrived home about eleven o'clock and prepared for bed. But he decided to read a few verses of his Bible just before retiring.

"I read just one scripture," he related, "but it seemed to have far more meaning than usual. So I decided to read another. I felt the same about that verse. Then I couldn't stop. On and on I read. Finally I closed my Bible and glanced over at the clock. I was shocked to see it was after four a.m. I had read God's Word practically the entire night. Never have I loved the Bible more."

Every generation has its social and political critics. It is the same with every generation of revival. There will always be those who question the necessity of such emotional occurrences as those mentioned in this chapter. So to those who ask, "Why didn't Jesus minister more with the laying on of hands?"[2] or, "How many instances in Scripture did Jesus pray for people who fell prostrate?" we have only a simple answer. It's an answer that comes from the words of Christ Himself.

Jesus made this unusual statement in the Upper Room during the Last Supper. Frankly, I have never fully understood it. Most commentators, likewise, have difficulty with it. It does, however, offer possible help in answering questions about manifestations or miracles that happen in our generation.

Jesus declared, "I tell you the truth, anyone who has faith in me will do what I have been doing. He will do even greater things than these, because I am going to the Father" (John 14:12).

Here Jesus promises much. Indeed, He promises "greater things." Perhaps this verse alone explains some of the unusual occurrences we are witnessing and may continue to witness during these final hours of history.

There is a final thought that should be shared concerning this subject of man's response to God. God has chosen varied methods to accomplish His work, and it can be dangerous to judge these methods or those using them. This is, of course, not to say we should throw caution to the wind and allow heresy or false teaching to go unchecked. Yet at the same time let us remember a fundamental premise of the teachings of Christ: "Do not judge, or you too will be judged" (Matt. 7:1). In that same discourse our Lord sets forth the real criterion for evaluating ministries: "By their fruit you will recognize them" (v. 16). The key, then, is to wait for the fruit of a ministry before we pronounce judgment. And real fruit is something only a genuine ministry of God can yield.

Paul also provides an interesting thought. He once addressed the Corinthians bluntly for their carnality in being followers of "man" instead of Christ. Paul preached, "You are still worldly. For since there is jealousy and quarreling among you, are you not worldly? Are you not acting like mere men? For when one says, 'I follow Paul,' and another, 'I follow Apollos,' are you not mere men? What, after all, is Apollos? And what is Paul? Only servants, through whom you came to believe—as the Lord has assigned to each his task. I planted the seed, Apollos watered it, but God made it grow" (1 Cor. 3:3–6).

No message could be more basic or clearer. Different people have different responsibilities in the body of Christ—some plant and some water. And even among those who plant there may be different methods used in the planting. Then, following the planting, someone else comes along to water. Why argue with how one drops the seeds or holds the hose? In the end, after all, the goal is fruit. Paul told the Philippians, "I desire fruit" (Phil. 4:17, KJV). And only God can give the increase.

Never has there been a greater need for good theology—sound theology. And yet, never has there been a greater need for experiencing the manifest presence of God. Experience apart from theology can lead to fanaticism. Theology apart from experience can bread legalism. Perhaps a proper conclusion to the matter is a merging of good, old-time religion with solid Bible teaching. In other words, we need a sound theology with an explosive experience. And amid all this we need to cease arguing.

George Verwer, founder of Operation Mobilization, said in a consultation I attended, "In England alone, the church is arguing over one hundred separate issues while millions are going to hell."

In the early 1970s, there were those who labeled the Jesus movement a "fluke" because it "just doesn't have enough good theology." Meanwhile, the movement proceeded to make headlines, and masses of troubled young people were transformed for Christ. Several hundred thousand conversions were reported in just a matter of months during those days of visitation. Church people were soon sneaking out of regular services to visit places where the Jesus people worshiped. They enjoyed meetings where one could actually "feel something." And that's the kind of experience we can expect more of in the future.

Vance Havner, a Baptist revival preacher, described it thus: "Sometimes I have thought I'd like to go back again to the old days at Corinth Baptist Church where I grew up, where we used to enjoy the spiritual food without arguing too much about the recipe." Looking back at his most zealous years, Havner recollects, "Though I didn't have much theology in my head, I had a lot of doxology in my heart."

That's what we need today. O God, give us both the Book and the blessing!

Chapter 19
ROMANCING THE WORD

S EVERAL MONTHS AFTER OFFICIALLY launching the Prayer Corps ministry, I traveled to another California college campus for a series of spiritual emphasis meetings. The Prayer Corps was not yet a year old. God would use this ministry assignment to bring balance to my life when it came to the issue of seeking manifestations of God as compared to merely seeking God—and particularly seeking God through cultivating an intimacy with His Word.

Many Christian colleges, especially Bible schools, have a fall and spring spiritual emphasis week, as was the case with the college in Minneapolis I referred to earlier. These meetings usually feature a well-known pastor or evangelist who comes to speak to the students. This not only serves to develop spiritual qualities in the students but also exposes them to older veterans of ministry who might set an example for young students. But I was clearly no veteran and far from being a gifted preacher. So I had good reason to feel underqualified.

This also was the season of my life when I had very few formal sermons, but rather I would spend a good deal of a day in prayer and searching Scripture to get a sense of what I might share during any particular meeting. It's humorous to say today that during those days more than once I honestly didn't know what I was preaching on until midway into a message. It was an adventure to say the least. Indeed, at this very college a professor assigned his homiletics class (homiletics is the study of developing sermons) to select one of my messages, evaluating the various points in outline form. Later I heard that several of the class turned in papers that began something like this: "The speaker had no points—he just read scriptures and told stories." Class members then tried to retell some of the stories in their papers. The professor eventually cancelled the assignment.

Still, in spite of my shortcomings, God would move in mysterious ways. At this particular campus all classes for the week were cancelled by the second day as many students prayed whole nights—some not leaving the chapel for thirty-six to forty-eight hours except to use a restroom. Many fasted, not because it was suggested, but because they were so caught up in what God was doing that food didn't matter.

But when I arrived on the campus that first day, I had no idea all this would happen. I just had that same empty sensation that I really didn't know what I should speak on or what God might do that particular week. Today I can look in retrospect with thankfulness for all God did at that campus, but at the time I was desperate.

This particular college had recently constructed a prayer chapel near the much larger main campus chapel. The prayer chapel was less than the size of a small bedroom, possibly 200 square feet. It had a beautiful atmosphere with a kneeling bench surrounding the room except for the entrance. The tiny chapel also had numerous colorful stained-glass windows that during the day would scatter rainbow rays of color throughout the room. It was here that first afternoon that I would spend several hours prayerfully preparing for the first meeting that night. It would also be here that God would do something profound and unexpected that would impact my ministry and personal walk with Him for the rest of my life. I was about to fall in love with His Word.

By late afternoon the sun was setting, and I was kneeling at the altar bench on one side of the chapel. Where I was praying was only about eight feet from the other side of the room.

I lifted my head from prayer momentarily and happened to gaze at the kneeling bench on the other side of the room. There my Bible lay open, resting on the cushioned altar. An array of colorful hues from the stained-glass windows sparkled on the pages. Something unusual came over me that I can only describe as an intense love for God's Word. It was something supernatural.

Because the distance to the opposite kneeler was so short, I didn't stand up and take the couple of steps to the other side but instead crawled on my knees to where my Bible lay. As I gazed at the open pages, with numerous passages underlined and handwritten notes beside them in the margin, my passion for the Scriptures intensified. *I was falling in love with the Word.* Suddenly I did something unexpected. I bowed down and kissed each of the open pages and began to weep.

"Lord," I said, "I love Your Word because Your Word is You. Your Word is a living extension of Your nature and character."

Something extraordinary began in those moments. Following that encounter, I began spending as much time in the Word as I did in prayer. Indeed, I saw very little difference in the two. To be in the Word was to be with God and hear His heart. Much of my praying soon was based on God's Word. I was learning to pray the Word.

As I began to cross-reference my Bible on a daily basis, a plan to be more systematic in the process emerged. That plan would eventually become a seminar titled "The University of the Word" that I would teach in many communities following my more evangelistic type of meetings. The University of the Word consisted of twelve biblical principles based on twelve significant foundational passages of Scripture. Each of the twelve foundational passages served as "home base" for other verses or passages that might be related to a main principle or theme.

For example, one of the principles was the respect principle, which focused on cultivating a reverence or respect of the Lord. So anytime I came across a scripture that had to do with a deep awe or reverence of the Lord, I would go back to that "home base" scripture and write the newly discovered verse in the margin of my Bible beside that main verse. In this way I began cross-referencing my Bible in a personal way. True, you could purchase Bibles that did this for you, but this was more exciting and fruitful.

As I read God's Word daily, I would carefully study each verse with an eye to see what principle that verse might relate to. If it related to the third of the twelve principles, I would write a number 3 in the margin beside the verse and circle the number. Soon almost every page of my Bible had numbers beside most of the verses.

I also discovered a way of color-coding verses relating to the twelve themes. I purchased a large box of crayons and, after doing some experimentation, discovered that lightly shading over verses with certain colors made it easy to distinguish the various themes. I selected twelve appropriate colors for the task. Over the following several years I personally enrolled in my own University of the Word. The word *university* means "a place of higher learning." God was taking me to a higher level of learning in a daily, systematic study of His Word.

We soon implemented these methods of Bible study at the Prayer Corps. The interns who participated were required to spend no less than two hours a day praying in the Gap, as well as two hours minimum in God's Word. We wanted these young intercessors not only to experience fervent prayer but also to cultivate an intense passion for the Scriptures.

I also would soon learn that saturating oneself in God's Word was the most significant asset in the entire matter of seeking divine guidance. By this time I had personally cultivated a growing sensitivity to hearing God's voice. As I shared in chapter 16, "Moses and Me," God wanted me to know He would speak to me from within, and do so very specifically. But it was Scripture that would confirm when God was speaking. One particular occasion comes to mind. And once again some stained-glass windows would play an interesting role in the encounter.

The Prayer Corps ministry had not yet begun, but my vision-encounter for the coming ministry had just happened a few weeks earlier in a storage area of our church. It was that afternoon that I was to hear the still, small voice of God speak to me about the future ministry in very specific ways.

Hearing God's voice in such a way was rather new to me. Until then much of what I felt was God speaking to me was more in the form of heart impressions. But now I was actually hearing His voice. "Wow," I thought, "God can speak in whole sentences."

I was most influenced in this regard by Joy Dawson, an anointed Bible teacher from New Zealand who later would become significantly involved with the ministry of Youth With A Mission (YWAM). Joy's teaching on "Hearing God's Voice" impacted many, including leaders like Mike Bickle of the International House of Prayer (IHOP) and Loren Cunningham, founder of YWAM. In fact, Loren would later pen one of the best books I've read on this subject, titled *Is That Really You, God?*

It was Joy who strongly urged those who believed God had spoken to them to first confirm it with His Word before taking specific action as the result. And this was the context in which a memorable, if not somewhat humorous, experience happened to me as the Prayer Corps was about to be birthed.

Just days after my vision to step out in faith and begin this new venture, I suddenly had strong doubts. We had no money and no indication that young people would even respond to such a 24/7 prayer ministry. Further, we had no prospect of a location for the center itself. Basically, we had nothing. I decided to have a heart-to-heart talk with God.

The church where I had been serving as youth pastor was a large rotunda-type of building. The outer area of the rotunda included Sunday school rooms that circled the building. In the center was the fifteen-hundred-seat auditorium. Small stained-glass windows dotted the walls of the various classrooms. I was in one of these rooms, where I would sometimes come for private prayer during the week.

When I first entered the room that afternoon, the sun was still shining brightly through the colorful stained-glass windows. It was therefore unnecessary for me to turn on any lights. Walking into the room, I placed my Bible on a lectern that the class teacher would use on Sundays and began pacing the room in prayer. Prayer-walking a room was not uncommon for me in those days.

My prayer-pacing had gone on for some time. Suddenly I felt the strong sense that God wanted to speak to me. The words I heard were, "You are making the right decision to begin the Prayer Corps ministry. I have given you the vision and I am confirming it today." God, indeed, was speaking in whole sentences!

I began to rejoice at what I was hearing. But suddenly doubt again filled my mind. How could I be sure I wasn't simply manufacturing the words I'd just heard? Could it be my flesh had made up those impressions and it wasn't God really speaking after all?

By now the sun was beginning to set, and the room was growing darker. Yet I could still see my Bible on the lectern, though barely, and began to make my way toward it. The light switch was on the far side of the room, so I didn't bother to walk over to the switch and turn on the lights. Approaching the lectern I prayed, "God, I need a confirmation that You really did speak. Please confirm it with Your Word."

I decided to open my Bible at random, point at a verse, and see if God might confirm directly what I had just heard. It was a little unorthodox, but I was desperate.

So I shut my eyes and reached into my closed Bible, preparing to open it at random and point. I would then accept what I pointed at as God's confirmation.

But I stopped suddenly, realizing that the placement of my fingers was near the Old Testament and not the New. "What if," I thought, "I reach into the Old Testament and point at a verse somewhere in First Chronicles where all those people are 'begetting' each other?"

So I promptly pulled my fingers from my Bible in order to place them in a better location closer to the New Testament. God must have been shaking His head by now! So I closed my eyes and prayed once more, "Lord, give me a verse to confirm that it really is You speaking."

With my eyes closed, I opened my Bible and pointed. I had to move my face much closer to the lectern because the sun had now almost set.

I couldn't believe what I saw. I didn't know whether to laugh or cry or just start over. I had placed My Bible upside down on the lectern when I entered the room. I had, after all, opened it to the Old Testament.

But what most startled me was that my fingers were resting directly on Numbers 23:19–20, the very scriptures God had given me a few months earlier in Minneapolis when that first wave of sacrifice occurred. Tearfully I read, "God is not a man, that he should lie, neither the son of man, that he should repent: hath he said, and shall he not do it? or hath he spoken, and shall he not make it good? Behold, I have received commandment to bless: and he hath blessed; and I cannot reverse it" (KJV).

In an instant, with a touch of humor to boot, I had my answer as to whether God had spoken to me or not about stepping out in faith to launch the Prayer Corps. And He had used a most remarkable passage to confirm it.

These were the occasions that caused me to cultivate a passion for God's Word. Eventually I would change Bible translations every few years and start again with a new personalized plan of marking and cross-referencing that particular translation. In each translation, I would discover new things I hadn't seen before. It would become clear that one of the greatest ways to practice God's presence, and to pray with power, is to fall in love with His Word.

Chapter 20

THE TITLE DEED

A N ONLOOKER MIGHT THINK all lessons learned at our prayer center in those early years focused exclusively on prayer. This is far from accurate. Perhaps even more was to be learned about faith. It had not been altogether out of the ordinary for discouragement to settle in the Prayer Corps ministry, especially in those early months when most often these trials concerned finances. From the very beginning new lessons had to be learned concerning faith. Faith was no longer just a biblical doctrine; it had become a way of life.

I would be foolish to attempt an in-depth theological explanation of faith. Like some of the manifestations mentioned earlier, faith is something difficult to explain. It is—by simplest definition—a quiet confidence *in* God. We read in Hebrews, "What is faith? It is the confident assurance that something we want...is waiting for us, even though we cannot see it up ahead" (Heb. 11:1, TLB).

In my encounters with faith, one of the most fitting definitions comes from a single phrase in the Amplified Bible. It includes three simple words: "the title deed" (Heb. 11:1, AMP).

Our faith possesses "the title deed" to property we have never seen. Whether it involves eternal life, healing, needed finances, or strength for tomorrow, we have a deed that declares it to be ours. That deed is our faith. Take, for example, Peter's explanation of our heavenly inheritance. According to Scripture, this inheritance is being "kept by the power of God through faith unto salvation ready to be revealed in the last time" (1 Pet. 1:5, KJV). *Kept*, say the commentators, is better rendered "reserved" or "guarded." Thus heaven is our property. We hold the title deed. And faith is that deed.

Confident Faith

I especially recall the circumstances surrounding Nancy's arrival at the Prayer Corps from Michigan. She was one of our very first members. It was a Tuesday afternoon when her plane set down in Sacramento. Two days previously, on Sunday, Nancy was still short the necessary airfare. She had, however, committed the need to God in prayer. During the morning service, Nancy's pastor asked her to sing and testify about her "calling" to this new prayer ministry. After her song and testimony, the pastor was struck with a sudden thought. Nothing really tangible had been done to help Nancy in her new venture. So, calling for the ushers, he received an offering. It totaled exactly what Nancy needed, plus eight cents.

When handed the money, Nancy joked with her minister, "What's the extra eight cents for?"

He answered, "That's to write us a letter when you get to the Prayer Corps to let us know what God's doing out in California." (The cost of a postcard back then was exactly eight cents!)

Faith, as we have shared, is a calm confidence in God that a thing will happen. There are times, however, that it doesn't always transpire in this manner. Sometimes our faith emerges from hearts of desperation rather than from hearts of confidence.

Desperate Faith

An example of desperate faith comes to mind. It involved a former Muslim man, now a Baptist pastor. The man's testimony was relayed to me by a Bible school student in Europe who also converted to Christianity from Islam. The student spoke of an older minister, a personal friend, who reached a point of desperation while praying at the altar of his small Baptist church. It was the middle of the day, and the man was crying out to God for revival. Just shortly after noon several children entered to pray. Not content to keep their prayers to themselves, they stood beside the kneeling minister and began praying for him. As one of the children reached out to touch him, he was immediately filled with the Holy Spirit. And along with great waves of joy flowing from his heart came what Charles Finney described at his similar encounter as "unutterable gushing of the heart" flowing in a joyful spontaneity of worship.

Crazy Faith

In addition to confident faith and desperate faith, we need to mention what might be defined as crazy faith. Crazy faith is a kind of faith that may seem crazy to our human reasoning but doesn't seem crazy to God. When Jesus saw the poor widow casting her last two "mites" (the smallest of coins in her culture) into the temple treasury, He didn't tell the disciples she was crazy. On the contrary, He was so pleased that He called His disciples together to preach to them (Mark 12:43–44). He said, "I tell you the truth, this poor widow has put more into the treasury than all the others. They all gave out of their wealth; but she, out of her poverty, put in everything—all she had to live on."

Peter is another good biblical example of this type of faith. What Peter did while in a boat with his fellow companions might be labeled crazy. He jumped overboard. It is, of course, pure insanity from a human standpoint to expect to walk on water. Only *crazy faith* made it possible for Peter to both leap out of the boat and then walk on water.

It's comforting to remember that even when Peter's crazy faith faltered (and he started to sink), Jesus didn't scold Peter for jumping out of the boat. Instead, He chided him for losing his faith: "Immediately Jesus reached out his hand and caught him. 'You of little faith,' he said, 'why did you doubt?'" (Matt. 14:31).

I well remember the night a woman in California—whom we will call Esther Johnson—decided to "jump overboard." A wave of sacrifice had settled upon the congregation, and she was repeatedly impressed to give the church her "car payment money"—due just two days later. Such an act would seem totally unrealistic, especially considering Esther had no money at home to replace that which she would give. But suddenly Esther was captivated by crazy faith. She believed that God would not fail her.

Deeply stirred, the weeping woman walked to the Communion table near the altar of the church to deposit the money. Like the poor widow, she had given all she had.

As Monday morning arrived, the young woman felt the joy derived only from total obedience. She knew she'd done the right thing. However, it was now a mere twenty-four hours before her car payment was due. And that's precisely when the miracle began.

At work, Esther was given an unexplained bonus check. It was weeks away from any holiday, and no one else in the large office of secretaries received anything similar. She was excited, though the amount was still far short of the needed finances. Upon arriving home Monday night, additional unexpected funds had come in the mail from six different sources. By eight o'clock that same evening all but seven dollars had arrived.

Then the phone rang. It was the wife of a young couple who had moved into the apartment vacated by the Johnsons several weeks earlier. While cleaning out the cupboards the lady discovered a sealed envelope on a top shelf with no name on it. The finder offered to bring the envelope by the Johnsons' new house that very night. Several minutes later Esther held the wrinkled envelope in her hands, arguing that it really couldn't belong to her since she didn't remember leaving it there.

"Well it's not mine either," retorted the visitor, who insisted Esther take it. Stepping backward through the door she smiled and said, "God bless you." It was amazing the extent to which the new tenant went to take such an envelope to a former occupant of the apartment.

Esther Johnson didn't know what to think. She momentarily gazed at the envelope before looking in. She was amazed. There were exactly seven one-dollar bills in the envelope. God had honored her crazy faith, and He did so in a seemingly "crazy" manner. It was exactly what she needed.

Unconscious Faith

In those early years reports were coming in to the Prayer Corps from all over the country of something that seemed to be happening everywhere with almost no explanation. People were being physically healed and relationships restored in meetings, even without prayer. As worshipers exalted the Lord or were simply enjoying the presence of God in a meeting, the Lord just came beside them and touched them in a sovereign manner. We might call this unconscious faith.

In meetings where participants had been healed in this manner, it seemed that people were so wrapped up in their worship of the Lord they were unconscious of any great effort of faith on their part. In fact, there may have been none. Perhaps the only thing that is really necessary under these conditions is not the presence of any great faith but merely a simple absence of unbelief. I'm convinced the greater the worship, the less there is room for doubt.

Several years after the Prayer Corps began, I conducted a weeklong Celebration of Jesus crusade in Des Moines, Iowa. So amazing was God's presence that a second week was added, then a third, a fourth, and, before it was over, ten consecutive weeks had passed.

One Sunday night God touched a lady named Helen who was standing in the lobby of the church waiting for prayer. (So many were waiting for prayer that the line stretched out into the foyer.) Behind Helen stood a friend from a local Lutheran church. She too was waiting for prayer. In her case it was for a painful knee condition. Suddenly, Helen fell to the floor as God touched her, her head striking her Lutheran friend's very painful knees. But instead of feeling unbearable pain as would be expected, the woman's knees were instantly healed. Neither Helen nor her friend had been specifically prayed for. I was in the main sanctuary at the time and nowhere near the two women.

That same night a couple named Bob and Angela of Muscatine, Iowa, made the 160-mile trip to the Sunday night rally simply because they had heard that God was moving in an unusual way in the meetings. Indeed He was! When Angela joined the prayer line, it wasn't merely for healing but also to draw closer to the Lord. The line was so long that Angela was standing near the door into the vestibule. Suddenly Angela fell to the floor as the power of the Holy Spirit came upon her. When she arose, a nerve deafness of twenty-nine years was gone. She could hear clearly in the once-deaf ear.

Relaxed Faith

Still another type of faith was experienced often in those early years at the prayer center. We referred to it as relaxed faith. It is a special faith for those extremely trying circumstances. It's a faith that says with the classic hymn, "It is well with my soul."

While I was visiting Europe during the founding months of the Prayer Corps, a missionary to Austria told me of a friend who had recently lost his wife and three young children in the Middle East. His friend had been driving late one night with his entire family when their car slammed into an unlighted tractor moving slowly along a narrow road. The father stood by helplessly watching his wife and three young children die.

According to the young minister relating the account, friends of the missionary heard of the tragedy and congregated in his home awaiting his arrival. As the door opened, in walked a man tested by the worst of tragedies. Not stopping to say hello to those gathered, the musically gifted missionary walked directly to his piano and with a look of confidence, free of tears, lifted his face toward heaven and began singing the great hymn "Great Is Thy Faithfulness."

In the midst of his profound personal tragedy, this missionary maintained a relaxed faith, holding firmly to his title deed, a document of faith that seems to begin with the words, "And we know that in all things God works for the good of those who love him, who have been called according to his purpose" (Rom. 8:28).

In the young Prayer Corps ministry, our greatest lessons concerning relaxed faith came during the third and fourth months of our full-scale operations. If any faith existed previous to this season, I suppose one would define it as tense faith. By early August finances were so low, there was no way out but a miracle. I finally decided nothing could be done but relax. "If you're going under," I thought, "at least you'll go under relaxed."

It was a discouraging August night that I chose to examine the unpaid bills. For August alone the total came to $5,877. Several days later, however, I discovered an error. My calculations were a thousand dollars off. We actually needed $6,877.

By August 15, midway through the month, a total of $2,036 had been received. We were approximately $5,000 short. To make matters worse, I was ministering hundreds of miles away in Dallas, Texas, and had called Dee in Sacramento the night before, and she was in tears. We needed $300 for personal expenses that next day, and we were flat broke.

David Wilkerson invited me to his Dallas office that sunny August afternoon for lunch. I was anticipating sharing with him more about the new prayer ministry God was leading Dee and me into and how much he had inspired us. During the conversation, which lasted several hours, Brother David spoke of an unusual discernment God had only recently given him concerning the needs of various individuals. By the time our conversation ended, I had forgotten those remarks. As I was walking from his office, David's business manager handed me a check, explaining that Brother David wanted me to have it. As the glass door swung shut behind me, I quickly looked at the gift. It was written to me personally, and it totaled exactly three hundred dollars.

By now I believed almost anything was possible. Finally, it was Friday night and our last service in the Dallas area. Sitting alone in the motel, I added up the checks for the month. My heart sank as I counted only $2,800. With a single service remaining, there was nothing to do but relax in Jesus.

En route to the church a strange feeling came over me. Someone somewhere was praying for our ministry. I had a surge of faith. God could meet the need. In fact, God *would* meet the need.

Once in the service, I said nothing about money. The pastor spoke only of people giving a love gift as unto God. It was a night of many miracles. And the following morning, I boarded the plane rejoicing. That previous night God had multiplied the loaves and fishes. Instead of the $2,800, I was bringing back $7,200 for the ministry. One thing was now clear. Faith is a miracle, and faith works. It was a lesson I would need for the future. In those early days we had to trust God for about $230 a day, or $7,000 a month. Today our ministry requires nearly $70,000 a day—and God is always faithful. What an exciting adventure in answered prayer.

Chapter 21
THE VICTORY BOARD

Fʀᴏᴍ ᴛʜᴇ ᴏᴜᴛsᴇᴛ ᴏғ establishing the Prayer Corps ministry, the highlight of our prayer center was the Gap. It was the focal point of power and praise. And yet, within the Gap was the "highlight" of this highlight. It was the victory board. Here the miracles of answered prayer phoned to us were briefly noted on a day-by-day basis.

It was, in fact, the victory board in our Sacramento Gap that first caught the attention of the city. A team of NBC cameramen flew in from their West Coast headquarters in Los Angeles to film what was happening. How they heard about us I do not know, but it was the Gap that most fascinated the reporters. They were first surprised that prayer never ceased, not even during the filming. But what most fascinated them was the victory board. On it were recorded numerous miracles (a couple of days' worth), including several cancer healings. Such reports of healing were not new to our visitors—who had previously filmed large meetings conducted by "healing evangelists" and other preachers. These were the days of the Jesus movement, and people seemed fascinated by how young people were being transformed by Christ. They had heard about the Prayer Corps and wanted to see for themselves what was happening. What surprised them was the simplicity of these clean-cut young people, ordinary teens, who were so devoted to such an effort. This was a small band of committed young people who were fighting daily battles for people of all faiths. And the victory board made it clear they were winning some key battles.

It was, indeed, the victory board that kept the prayer ministry going with joy and intensity. These daily victories made it clear to these young intercessors that prayer truly works.

Late one October afternoon, I slipped into the Gap for a time of prayer and praise, careful not to disturb the others who were praying. I couldn't help but rejoice as I stood before the victory board. Crammed on the large whiteboard that particular day were these reports of answered prayer:

- Arlene's mother came through her operation beautifully: Praise the Lord!
- Two people were saved at the mall.
- Ann received victory over her drinking problem.
- Mrs. Smith had her brain tumor removed. Everything is normal. Praise the Lord!
- God has given us a new piano. We've been praying for this for several months.
- At least five more people saved at the mall. Praise the Lord!
- Praise the Lord, another church has started twenty-four-hour prayer.
- Two more saved at the mall.
- The Lord healed my body—Steve.

Unfortunately, we did not always receive the complete details of every miracle, though these one-line statements on the board still provided welcome encouragement to the young intercessors. In some cases, however, more complete reports of victory came our way.[1]

A case in point involved a Lutheran woman who submitted an urgent request for her church. It was "ultra modern and quite liberal," she explained, "with little emphasis being placed on truly important spiritual matters." According to the request, nothing was ever mentioned about the Holy Spirit in her church, whereas other denominational churches of the city seemed to be coming alive in the Holy Spirit. Prayer began that afternoon and continued seven days for that request. The following Monday the phone rang in the Gap. It was the same Lutheran lady with an exciting testimony. She described her pastor's words, spoken the day before (Sunday) from the pulpit:

> I'm going to do something most unusual this morning. I'm laying aside my prepared sermon notes to discuss something that has troubled me all week. I speak of the renewed emphasis of recent years on the work of the Holy Spirit. We have spoken too little of this topic in our church, and I want to change that.

The Lutheran minister then shared from his heart the urgent need to give the third Person of the Trinity, the Holy Spirit, a rightful place in our lives. To the caller, this was an extraordinary answer to prayer.

A single line appeared on the victory board one day concerning the cancellation of an eleven-hour operation. I especially rejoiced when the opportunity came to hear the rest of the story.

A lady in a Southern California hospital several hundred miles away was in need of a miracle. She had been ill for quite some time and a few months earlier had undergone an eight-hour operation for her condition. When severe complications resulted, tests determined that another, even longer operation would be required. It was scheduled for 8:00 a.m. that Friday morning. But shortly after midnight, very early Friday morning, a concerned relative called our Fire House for prayer. Those in the Gap prayed through the remainder of those early morning hours. At 8:00 a.m. the extremely weak woman asked the doctor to run the test one more time.

"I'd rather die than go through surgery again," the lady told her doctors. To this comment the chief surgeon answered, "Lady, you will die if you don't. Those tests were taken just two days ago, and two days can't change a condition this severe."

But the doctors were promptly informed by the woman that no operation would be allowed unless all the earlier tests were redone. Then, if the second battery of tests indicated the operation was necessary, she would endure it.

Reluctantly the doctors repeated the series of tests. When the tests were completed, they returned to her room stunned. The senior physician stood before the patient a good deal perplexed and somewhat embarrassed.

"You can go home soon," he explained. "It looks like the operation won't be needed after all." She had been healed.

These kinds of more complete reports led to a special addition in the Gap, placed on the wooden altar just below the victory board. We called it the miracle box. Miracles—as they were phoned in—were written out in greater detail on a miracle card (or on several cards if the details required such). The basic answer to prayer was first put on the victory board, while the more detailed information was written on the cards and placed in the miracle box. While praying, corps members always enjoyed thumbing through the scores of miracle cards. It increased their faith and stimulated praise.

Not long ago while praying in the Gap, I took a handful of these cards from the miracle box and read several of the exciting victories. You may be blessed by this small sampling:

Mrs. Wilson called. She's rejoicing over her husband's salvation. He's been in our prayers at the Fire House for several months. Last weekend he unexpectedly decided to go to a couples' retreat sponsored by our church and was saved.

Praise God for answering prayer. The lady whose four small children disappeared last Tuesday morning reported they have been returned home safely. She had called for prayer Tuesday night. They were all found the following afternoon.

Word came today that the elderly Jewish man we interceded for over a two-month period accepted Christ. It happened suddenly right in his home. Praise God for miracles.

Mrs. Stone called rejoicing about her husband's healing. Praise God! He was healed of a gout condition in his legs.

Praise the Lord. A Bible school is starting a Prayer Corps ministry on campus. Over two hundred students already are participating. They're now praying twenty-four hours a day in two separate Gaps, one in the girls' dorm and one in the guys'.

Chuck, a heroin pusher on his way to Mexico for a shipment of drugs, was saved on the streets this week as Prayer Corps members witnessed to him. Though people are now out to kill him, he won't turn his back on Jesus. He's already excited about helping us witness.

Sally R. called earlier this week requesting prayer for her six-month-old son. He was so sick with pneumonia they didn't expect him to live. Today he is completely well. Praise God!

Gloria D. accepted Christ on the phone today and was delivered at once of a mental oppression. Then she was filled with the Holy Spirit, right over the phone.

A lady with diabetes who was expecting a baby came through the ordeal perfectly. When a friend called Wednesday about her condition, doctors said both mother and unborn child were in serious trouble. But today the infant had a natural birth. Both mother and baby are doing fine.

Yesterday during the bad rain and floods a lady in Rio Linda called. Her daughter's home was flooding. We commanded the flooding to stop in the name of Jesus. She called back to tell us the rain and flooding stopped right while we were praying.

Mrs. N. had a tumor removed from her brain this week. The call for prayer came in last Monday. Today she's doing much better. In fact, the doctors say she's a living miracle. Praise the Lord!

The victory board in the Gap frequently transformed our prayer center into an old-fashioned house of praise. Hours daily were spent praising God for miracles. And from the first days of continued prayer this had been the case. Often people stopped by the center just to join us in praising God.

In reflecting back on those earliest days of the Prayer Corps, I have often referred to it as a "baby IHOP," a reference to the International House of Prayer in Kansas City. Indeed, I've sometimes wondered if these praying young people, way back in the early 1970s, somehow helped birth (at least in the heavenlies) such ministries as IHOP and other 24/7 movements.

I particularly recall the night a businessman who was one of our supporters was alone wallpapering at the center. Two elderly visitors stopped by to see if it was really true that Sacramento was about to have a 24/7 prayer center. He showed the ladies our newly acquired facility and explained its unique spiritual purpose. He took them to the temporary Gap upstairs and explained that our resident intercessors were planning to build a new, permanent Gap below the house.

As our supporter shared, these elderly saints listened carefully. Their eyes sparkled with enthusiasm. "We've been praying for this," one of the ladies explained. "Praise God," the other quickly added, as she inspected the work being done in preparing the new center for its mission.

It was nine o'clock that night when the two visitors departed with a "God bless you." My friend continued working another ninety minutes on the wallpapering before calling it a day. Leaving the center he was thrilled—though surprised—to discover the two ladies hadn't gone home. They were on the sidewalk in front of the center, walking up and down the street—hands lifted toward heaven—praising God. The guests seemed totally oblivious to their surroundings. They were unashamedly worshiping God over this new prayer venture.

It was one of our first real lessons in the power of praise and worship. From then on our motto was more than just "Prayer Power." Praise power, we soon learned, would keep the center alive during times of discouragement. Worship-filled prayer quickly became a highlight of the "other miracles" in this new ministry. Praise, after all, is the miracle of thanking God for miracles.

Chapter 22
A BUG ON THE MOUNTAIN

LOOKING BACK AT THE first twelve months of that exciting new prayer adventure, I knew God had undeniably charted the way. It was clearly a birthing time for other prayer ministries and movements to come. But somehow my presence in Europe confused me. In every regard the trip seemed to be a failure. The finances for our new ministry were too depleted to make the journey, and there were no speaking engagements scheduled once I arrived. I wished I were back in Sacramento with the Prayer Corps.

These first several days in Europe left me bewildered. And though I was able to share the vision of 24/7 prayer with several missionaries, the trip remained in my mind a colossal mistake. So I decided to return home early.

Two days later I was standing in a European airline office exchanging tickets so that I would get home in time for Thanksgiving. But God evidently saw things differently, as I was soon to discover.

An hour passed while the agent worked out the details. I was informed there would be a one-hundred-dollar refund because I was taking a shorter route home. This excited me. Surely it was the will of God to go home. We needed that hundred dollars. After all, since finances were so low, it would be foolish to consider this anything less than a confirmation from God.

Placing the ticket in its folder the agent suddenly hesitated. There was an apparent error. He gazed at the original date of purchase for several seconds. Then, looking up, he slowly explained, "Sir, I believe I've made a terrible mistake. I've forgotten to check the length of your stay in Europe. Your original ticket was purchased at an excursion rate. You must stay in Europe at least twenty-two days to receive this rate. According to your ticket, it will cost you an additional three hundred dollars if you depart early."

I had little choice in the matter. Three hundred dollars was out of the question. I just didn't have it. My anxiety increased as I tried to figure out what was happening. That day, however, things began piecing themselves together. Unable to return early, I could now visit Christians behind the iron curtain and share this prayer vision with them. The trip would take two or three days, depending on the weather.

I slept little that night, only an hour or two. I was excited to see what God had planned. As it turned out, He wanted me to visit a Communist nation for a crucial reason. Only then could I adequately sense the world's desperate need for intercessory prayer.

The next day I was to leave with my brother and cousin for the trip into Eastern Europe. From the outset of the journey one thing was strangely clear. Satan didn't want us planting a prayer ministry in his territory. He had already tried talking me into returning home early, and now that we were under way, various discouragements were thrust upon us.

In the towering Alps a vicious blizzard caught us totally unprepared. It appeared we were doomed to several days of delay—snowbound. Even cars with chains had difficulty climbing the icy grades. We had no chains. As we climbed still higher, the ice and snow reduced our speed to a crawl. We were suddenly on glare ice. Cars everywhere were stranded.

Having been appointed the driver for this treacherous journey, I carefully tried inching the car forward while my brother and cousin climbed from the motionless vehicle to push it. Finally enough momentum was achieved to climb a grade, and then another. But we were still in danger, since a much steeper hill awaited us in the distance.

Several times the pushing procedure had to be duplicated. As the car slowed to a halt for the fourth time, I seriously contemplated turning back and heading down the mountain, but something inside provided the faith to tackle one more grade on the mountain. That something proved to be the Spirit of God. The "one more grade" brought us to the lengthy tunnel at the summit of the mountain, and we were soon on our way down.

Score one more for faith. We had, so it seemed, conquered both the mountain and Satan. Though the storm was equally troublesome on the opposite side of the tunnel, traction was no longer a problem. We could make it with ease—I thought.

Going down the icy grades, however, produced another problem— my improper use of the brakes. Suddenly we found ourselves in the middle of an unusually steep one-lane construction area with heavy-equipment vehicles parked everywhere. Ahead, a Volkswagen bug (the Mini Cooper of our day) was inching its way up the mountain, having the same difficulty we had experienced in climbing the other side. In those days a good sneeze could blow a Volkswagen bug halfway across a highway, and the winds at this altitude were howling.

Two cars now occupied the same lane of an icy highway, traveling on a collision course. The VW bug climbing toward us could do
nothing. Traction ruled out his going anywhere. It was up to me to act.
So I slammed on my brakes, throwing the car into a sudden skid. The
thought of a Volkswagen bug forcing us off a narrow mountain highway
in Eastern Europe was ironic if not embarrassing.

My brother started yelling, "Pump 'em! Pump 'em!"

My cousin quietly mumbled, "Oh, Jesus!"

I just held the brake pedal to the floor as we skidded headlong toward
a frantic, potential traffic fatality coming at us in his bug.

Suddenly I released the brake. It seemed crazy at the time. The car
quickly skidded to the left. We were going to hit on my brother's side. I
touched the brake again, just slightly. Back to the right we veered. It all
happened in seconds. Now we were headed directly toward a piece of heavy
equipment parked by the side of the road. Volvos are sturdy, but so are
bulldozers! Through it all, my brother kept yelling, my cousin continued
mumbling, and the other driver appeared to just close his eyes.

I don't recall moving my hands to steer the car—though they certainly
moved. God had obviously become the driver. A quick though very slight
turn back to the left brought us to within inches of both the oncoming
car and the piece of construction equipment. Somehow, though on glare
ice, we slithered through. My brother quietly declared, "I don't believe
it." My cousin just kept mumbling, "Oh, Jesus."

Five hours later, we were at the border of the then Communist country
of Yugoslavia. None of us had ever visited a Communist country, even as
tourists. Since we had no visas, our party was quickly diverted to the side
of the road while others were allowed to pass. Thirty anxious minutes
slipped by as we waited for our passports to be checked against a "master
list" of past troublemakers, a fact we learned later from an area pastor.
This was done to determine if any of us was a known agitator.

Because of the increased intensity of the storm, numerous cars were
now backed up at the border gate. Excess traffic is usually a heaven-
sent blessing, we were later informed, because cars are allowed to pass
through much more quickly. In moments, we were given our visas and
sent on our way. The guards, though checking others carefully, never
even opened our trunk. Breathing a sigh of relief, we were on our way.

The storm grew much more intense as early evening arrived. And there were already an unusual number of cars stranded along the side of the road. We already had counted five accidents. Later we learned that the Communist people had been able to own automobiles only recently, so they were relatively inexperienced drivers.

Coupled with inexperienced drivers and poor road conditions was the worst storm the populace could remember. I suddenly realized how earnestly Satan desired to hassle us. He knew now that we wouldn't turn back, so he decided to make the whole trip as miserable as possible. Satan has always aimed similar disruptions against those doing God's work. Paul once spoke of his thorn (or hassle) in the flesh. The apostle explained it was "a messenger of Satan, to torment me" (2 Cor. 12:7). *The Message* Bible uniquely paraphrases this thorn as "the gift of a handicap to keep me in touch with my limitations."

Certainly God could remove such spiritual obstacles if He so desired. Yet to keep us dependent on His grace for every need, He sometimes allows these hassles. Remember, Paul prayed three times for victory, and when this choice apostle asked God to deliver him from his thorn, God simply replied, "No. But I am with you; that is all you need" (2 Cor. 12:9, TLB).

By now two things were clearly evident concerning our trip: God was with us, and we were being hassled. That's when another thorn suddenly appeared. This time our Volvo became the object of the buffeting. A faint screeching in the engine seemed to be getting worse. My brother suggested it sounded like a fan belt problem. To me it sounded like the devil laughing at us.

Before long the car lights became unusually dim, and the engine was missing badly. It was now apparent that the generator was malfunctioning. My brother had been right. The fan belt was seriously loose, and even if we had had the proper tools it would have been too dangerous to stop the car and tighten the belt. There was obviously little electrical current remaining in the battery. I could only pray we would make it to the next town where help might be available.

Twenty minutes later we arrived at the outskirts of a large Eastern European city. We were delighted to find a small service station open, though the delight soon disappeared when we tried to explain our problem to one of the attendants. None spoke English. Neither did we understand a word of their language. No one knew what to do, as we stood for a moment silently staring at one another.

Our final course of action was a makeshift game of charades. Waving arms and uttering strange sounds, we eventually sent the man into his garage for the necessary tools. After several minutes, the fan belt was tightened enough to make the final leg of the trip. By now, however, the battery was completely dead, and the car wouldn't start.

Several charades and a significant number of mumbles later the young attendant found a twelve-volt battery, well charged, to replace ours long enough to start the car. With the car running it was possible to change batteries again, putting the original back in its place. Once on the road the battery would gain back its needed energy from the now-functioning generator. So in minutes we were on our way. Satan's hassles, though very real, had failed. Late that night we arrived at our destination, ready to minister for the first time behind the iron curtain.

Chapter 23

BACK TO BACK

Iᴛ sᴇᴇᴍᴇᴅ ꜰɪᴛᴛɪɴɢ ᴛᴏ celebrate the first birthday of the Prayer Corps ministry in this challenging part of the world. Here, as much as in any other dark place on our planet, prayer's value was cherished by believers. Christians behind the iron curtain greatly depended on this prayer help. They would, of course, ultimately see these prayers answered in dramatic ways as Communism would fall throughout the region, including in the Soviet Union.

We were welcomed to the country by a fine congregation of worshiping believers. Worship in Communist countries, we quickly learned, is much like ours. The people are not ashamed to praise and adore God vocally, although they often must do it in secret. The first service we visited began at 8:00 a.m. and continued until noon. It was easy to see how much these Christians enjoyed simple "New Testament" worship.

That night opportunity came to share about our year-old prayer ministry with the congregation. When we explained to them that concerned American young people were interceding for them around the clock, the people began weeping. It was one of the most lasting impressions from the entire trip. They clearly coveted the prayers of concerned Christians. Simply saying, "We pray for you daily," caused them to break into tears.

During the first evening rally God impressed me with a deep sense of need for these people. I suddenly realized how desperately all Christians need each other. Real spiritual battles will never be won by lone individuals; these battles are simply too great. True, some Christians may appear spiritually stronger than others, but each needs the rest of "the body."

As I stood in the well-worn pulpit, God reminded me of a scripture I had only recently discovered in my daily Bible reading. It seemed to tell the whole story of the Prayer Corps in several poignant words: "And one standing alone can be attacked and defeated, but two can stand back-to-back and conquer; three are even better, for a triple-braided cord is not easily broken" (Eccles. 4:12–13, ᴛʟʙ). Back-to-back, I reasoned; that's the key. We need to unite all the body of Christ to stand back-to-back in prayer for the nations.

Brushing elbows and chatting with these Slavic people (through Peter, our interpreter) we were taught much about the plight of Christians in an atheistic land. Peter himself has a story well worth sharing. It is one of dynamic dedication and unselfish sacrifice.

According to a veteran missionary, Peter was from the elite upper level of academic brilliance, which is most unusual for an outspoken evangelical Christian in a Communist country. To a great extent, Peter was self-taught. Speaking seven languages, the young man also could read Greek and Hebrew. His personal library, I was told, contained in excess of five thousand volumes. Once, because of his brilliance, Peter was offered a respected position in the Communist Party, but he refused it on the grounds that he would not take the required oath of atheism.

Peter's Christian heritage was passed along from godly parents in a remote peasant village where he grew up. A pioneering missionary passing through for a rare visit shared the story of Jesus with Peter's parents. Both parents accepted Christ during that visit and later received a powerful infilling of the Holy Spirit. Observing their example of sacrifice, Peter himself decided to receive Christ as Lord of his life.

Together this Christian family learned the meaning of sacrifice. Very early each Sunday, while it was yet dark, they would embark on a thirty-mile walk to the nearest church. It was impossible to arrive in time for the morning service, but they seldom missed the afternoon meeting. Peter's family then would remain through the evening service and walk home after it concluded. For years they kept this rigid weekend schedule—walking all night and arriving at their home at dawn on Monday morning, having sacrificed an entire night's sleep every weekend.

Hearing these accounts and visiting with these oppressed people first-hand revealed just how very much these Christians really do sacrifice for Jesus. The shortage of Christian literature was only one example. Bringing evangelical literature in from the West was always shaky business. It was only attempted with plenty of prayer and persistent courage. Little could they have known that this diabolical curtain of oppression would come crashing down in just a couple decades in answer to the prayers even then being mobilized.

Of all Christian literature they lacked, however, the most coveted possession was the Bible. Christians there had a passionate obsession with this supernatural Book so often neglected by Western believers. A young missionary from the United States serving in this region spoke to me of an unusual personal encounter she had with one of the students at a newly established Eastern European Bible institute. It well illustrates this deep love for Scripture in oppressed lands. During a study period she observed the young man seated in front of her reading the final few chapters of the Book of Revelation. As he finished his reading, he turned to the last page of his Bible and added a check mark. She noticed the page was filled with at least fifteen similar markings. When she asked about these markings, the student answered, "Oh, that's how many times I've read through my Bible from Genesis to Revelation."

Amazed at his reply, the missionary asked, "And how long has it taken you to do this?" He quietly replied, "Since I was saved two years ago." He was reading completely through his Bible approximately every six weeks!

At no time did I become more conscious of the need for prayer than during our visit with an older evangelical pastor. For years he had served a fine congregation in a large Eastern European city. Like others we met behind the iron curtain, the pastor appeared nervous when questioned about Communism and its oppression of religion. Rubbing his hands nervously and shifting his eyes from one side of the room to the other, the pastor spoke tentatively. "You can't feel what we feel until you live here," he told me. "A single visit will never do. You must wear our skin to fully understand the horror of this satanic rule."

Sitting quietly and listening to a brother surrounded by the oppressive forces of spiritual darkness made me search my own heart. He spoke of his years in prison, just for giving a single Bible to a soldier. At one point during his prison days he was almost executed.

"The guards asked me to kill a political prisoner who had been sentenced to death, but I refused. They wanted me, a minister, to be his executioner. I told them it would be impossible for me to kill a man. Many in the prison knew me. What would become of their faith if they saw a minister commit murder?"

The pastor paused to pour his guest a second cup of tea. Quietly he resumed his reflections of prison days: "So they said they would kill me if I refused to execute the man. One of the guards even handed me a gun and ordered me to shoot the condemned prisoner right then. I refused again. It was decided I must die at five o'clock the next morning.

"At first my heart was filled with fear, great fear, because I knew that many had unjustly died in our prison already. I really believed my time had come to die. But during the night I began praising God. I walked around my cell lifting holy hands toward heaven, praising God that at five o'clock I would see my Jesus face-to-face. But no one came to take me in the morning. I never knew what happened. For some reason the guards changed their minds, and I was kept alive. Many others died, but I was kept alive."

The conversation continued in these rather somber tones. I asked him about prospects for the future. The pastor's words penetrated my heart as he answered, "Things are getting worse now. For a while we had some religious freedoms, mostly in the mid-sixties. The government appointed a commission on religion. And the Catholic as well as Protestant churches seemed to gain special favor with this commission. Then the Russian government declared new war on religion, and the other Communist countries felt the pressure. One day our government officials turned against the very religious commission they had appointed. So here we were, on good terms with a religious commission that was on bad terms with our government. It has left the church in serious trouble. So we expect things to get much worse. I wake up each morning wondering if this day I shall die for my Jesus."

The pastor paused again before speaking. He appeared uneasy, as if he couldn't share all that he wished. Concluding his remarks, this veteran of oppression added a rather desperate plea: "Pray for us. Prayer is our only hope."

Since it was only possible to visit these faithful Christians for a short time, we found it essential to use each day wisely. We heard of a "Jesus revival," similar to our Jesus movement, impacting a town several hundred miles away. We decided to visit the church responsible for inspiring the revival. While en route we felt again the unseen oppression of the enemy, which seemed to be everywhere. Truly we were in Satan's territory.

Arriving at the city we found housing in the most unusual hotel I've ever seen. For centuries it had served as a key military fortress for those who controlled the mountain overlooking the vast valley below. I decided to set aside an afternoon to give myself a personal tour of the fortress.

It was a beautiful day as I made my way to the edge of a granite lookout constructed high on a cliff. Below, in a gentle valley beside the flowing Danube River, lay a city clearly in Satan's grasp. Yet for some unusual reason I felt protected in this fortress. In my heart an invisible choir seemed to be singing Martin Luther's powerful anthem, "A mighty fortress is our God, a bulwark never failing."

Gazing below I saw a lone navy vessel following the curving river. Soon it was gone, and the river was again silent—a river that seemed out of place in the picture before me. It was too quiet, too peaceful.

I was praying and thinking as I sat alone on the towering lookout. Suddenly I discovered a hidden truth in what I was observing below. A quiet river was indeed beginning to flow across these oppressed lands, the river of the Holy Spirit. Only a month earlier the Communist leaders in Russia were so alarmed about the increased interest in Christianity that a new war was declared on all forms of religion. It was a front-page story in *Pravda*, which at that time was the primary voice of Soviet Communism in the former Soviet Union and all of Eastern Europe. That very week a Romanian evangelist spoke to us of a Holy Spirit revival in his country unlike anything he had witnessed in his lifetime. Two hundred thousand Christians had become involved, with an estimated fifty thousand being young people under the age of twenty-five. (Reports from two other national pastors on our trip confirmed these figures.)

"Supernatural revival for these people," I joyously thought to myself, "is indeed on its way. But it won't come without a price, and everyone will have to work together. God's prayer army must be put on alert."

It was time to leave the lookout. In several days I would be back in Sacramento, comfortably praying in an atmosphere of spiritual freedom with a band of radical young intercessors. I took one final look at the valley below before returning to my room. Twilight was setting. Distant mountains were shrouded in a blurry mist as the sun soon hid behind a hazy horizon. Fog slowly covered the city below. It was only four o'clock in the afternoon. I remember thinking it was unusually dark for that time of day. Again, my heart listened for the lesson God wanted me to hear. It came quickly as His Spirit spoke. "Twilight is settling. It has, indeed, become dark early. And spiritual action must be taken swiftly."

Each of us is being challenged to ask three basic questions.

First, am I yet out in the fields waiting to be harvested, or am I engaged in the harvest?

Someone has said we are either missionaries or mission fields. What is my condition as I read this? Am I a mission field, waiting to be evangelized for Christ? If so, this is the day I must claim Jesus as Lord. I must act now, before the mist of oppression obscures my spiritual vision and clouds my real condition. The Bible declares, "If we say that we have no sin, we are only fooling ourselves and refusing to accept the truth. But if we confess our sins to him, he can be depended on to forgive us and to cleanse us from every wrong" (1 John 1:8–9, TLB).

Second, am I praying that the Lord of the harvest will send out new laborers into the harvest? There is no higher act of Christian service than prayer. The renowned Boston preacher S. D. Gordon said, "Prayer isn't the only thing, but it is the chief thing. The great people of the earth are the people who pray." Jesus declared, "The harvest truly is plentiful, but the laborers are few. Therefore pray the Lord of the harvest to send out laborers into His harvest." (Matt. 9:37–38, NKJV).

Finally, have I helped answer the above prayer—at least in part—by becoming one more laborer in Christ's harvest or by sending those who are willing to go? Jesus said, "You did not choose Me, but I chose you and appointed you that you should go and bear fruit, and that your fruit should remain" (John 15:16, NKJV).

The challenge is clearly before us. The task of global evangelism will be accomplished. But we need each other. Every Christ-honoring Christian ministry is necessary. The gap cannot be left unattended. And we must work together. Alone, we will be defeated. It is in standing back-to-back that we will conquer.

AUTHOR'S NOTE: I could never have imagined during this visit to Yugoslavia what would happen in the years to come in answer to the prayers that were prayed during this trip and at the Prayer Corps once we arrived back home. I would visit the nation of Yugoslavia numerous times in subsequent years and with the demise of Communism in Eastern Europe by the early 1990s see it divided into six different nations—Croatia, Kosovo, Serbia, Slovenia, Bosnia-Herzegovina, and Macedonia. At the breakup of Yugoslavia, Every Home for Christ would begin home-to-home campaigns in all of these new nations. Since those days an amazing 5,075,004 homes have been visited with the gospel, and more than 23,659 people have made a decision for Christ as the result or have asked to be enrolled in our Bible correspondence course to learn more about Jesus. There is little doubt those prayers made a difference.

Part 6
BEYOND THE PIG

Chapter 24
A VISION OF JERICHO

I JOINED THE MINISTRY OF Every Home for Christ (EHC) in mid-1976 to serve as director of prayer mobilization. My invitation to lead EHC's prayer ministry was the result of the ministry's founder, Jack McAlister, hearing about the Prayer Corps and inviting me to take what we had learned through the many thousands of hours of prayer at our first Fire House and to develop training that could be taken to the nations. Every Home for Christ, a ministry founded in 1946, has been reaching millions of people annually with the gospel by taking a printed salvation message for both adults and children to every home in scores of nations. (I describe this ministry more in-depth in chapter 30, "An Accelerating Harvest.") By 1988 I had become the international president of the ministry, a position I hold to the present.

During the early years of our involvement in this ministry it was headquartered in Southern California in the Los Angeles suburb of Chatsworth. I assumed the ministry would be located there until Jesus returned. However, two years after my appointment as international president, our executive vice president, Vince D'Acchioli, came to me with a question. For both practical and economic reasons, he wondered if there might be a better location for our ministry to be headquartered. Operational costs were becoming increasingly expensive in the Los Angeles Basin.

Frankly, when Vince brought up the subject of relocating, I inwardly rejected the idea immediately. I just didn't tell him. I felt a major move such as this would be too disruptive. But I did agree to pray about the matter.

During this season something else was happening on the global scene that consumed much of my attention. It was the opening of once-closed doors to the gospel where proclaiming the Good News of Jesus had been severely restricted for generations. But that was all changing. The influence of Communism, for example, was diminishing rapidly throughout Eastern Europe and the Soviet Union. Walls had begun to fall everywhere, including the Berlin wall itself, which had been torn down in

November 1989. Now, a year later, the door to the former Soviet Union
and all of the former Eastern Bloc nations had opened in amazing ways.
Only a few years earlier this was unthinkable.

A consultant working with us during these days referred to this season
as "the Jericho Hour." That phrase would become the title of a book I
would write on the subject of strategic level prayer a few years later. One
of the chapters in that book included a subtitle that read "Capturing the
Momentum of a Season of Suddenlies." In the chapter I referred to the fact
that in Scripture there are numerous occasions where "divine suddenlies"
occurred. Most notable was on the Day of Pentecost, when "suddenly from
heaven" a mighty rushing wind driven by the Holy Spirit swept across a
small group of some one hundred twenty worshipers. In a single day their
number increased by three thousand. (See Acts 2:1–4, 41.) I was convinced
the church globally was entering such a season. We could expect many
suddenlies and *falling walls of opposition to the gospel* all over the world.

It was at this same time (August 1990) that I was praying about the
challenge Vince had brought to my attention about possibly relocating.
I finally agreed that we should look into the matter. Several cities in
different parts of our nation were considered as a relocation site.

A close friend of Vince, an architect named Gary Larson, heard of our
thoughts of making such a move. Gary happened to be the architect for
Focus on the Family, a ministry also considering moving from the more
costly Southern California area. Focus, in fact, had already decided on
moving to Colorado Springs, and Gary had made numerous trips to the
city to do research on their behalf. He knew as much about Colorado
Springs as anyone, other than a resident of the city.

In discussions with Vince, we agreed that we should invite Gary and
his wife, Sherrill, to go with us and look at possible opportunities for Every
Home for Christ relocating to that community. As we contemplated this
visit, God put on my heart the vision that we now know as "the Jericho
Center." That vision was to become a significant culmination to the Prayer
Corps vision given so many years earlier.

In my vision I saw a picture of Jericho as a significant symbol for several
reasons. For one, Jericho represented all the tribes of Israel coming together
in unity toward a commonly agreed-upon focus. The tribes had been
wandering in the wilderness for forty years, murmuring and complaining
all the while. But then, at Jericho, they had come together in what essen-
tially was a worship strategy. The end result was the falling of the walls of

Jericho. This reminded me that when Christ's body unites, walls fall. It was a phrase that stuck in my mind and was to become our motto for the eventual center: "Where Christ's Body Unites, Walls Fall."

Jericho also was a picture of a total sacrifice to the Lord. Although some might look at what happened at Jericho as a picture of total destruction, Jericho actually represented the firstfruits of all the cities that were to be conquered when Israel finally possessed their Promised Land.

God has always required the firstfruits of our increase as a reminder to us that He is truly our primary source of supply. (See Exodus 13:2–15; Deuteronomy 26:1–3; Proverbs 3:9–10.) Thus the very picture of Jericho is of something fully devoted to the Lord. I was sure this was what God wanted in our future facility. It was to be a place that existed for the purpose of enthroning God in all our strategies to reach and disciple the nations. Perhaps God intended to fulfill the vision in Colorado.

So, in early August of 1990, Vince and his wife, Cindy, joined Gary Larson and his wife, Sherrill, and my wife, Dee, and me in traveling to Colorado Springs from Los Angeles to consider the Springs as our possible new home. We had decided to look at numerous empty buildings where our headquarters might reside if we did choose to move there. We rented a car in Denver and drove to Colorado Springs, and on the day we arrived we spent a good part of the afternoon visiting some of these vacant buildings.

Several years earlier, President Reagan had established a program dubbed Star Wars that was to establish a defensive missile system. Colorado Springs was to be the headquarters for this program. Many buildings were built at a high cost during those years, but when the cold war ended, the Star Wars initiative died. Now, many of these buildings were empty. Of course, my dream was to build our own facility, but perhaps a miracle deal awaited us!

So we visited as many buildings as possible that first afternoon. But at the end of the day, Gary Larson looked at me and said, "Now I would like to take you to the place where I think God wants you to be."

I had no idea what he meant. In moments we were driving our rental car to yet another location—a knoll of about seven acres overlooking a beautiful pond in north Colorado Springs. There was no vacant building on the land. Gary explained that Focus on the Family had looked at this property and really desired it, but it was too small to fulfill their needs. Gary firmly believed God had saved this land just for us and that we should consider building our own building to meet our unique needs rather than attempt to adapt an existing building for our purposes. He looked at me and said, "I think you should pray about this."

We stood on the top of the hill overlooking the pond and did pray. If this was to be the place God wanted us, then we asked Him to make it happen. Little could I have known that more than a decade later this would indeed be the very spot where the Jericho Center would be constructed.

None of the other buildings we had looked at, no matter how inexpensive, met the requirements of all we needed in order to have continuous worship and intercession as well as a functioning international headquarters for our global ministry.

Upon returning to California, a board meeting was conducted, and we shared our findings. The board voted unanimously to relocate to Colorado Springs the following year. By July 1991 we had relocated and occupied leased office space until we could build.

We soon began developing plans for the Jericho Center. We asked Gary Larson, the architect of Focus on the Family, to be our architect as well to help design our facility. My first mental picture of the center was sketched on a small three-by-five card. To this day I can look at the front of our building, with two special rooms devoted exclusively for intercession and worship, and still recall with vivid detail that initial sketch. Gary's unique gifts eventually made those scribbles a wonderful reality.

During the months that followed our move, a gift came to the ministry allowing us to purchase the land Gary believed was to be the location for our permanent headquarters. During these same days I received much insight from the Lord regarding the purposes of the future center. I especially felt that at the heart of the Jericho Center we needed a ministry of continuing worship and intercession. This was essential, I felt, to enthroning Him in our planning. God used Revelation 5:8–10 as a basis for this. It is in this passage that "elders" and "living creatures" come before the Lamb (Christ), each holding a harp (a symbol of worship) and a bowl (a symbol of intercession). Following this symbolic act of intercession and worship, a new song is sung. That song describes how redeemed humanity was being called out of "every tribe, tongue, people and nation." I, of course, am very partial to passages of scripture that include the word *every*.

Little could I have known that it would take more than a decade to see the reality of this center fully unfold. God had so much to teach us. It would not be until the third Saturday in September of 1999 (eight years after our move to Colorado Springs) that we finally broke ground for the new facility. Then it took four more years to finally complete the project. Years later I learned that our groundbreaking ceremony was held on the exact weekend (indeed, the exact day) that 24/7 worship and intercession officially began at the International House of Prayer (IHOP), founded by Mike Bickle. I would soon see a profound prophetic significance in these two simultaneous events. God was surely up to something. He was linking prayer and worship movements to the harvest!

In the visionary planning stages for the Jericho Center, God impressed on my heart that this center would focus on four *links* that would help lead to the fulfillment of the Great Commission. The center was to host consultations that would bring like-minded ministries together regarding these four focuses, just as the tribes had come together at Jericho before entering the Promised Land.

1. The *planning* link would include everything from gathering critical research data for potentially united evangelism and discipleship projects, to organizing prayer teams and intercessory worship networks to saturate these projects in prayer.

2. The *equipping* link would involve ministries, agencies, and denominations that specialize in training or equipping for the tasks of evangelism, discipleship, and church planting for that specifically agreed-upon project. This link also would include those who provided tools to help in the process of spreading the gospel.

3. The *going* link would link ministries, agencies, or groups, focusing on both mass and personal evangelism (i.e., anyone who goes with the gospel). This, of course, might include a vast array of possibilities since almost all ministries somehow view their mandate as contributing to this category.

4. The *discipleship* link would represent those ministries that focus on the ultimate goal of the entire process of these various consultations, that of planting self-sustaining churches everywhere in the agreed-upon region of focus.

I could only imagine what might result if regular consultations were conducted at our future center that focused specifically on each of these four links as they touched a particular geographic region or nation. Further, imagine aligning numerous participating entities into a cohesive, strategic Great Commission force. I specifically pictured Ethiopia at the time, because there had been a discussion among Bible societies and literature ministries of doing a cooperative work in that nation, but in the end it was only minimally successful because most groups didn't cooperate. I wondered what might have happened if a process had been followed using this four-link strategy, where every step was saturated in day-and-night worship and intercession—24/7.

This is what I envisioned happening at the Jericho Center. But one thing was absolutely critical. All of these strategies had to be enthroned in sustained worship and intercession. Mike Bickle of IHOP would coin the expression *intercessory worship* in describing such a prayer strategy.

Interestingly, within weeks of breaking ground for the Jericho Center, which, as stated, was the exact day IHOP began its 24/7 ministry, I ran into Mike Bickle (quite literally) at the Denver, Colorado, airport. He was rushing to make a connection, as was I. In those brief moments I explained to Mike that we were now beginning the Jericho Center project and that our ultimate goal was 24/7 worship and intercession saturating all of our global projects. As Mike turned to head for his connection, he shouted, "You're right on target, Dick!" He then added repeatedly, "It's harp and bowl, harp and bowl, harp and bowl!"

It was after that chance meeting that I began using the term *harp and bowl* when I spoke about the coming prayer focus of the Jericho Center. I would be deeply impacted in the days to come by the prophetic symbolism of these words and the impact of the Revelation 5:8–10 passage.

In the early months of 2000, God would further cement the significance of this harp-and-bowl focus by calling me to a forty-day fast. I had done this once before in my life (in 1996), and I just assumed it was to be a season of fasting and prayer. But it would be on the first day of that fast that God startled me by saying that He was not calling me to forty days of "fasting and prayer" but to forty days of "fasting and worship." I had never really heard that expression before.

When I asked God what this meant, He reminded me of Acts 13:1–2 where it tells how early disciples "worshiped the Lord and fasted" before they commissioned Paul and Silas to go forth and turn entire cities and regions upside down for Christ. (See Acts 13:44, 49; 14:1, 21.) I quickly realized there was a profound significance not only to fasting and prayer but also to fasting and worship. When I asked the Lord how such a fast was to be carried out, He made it clear that I was to sing all my prayers to Him daily throughout the forty days instead of praying my petitions and intercessions as usual. The weeks that followed were some of the most amazing of my entire walk with the Lord. These experiences were to result in the writing of a three-book trilogy, including *Heights of Delight, Pathways of Delight,* and *Rivers of Delight.*

Today everything I saw in those visionary months before the Jericho Center was completed has transpired. We now have the facility with the harp-and-bowl worship and intercession rooms. Further, as I describe in my final chapter, "A Call to the Wall," we now have the additional Watchman Training Center as well as a literal Wall of Prayer with numerous "prayer grottos" where people can seek the Lord intimately. And even that hypothetical illustration about Ethiopia came true just a few years after we occupied the Jericho Center. Consultations were held over several months involving several ministry partners who had burdens for Ethiopia. In less than two years following those consultations, more than twelve hundred new churches were planted (and church buildings built for them), and fifty thousand Ethiopians had been led to Christ. Enthroning God, indeed, has proven to be the key to advancing God's kingdom strategies.

Yet, as I reflect back on how all this has unfolded, I have been reminded more than once that it almost never happened. Three decades earlier, after first joining the ministry of Every Home for Christ, Satan tried to abort it all. I was about to quit the EHC ministry in a very weak moment and may well have done so had it not been for two strange visitors I met but for a moment's time at O'Hare International Airport in Chicago and then never saw again. That encounter changed my personal theology on the subject of angels.

Chapter 25
AGENTS OF THE INVISIBLE

Mental weariness was taking its toll. I decided I couldn't go on.[1] "I'll just resign," I said to myself as I boarded the plane for yet another tiring assignment.

Every Home for Christ, the ministry I joined after turning the Prayer Corps over to a well-qualified young brother, was much larger than the Prayer Corps, with numerous vice presidents (of which I was one) and hundreds of full-time staff. I was barely thirty when I began. But now the frailties of some of the senior staff, mine included, were beginning to show. Leadership was in transition, and some in the organization were jockeying for position.

For months I had carried an unusually heavy burden that often kept me awake all night. On one occasion at work, long before dawn, I had found myself prostrate, all alone, just inside the office entryway of our ministry, weeping and crying out to God for personal and corporate cleansing. But for weeks nothing seemed to happen. My emotions were frayed.

I fastened my seat belt as the plane taxied down the runway for the three-hour flight to Chicago's O'Hare Airport. There I would catch a connection for the East Coast to appear on *The 700 Club* television program discussing the very work that now seemed to be robbing me of my joy. I felt even more depressed. How could I share testimonies of spiritual victories with integrity when I felt such defeat?

"I'll just resign," I said to myself again as the plane began its final approach into Chicago. "I'll quit, that's what I'll do."

I stared at the huge Sears Tower, which loomed over the skyline. Suddenly an unexpected spirit of determination flooded my mind. I knew God had called me to this ministry, and I knew He had not *uncalled* me. Indignation filled my heart against Satan, who must be trying to rob me of my joy. It was not God trying to *call* me out of the work but the enemy trying to *force* me out.

I began praying fervently in my spirit as the plane descended toward O'Hare. I grabbed both armrests firmly. So intense was my prayer against what I perceived to be Satan's harassing demons that I know my body was shaking noticeably, even though my prayers were silent.

Inwardly I shouted—"I will not quit. You can't make me quit! I will stay in the battle, no matter what the outcome."

Instantly my anxiety and depression lifted. It seemed that fresh oil began pouring over me. As I exited the plane, I felt almost light-hearted, renewed.

O'Hare was packed with people as I stood at the gate waiting for my connecting flight to board. A man with a dark pinstriped suit and attaché case came and stood beside me.

"Perhaps he's on the same flight," I thought.

The man never spoke. He just stood, staring straight ahead. Then another man came, wearing an identical suit and carrying a similar attaché case.

"Strange. They must work for the same company."

The new arrival stood directly beside the other man and, like the first, stared straight ahead.

For a moment it was just another O'Hare oddity—the kind of strange sight you see in busy public places when you're watching people. But suddenly I sensed this was different.

"Hey," said one man to the other, still staring straight ahead. "Whatever happened to that Eastman fellow? I heard he was going to quit the company."

I caught my breath and looked out of the corner of my eye to see if either one of them would acknowledge my existence. Could they possibly know my name was *Eastman* and that only a short time earlier I had thought of quitting my company?

The other man kept looking straight ahead.

"Oh, I have some good news," he said. "I just talked to headquarters. The Chief told me Eastman changed his mind. He was hanging by a thread, you know. We thought we were going to lose him."

Then, with a slight smile, he concluded, "Yeah, the Chief says Eastman's going to stay in the battle."

"I'm really glad to hear that. There's a great future for him in the company."

I am not sure what kept me from turning to either of those men and saying, "Hey, who are you guys, anyway?" But the next instant they walked away and went around a corner perhaps thirty feet away. I looked for them seconds later but couldn't find them.

Whether they simply blended into the crowd or literally disappeared, I do not know. And whether this was merely a very odd coincidence or a divine encounter, the incident became a great source of encouragement for me in an otherwise deeply difficult time.

Over the years, I have often wondered if those men were *agents of the invisible* (angels) who had come to deliver an encouraging confirmation for me to stay in the battle long enough to see victory. God clearly had a glorious future for me in this very ministry, and Satan wanted me out. Of one thing I became certain: there *are* angels out there, and they are clearly at work.

Dispensers of the Divine

Centuries ago John Calvin, writing in the *Institutes of the Christian Religion*, advised:

> Angels are the ministers and the dispensers of the divine bounty towards us. Accordingly, we are told how they watch for our safety, how they undertake our defense, direct our path, and take heed that no evil befall us.[2]

Billy Graham adds thoughtfully:

> I am convinced that these heavenly beings exist and that they provide unseen aid on our behalf. I do not believe in angels because someone has told me about a dramatic visitation from an angel, impressive as such rare testimonies may be....I do not believe in angels because I have ever seen one—because I haven't. I believe in angels because the Bible says there are angels, and I believe the Bible to be the true Word of God.[3]

There is little doubt biblically and experientially (my strange O'Hare encounter aside) that God does send angels on specific assignments to accomplish His will, especially regarding world evangelization.

Biblically speaking, we see angels involved in the work of evangelism from the very birth of Christ, when one of them announced the Good News to frightened shepherds:

> Do not be afraid, for behold, I bring you good tidings of great joy which will be to all people. For there is born to you this day in the city of David a Savior, who is Christ the Lord.
> —LUKE 2:10–11, NKJV

If we accept the definition of *evangelism* as "sharing the Good News," then this angel was involved in evangelism. In fact, this heavenly being was specifically dispatched to deliver the very first declaration in history that Jesus Christ, the Savior of the world, had been born.

The Bible says much about the ministry of angels, referring to them (in differing angelic categories) some three hundred times. Their functions are defined as twofold: service and worship. (See Isaiah 6:1–4; Hebrews 1:13–14; Revelation 4:8–11.) We may even infer from the rhetorical question of Hebrews 1:14—"Are not all angels ministering spirits sent to serve those who will inherit salvation?"—that *all* angels are involved somehow in the harvest of souls. This is good news for us on the ground who are sharing the Good News of salvation to the lost!

Angels Are Everywhere

Isaiah's vision of God's throne room (Isa. 6:1–4) involved unique angelic beings called *seraphs*, each with six wings, praising God for His holiness. Isaiah did not report how many seraphs he saw but simply referred to them in the plural. The apostle John specifically referred to four living creatures, each with six wings, likewise worshiping God for His holiness (Rev. 4:8–11). Perhaps Isaiah and John were describing the same angelic worship leaders orchestrating praise around the throne.

But no matter how we define angels—or differentiate between cherubim (Ezek. 10:8–15) and seraphs (Isa. 6:2), or between seraphs and archangels (1 Thess. 4:16; Jude 9), or between all of the above from the living creatures of Revelation (Rev. 4:8; 7:11), one thing is certain—angels are real, and they are everywhere.

In the Old Testament

Elisha and his servant saw hills filled with angelic beings described as "chariots of fire" (2 Kings 6:17). As Jacob slept on his journey to Haran, he saw a stairway leading into the heavenlies on which "the angels of God were ascending and descending" (Gen. 28:12).

In the early church

God's agents of the invisible, who sometimes showed up clothed in human bodies, were also significant in the emerging early church.

An angel opened prison doors, allowing the apostles to go free and continue evangelizing throughout Jerusalem (Acts 5:19–20). An angel gave Philip his Gaza Strip assignment, which led him into the desert to encounter and convert the Ethiopian eunuch (Acts 8:26).

God sent an angelic representative to Cornelius to commend the centurion for his faithfulness in praying and giving (Acts 10:3–4), and to instruct him to send for Peter (vv. 5–6), who would bring the message of salvation to Cornelius's family. Once again the preaching of the gospel to lost people is linked with angelic intervention.

An angel was sent to deliver Peter from prison while the disciples prayed for him "without ceasing" (Acts 12:5, KJV). And in the same chapter we read that Herod's death came at the hands of an angel (v. 23).

Paul was also touched by these agents of the invisible. For example, as he sailed to Rome, he was told by an angel that he and those aboard ship would be saved from drowning and that he would stand trial before Caesar (Acts 27:23–24).

A study of Revelation reveals a dramatic increase in angelic activity as this present age concludes. The seven angels sound seven trumpets of judgment that announce the establishing of Christ's kingdom on the earth (Rev. 8–9, 11).

Mission strategist Ed Silvoso reminds us:

> The reality of angels cannot be denied. The Book of Acts contains 20 references to angels. On almost every occasion, when the Church was in danger or in confusion, angels were dispatched to the battlefield to help. This is not something that ceased with the completion of the biblical canon. All over the Third World, where the Church is on fire, we find ever-expanding numbers of testimonies of dramatic angelic intervention on behalf of the Church.[4]

The idea of angelic ministry is indeed biblical, and angels *are* out there. And because they are "ministering spirits sent to serve those who will inherit salvation" (Heb. 1:14), we should not be surprised to see an increased level of their activity as the church advances toward completion of the Great Commission and the conclusion of this present age.

The Crocodile River

There is no biblical basis for praying to angels, but we can pray to God, asking Him to send His angels to work on our behalf. As the psalmist asked, "Let those be put to shame and brought to dishonor who seek after my life.... And let the angel of the LORD chase them" (Ps. 35:4–5).

Two Every Home for Christ field workers learned this lesson firsthand. Several years ago while on a remote mission assignment on a South Pacific island, they claimed the release of angels to *chase* a very formidable enemy! Jack and Andrew were doing systematic, home-to-home evangelism in villages throughout the western province of Guadalcanal, the main island in the Solomon Island chain. One settlement was located on a wide river that cut through the region where they were ministering. Jack and Andrew visited every home in that village, sharing the Good News with all who would listen.

In the afternoon, after visiting with the last family, they looked across the river and noticed another village almost hidden in the dense trees. That village too had to be reached, but they had no means of crossing the river. They inquired about the availability of a boat, but everyone who had a boat was fishing on the river. The workers waited for a boat to return, but none came.

It was now late afternoon, and Jack and Andrew realized that if they were to do any more evangelism that day, they would have to cross the river now. So they decided to tie some logs together as a flotation device to help them swim across. They would hang on to the logs and swim across.

As they tossed several logs into the river and prepared to wade in, a village elder rushed over shouting, "What are you doing?"

Jack explained their intention to swim across the river using the logs.

"Oh, no," cried the old man. "You'll be eaten."

"What do you mean?" Andrew inquired.

"The river is filled with crocodiles. In all my years in this village, we have never known anyone to swim across this river successfully."

Still Andrew and Jack knew they had to cross, and no boat was available.

"We'll just have to ask God to send His angels," Jack told the elder, "just as He did for Daniel in the lions' den."

The old man had no idea what the evangelist meant and stood bewildered as the Christian workers entered the water. Pushing several logs together, they placed their bags of gospel literature carefully in the center of the logs. Then, their bodies half submerged and their feet kicking furiously, they swam toward the center of the river.

The swimming evangelists could soon see crocodiles lunging into the water and moving toward them. The reptiles formed a small line of observers, eyes above the surface of the water following their moves, but appearing strangely uncertain about coming any closer. Andrew and Jack could also see a lone village elder getting smaller and smaller watching from the other side of the river.

As they approached the opposite shore and began to gather up their gospel literature, a villager from the other side rushed up and exclaimed, "You are the first people ever to swim across that river without being attacked by crocodiles! Even dogs that swim in this river never make it across. They're swallowed up."

Andrew and Jack thanked God for keeping the crocodiles at bay and set out to visit every home in the village, leaving gospel messages for those who could read and taking time to tell all who would listen the story of Jesus. By evening word had spread about how the young men had crossed the crocodile-infested waters untouched and how *unseen beings* must have protected them.

That night Jack and Andrew began singing gospel songs in the village center to a gathering crowd. Andrew was soon preaching, telling the story of Daniel in the lions' den and using the story to lead to a message about Jesus. It clearly was the message of the hour. Most in the village received Christ when his message concluded. The village chief then told the workers something that amplified the significance of all that had happened that day. He explained that the crocodile had been the *god* those villagers had worshiped for many generations. Now, he told them, they would be worshiping the one true God!

When the young men headed back across the river, they took a boat. Daniel had been in the lions' den only once, they reasoned, and they didn't want to be presumptuous! But they never doubted that invisible agents had crossed the river with them and had kept the mouths of the crocodiles shut. Yes, angels are everywhere!

Chapter 26
SEEDS OF PASSION

I SAT IN THE COMFORTABLE hotel chair with my feet on the bed and my Bible open in my lap. It was my most common prayer posture when spending extended times in prayer while traveling. I had arrived late the previous night in North Carolina to speak at a prayer banquet planned by a growing Southern Baptist church. A year earlier the church had hosted one of our Change the World Schools of Prayer taught by another of our ten full-time instructors who were teaching the course at the time.

So moved had the pastor been after the training that he decided to build an on-site, 24/7 prayer chapel on the campus of the church. In fact, he had stood before his congregation one Sunday and boldly declared, "If you want me to continue as your pastor, you will help me build this prayer chapel." Then he asked for the congregation to give an offering. Most came forward, laying their gifts on the altar. More than $50,000 was raised in just a few minutes' time.

Now the chapel had been completed, and the day-and-night prayer had begun. The pastor called me in California and asked if I would be willing to fly to the East Coast and speak at a Saturday night prayer banquet and then help dedicate the new chapel on Sunday.

So here I was, quietly praying about what to speak on that night at the banquet. My least desired venue for speaking on prayer (or any subject) is at a banquet. When it's time to speak, most attendees are usually still eating their dessert, or the service staff is picking up plates, accompanied by the clatter of dishes and the dropping of silverware. I call this noise "anointing killers."

I realized that I would have only about thirty minutes to speak at the conclusion of the banquet. By now I was struggling as to what message I might bring. In those days most of my messages had handwritten notes in the margin of my Bible alongside the main scripture text for that specific message.

So I was now randomly thumbing through my Bible for an appropriate inspirational challenge for the evening. I was getting nowhere.

Every passage I turned to and every message outline scribbled in one of the margins seemed inappropriate for the gathering. I was becoming increasingly frustrated.

Finally it occurred to me that I really hadn't specifically asked the Lord what He thought I should speak on that night. So I voiced my desire: "Lord, what would You have me share tonight?"

The response was startling.

"Pick anything you want. It doesn't matter."

"What on Earth does that mean?" I asked the Lord.

How couldn't it matter? And what did He mean by "pick anything you want"?

I heard His still, small voice again: "You can choose any passage you wish because I have sent you here for a purpose, and I am going to work that purpose no matter what message you choose."

I was bewildered. I had never heard anything like this before. But the Lord wasn't finished speaking. He added, "You really don't fully understand the nature of the ministry I have given you when you teach on prayer."

That too brought questions. I thought I understood the nature of my calling quite well.

But the Lord had more He wanted to show me. He showed me that the essence of my teaching ministry was that of sowing seeds. First, the teaching represented seeds for a passion of the Lord Himself. Second, they were seeds for a passion for the lost.

"I've called you to be a sower of seeds of passion," the Lord explained, adding, "Tonight when you speak, you will be scattering seeds for a hunger for My presence and a passion for the lost. These seeds are destined for the fertile soil of those willing hearts who will gather."

Never had I viewed my ministry in this way. I did recall times when I would be teaching a seminar or leading a prayer retreat or some other meeting when suddenly people would break down weeping, and I wasn't sure why. Sometimes I would pause momentarily and try to recall what I had just said to see why there might have been that kind of reaction. But I would quickly determine I had said nothing of any great significance. I concluded it was simply the work of God's Spirit and that I would never fully understand it. But I did sense that something had taken root in their hearts and that the impact was being made visible by their reaction.

I went to the banquet that night a bit bewildered. I didn't eat as the meals were brought to the tables. I was still thumbing through my Bible looking for something that I might share that would be appropriate for the occasion. I was understandably numb when I was introduced by the senior pastor of the church. To this day I do not recall what I spoke, nor did I record it in my daily journal the following day (something I always do after a speaking engagement). What I do recall with vivid detail is that midway through my message, a brokenness settled throughout the banquet hall. Dessert was postponed, and the service staff stood silent off to the side. God was moving. I suddenly realized that what God had spoken to my heart earlier that day was taking place before my very eyes.

All this would have been a simple though certainly unusual experience that might easily have been forgotten were it not for something equally profound that happened to me two years later. That subsequent experience would prove to me that our words, when anointed by God's Spirit (no matter the vessel), can become fruit-bearing seeds lying dormant in the fertile soil of willing hearts just waiting to produce God-honoring fruit.

I had been invited to Illinois for a statewide youth retreat focusing on prayer. Several hundred young people had gathered from throughout the state. It was to be a several-day conference, including one all-night session devoted exclusively to prayer.

The all-night prayer vigil occurred on the final night of the gathering. I was asked to lead that night's meeting, and I decided to conduct it in a similar fashion as the prayer retreats I had led so many years previously.

First, I would engage the young people in various group prayer models and methods designed to keep their attention for several hours. That would take us close to midnight. It would include forming small prayer groups of four to six young people who would pray together for personal needs, followed by asking participants to kneel and pray alone for a short period of time, then we would pray Scripture together in small groups, all of which would include a good deal of praise and worship sprinkled throughout. It all unfolded as I had imagined.

Then, just before midnight, an idea came. I was to invite young people to come to the microphone one at a time and cry out to God—quite literally. I was to tell them they were free to express verbally and intensely the deep hunger of their hearts for more of God. "Don't hold back," I was to tell them. I also was to encourage the larger group to agree verbally with whoever came forward to pray.

It all sounded a bit risky, but I knew I should do it. I sensed that as individual young people did this, it would motivate their peers also to cry out to God. Frankly, I had no idea the impact this was about to have.

The first to respond was a young man about seventeen. He started praying softly but then raised his voice as he continued praying. The level of intensity increased with almost every word. It was a deeply moving prayer. As I looked across the auditorium, I could see tears streaming down the faces of many. God was doing exactly what I had imagined.

Then a second youthful intercessor, a young lady, came forward. She seemed a bit tentative as she stepped to the microphone. But any hesitancy quickly vanished as she began praying. The emotion is hard to describe. She seemed desperate for more of God. I was amazed at her courage to pray so intensely in front of others.

"God, I have never wanted You more than I want You now," she cried out. "I love You so much I can hardly describe it," she added.

Then she prayed something that immediately caught my attention: "I feel like someone has planted seeds in my heart for a passion for Your presence, and those seeds are beginning to grow in my heart even as I pray. O Lord..."

Suddenly, the teen stopped mid-sentence. It was an abrupt interruption. All of us waited to hear her go on. But the pause continued. There was an eerie silence. Then, before the entire group, she turned to me and said, "Brother Dick, God just spoke to me about you." The crowd moved to the edge of their seats.

"What did He say," I wondered, "and how did she know it was God?" What she said next troubled and concerned me.

"I hope this doesn't embarrass you, Brother Dick, but He told me to tell you this in front of everybody."

A cold sweat came over me. What secret did she know? And why did she use the word *embarrass*? I had done some less than godly things in my teen years, but I really felt I had repented of them. What was she about to reveal? I knew if I tried to stop her, it would only make matters worse. For a moment I went numb.

When she spoke next, I wept.

"Brother Dick, God told me to tell you that the seeds you are planting are real. They are as real as any seed a farmer plants in the ground. When they reach the heart of a person, they begin to grow just as real seeds grow. And those seeds produce real fruit. From that fruit even more seeds come to produce even more fruit. Until now you have not truly understood or fully believed that. The Lord wants you to know those seeds are real."

Looking intently at me, the youth hesitated momentarily before concluding.

"I don't know what all this means, but God told me you would understand."

With that, she turned back to the microphone and finished her impassioned prayer. There were no dry eyes in the auditorium, especially mine.

I, of course, knew exactly what she meant. From that moment on I realized that when those of us who are pastors, evangelists, or teachers spend much time with the Lord in preparation for ministry, our words do indeed become seeds. They are seeds that, if watered by God's Spirit, can produce glorious fruit in which there will be even more seeds to produce even greater fruit. And most often these seeds are seeds for a hunger for God and a passion for the lost.

Chapter 27

A SONG OF CONCEPTION

TWICE IN MY LIFE I have felt compelled to spend a month in prayer. On two other occasions, inspired by the life of the late Dr. Bill Bright of Campus Crusade for Christ, I have felt led to devote forty days to fasting and prayer. One of those forty-day seasons of fasting was actually fasting and worship, as I described in chapter 24.

The two occasions of spending a month in prayer involved setting aside my usual office hours and other assignments (including speaking engagements) exclusively to seek God in prayer for an entire month. I would eat meals with my family, but the rest of these days were spent in prayer and worship.

The first of these month-long experiences occurred in December 1987. I had no idea at the time that this prolonged season of prayer would launch me on a unique journey to Eastern Europe to pray for the walls of Communist oppression to fall, nor that it would lead me to my present leadership role as international president of Every Home for Christ.

The experience that led me to spend that first month in prayer in December 1987 began with a simple impression a few days after Thanksgiving of that year. I was in prayer when I felt the Holy Spirit speak, "I want you to confront the strongholds of Communism in Eastern Europe."

I immediately saw in my mind that principal symbol of Communist oppression at the time—the Berlin wall. I sensed the Lord was calling me to travel the six thousand miles from Southern California, where we lived at the time, to West Berlin, Germany. Once there I was to lay my hands on the wall and simply tell it to come down "in Jesus's name." Even as I prayed about this assignment, I imagined myself standing at the graffiti-covered western side of the Berlin wall and praying, "In Jesus's name, come down!"

But it would not be until this directive was carried out that I would recognize the profound significance of prophetic acts in prayer. Of course, I realized I wasn't the only one praying, and I later learned that others had engaged in unusual prophetic acts of prayer. One brother I later met had prayer-walked the entire length of the wall! A group of Catholic nuns had come to the wall every Monday night for years to pray. But still I felt this was something I had to do, even if flying six thousand miles to pray a five-word prayer seemed a bit pricey.

When receiving this heart directive on that November morning in 1987, I assumed I was to board a plane immediately, or at least within a day or two, to carry out the assignment. However, the Lord made it clear that I wasn't ready yet. When I asked the Lord what I needed to do to get ready, I felt the Lord was asking me a question rather than giving me a directive.

"Have you ever thought of spending an entire month of just seeking My presence in prayer?"

I knew that by the very nature of the question the Lord was asking if I was willing to first spend an entire month in prayer before boarding an airplane for the six-thousand-mile flight to Germany. Within the next few days between Thanksgiving and the first day of December, I began mapping out in my mind how I might spend a complete month in prayer. It was not something I had ever done before. In fact, I had never spent an entire week in prayer. I also realized that once the month had passed, I would be much more prepared to head to West Germany to carry out my five-word prayer assignment at the Berlin wall.

Realizing that praying for an entire month would not be an easy task, I prayerfully thought of different methods of prayer that I might focus on for the different days of the month. Of course, I had to inform our staff that I would not be engaged in the usual activities that were normal for that time of the year, particularly during the office hours. I also felt that it would be good for me to spend some of those days with other intercessors and even staff who might care to join me. This, I believed, would give variety to the month and make it a little easier to do.

I decided that one of those days would be set aside to simply sing to the Lord for an entire day, something I'd never done in my life. I knew, of course, that it would be somewhat difficult for me to sing to the Lord alone for an entire day, so I informed our regular intercessors and staff that if they would like to join me, they were welcome. We would do it in our office prayer chapel where intercessors came daily to pray for our ministry. This was prior to my becoming international president of Every Home for Christ and during a time when I was directing a full-time prayer ministry called Change the World Ministries.

The appointed day for singing to the Lord arrived, and numerous intercessors and staff were brave enough to join me for at least part of day, with a few remaining the entire time. Realizing that some might find it difficult to sing to the Lord for hours on end, I had suggested that worshipers come at their leisure and leave as they felt led. They could join me for an hour, two hours, or the whole day.

We gathered at the start of the day, and I informed those participating that we would be singing a variety of songs, like the psalms and other passages of Scripture, familiar choruses, but most of all spontaneous songs that would come from our hearts—*heart songs* as I referred to them. We would, I suggested, "sing in the Spirit." (See 1 Corinthians 14:15; Colossians 3:16.) I encouraged them to make up their own melodies even if it seemed awkward. I believed God would bless us if we at least tried. True, at the start it was awkward, but as the day progressed, it became a wonderful new adventure in corporate worship. It was what is now very common in continuous worship in places like the International House of Prayer (IHOP) in Kansas City or at our own headquarters, the Jericho Center in Colorado Springs.

It was near the end of that day's worship that something most unusual happened. One of those who had joined me for the entire time was my assistant Wes Wilson, who helped me found our prayer ministry.

Wes began singing a personal song that at first seemed rather humorous. He sang, "O Lord, our culture has a saying, 'We make our bed and therefore must lie in it...'"

Before he sang the next line, I wondered where he was taking these strange lyrics, especially if it was to have anything to do with worship. His voice cracked, and he could hardly go on. But then he added, "Lord, we have chosen to make for You a bed of song, and we come with our melodies just to love You!"

As Wes sang the passion and desire of his heart, something came over me. When he finished, I began to sing a spontaneous song of my love for the Lord. I began to weep with a passion I hadn't felt for many months, perhaps years. I was absolutely consumed with the presence of the Lord. Surely this was something akin to the manifest presence of God. It seemed as if I was lifted into a heavenly sphere where I experienced God's presence in ways that I had not experienced before. It wasn't that I had never sung spontaneously in His presence before, but I had certainly never set aside an entire day to do it. Now I was being transported into

His presence as if to conceive something within me that could not have been conceived and ultimately birthed in any other way. It was a stunning experience. I wept for the rest of that day.

So powerful was the experience that when I arrived home that evening, I went immediately to our backyard prayer chapel. As I sat on my prayer cushions and continued worshiping, I noticed a calendar for the coming year (1988) pinned to my small bulletin board. So profound was the sense that something had been conceived that day that I counted nine months from that day in mid-December and marked the date in September 1988 on the new calendar. Why nine months? I thought of a baby in the mother's womb maturing from a fertilized speck of life and then emerging from the womb nine months later to express its fullness in life. This is what I believed was happening. I looked at the date on the calendar. It was September 12 of the following year. In the small square for that date on the calendar I wrote these words with a green felt-tipped marker: "Something new will be born today." I was certain it had to do with my personal destiny, and especially regarding taking the gospel to all the nations of the world. I felt I was pregnant with some kind of unusual blessing that had come as the result of those unusual moments of divine conception through song. I can find no other way to describe it.

Little could I have known all that was going to happen in the months that followed.

For one thing, I would indeed travel to West Berlin to fulfill the directive that had set all this in motion just prior to that month of prayer. By mid-January 1988 I arrived in Berlin and went to the Berlin wall, exactly as I had imagined more than a month earlier when I felt the Holy Spirit say, "Confront the strongholds of Communism in Eastern Europe."

I vividly recall that day as I walked to the Berlin wall. It was a rather chilly experience (freezing, to be honest), because coming from California I forgot that their winters in Berlin were much colder, and I was wearing a light jacket. I'm sure people noticed. They could tell I was shaking, and it wasn't the anointing! I was freezing.

But I had an assignment to fulfill. I walked to the wall and laid my hands on it. Somewhat embarrassed, and thinking that others might be observing me do this, I pulled my hands back and looked in different directions to see who might be watching. But then I realized I had a very specific prayer assignment, and I laid my hands on the graffiti-covered wall. I spoke authoritatively, my face less than a foot from the wall, "In Jesus's name, come down."

In seconds, my six-thousand-mile, five-word prayer assignment was completed.

I caught a plane that night and headed for home. Within two weeks of arriving back in Los Angeles, I picked up the *Los Angeles Times* and noticed an amazing editorial titled "The Wall Behind the Wall Is Falling." Of course, I clearly understood that my prayer assignment at the Berlin wall wasn't to confront *brick and mortar* but invisible powers of demonic darkness that had caused that wall to stand as such a formidable obstacle to freedom for so many years. Little could I have known that already something had been set in motion that all the political forces of Communist Eastern Europe could not stop.

That editorial in the *Los Angeles Times* explained that "brick by brick" the ideology of Communist Eastern Europe was beginning to come down. The author suggested that it might be just a matter of months before the Berlin wall itself would be history. Interestingly, within just a few months Hungary would be the first Eastern Bloc nation to begin cutting the barbed-wire fences that had been a continuation of the actual Berlin wall and what Winston Churchill coined as "the iron curtain." Little more than a year later, the Berlin wall itself would come crashing down.

Later, in a visit back to the now-crumbling wall in November 1989, I would hear the amazing story of how just a few days before a huge bulldozer broke the first opening in the wall a group of scores of young German believers had come to the wall for worship. They had boosted one another to the top and were singing spontaneous *heart songs* to the Lord. I was told by Christian leaders who knew the whole story that when the wall finally was broken down, that first bulldozer slammed into the wall at the exact spot where the young people had been worshiping. (I had often wondered, though I couldn't prove it, if that might have been the exact spot where I had prayed a year earlier!)

Upon arriving home from my five-word prayer journey to Berlin, I felt another strong impression. The Lord was urging me to take a team of intercessors the following summer to pray at different Communist strongholds in other parts of Eastern Europe. At first I thought God wanted me to mobilize veteran intercessors, perhaps even some key pastors and other ministry leaders to accompany Dee and me.

But immediately the Lord clarified that He wanted all these intercessors to be teenagers. This both amazed and confused me. Where would I find young intercessors who would understand such spiritual warfare? But I was certain the Lord was speaking.

I went to my pastor at that time, Jack Hayford, who suggested we mobilize select youth from the church and train them over a period of weeks in principles of spiritual warfare. Over the next several months this was done, and a team of twenty young people responded and were trained for this unusual prayer mission. The average age of the team members was just sixteen.

That following July we were on our way to Eastern Europe. The trip included unusual prayer encounters in various places still under strong Communist control. We visited cities like Bucharest, Romania, where Nicolae Ceausescu, one of the most ruthless Communist rulers, had ruled Romania for decades. We were only able to visit the country as tourists because they wanted our foreign dollars. Little did they know that we were actually there to pray for Communism to crumble.

On one occasion during our Romanian visit we told our tour guide (who was required to stay with us at all times) that we would appreciate some time free just to walk around the center of his beautiful city. He had no idea that our true intention was to prayer-walk seven times around the Communist Party building in the center of Bucharest, claiming that the spirit of Communism would lose its grip in this Balkan nation of oppression. The guide was happy to release us for several hours as he took a long nap on the tour bus.

The following year after our prayer journey, tremendous political upheaval came to Romania. The very building we had marched around seven times was seen in flames on international television. During those same days Ceausescu was arrested and detained. Within a few weeks the dictator and his wife would be executed by a firing squad. Ironically, their executions would take place on Christmas Day.

On that same journey to Eastern Europe, we traveled from Romania to Bulgaria and spent numerous powerful prayer times across Bulgaria, including a most memorable encounter in the central park of the capital of Bulgaria, Sofia.

At one point in the park, Wes Wilson, whom I mentioned earlier regarding our day of singing to the Lord (and one of the adult chaperones on our Eastern Europe prayer journey), saw an interesting prophetic picture in his mind. He envisioned our group planting seeds of God's glory in the soil of the park. Those seeds, he believed, would grow to produce a revival that would free the people of Bulgaria from Communist dominance. At that time, possibly the most ruthless dictator in all of Eastern Europe, even worse than Romania's Ceausescu, was Todor Zhivkov of Bulgaria, a strict Stalinist. Zhivkov had been in power longer than any dictator in Eastern Europe since Stalin himself.

We were in a large clearing of Sofia's Central Park at the time, and no other locals were anywhere nearby. Wes felt comfortable in sharing his unusual vision and led the group through the prophetic exercise of planting invisible seeds in the soil of the clearing. He boldly challenged each teen to dig a small hole with his or her bare hands and then plant their imaginary seeds of God's glory, covering them up as they finished. It was an unusual exercise to say the least, and the teens responded obediently, though some kept looking in every direction as they dug their holes. They were somewhat reminiscent of Gideon's troops who, while lapping water from the brook, kept looking around to make sure no enemies were watching! Little could we have known that we were watching history in the making.

"I believe these invisible seeds will bear the fruit of transformation in the days to come," Wes suggested. He then added a simple statement, which, months later, would prove to be amazingly prophetic: "I believe that some day a revolution overthrowing Communism will come to Bulgaria, and I believe it will begin right here on this very spot." But Wes didn't stop with that statement. He concluded, "I also believe that someday I'll read the answer to this prayer on the front page of the *Los Angeles Times!*"

After we arrived home from leading this team of teens to Eastern Europe, the Board of Directors of Every Home for Christ contacted me about the future of the EHC vision. They asked if I would consider allowing my name to be submitted to serve as international president of the ministry. Within a few days I felt a release from the Lord to say yes, and within a few additional weeks, the board graciously voted to invite me to serve in this capacity. When I asked the board chairman, Andrew Duda, when the board wanted me to assume my new role, he gave me the date. I was expecting it to be at least several months later in the year to transition from our present ministry. But they wanted me to begin almost immediately. As I looked at Andy's start date in my Day-Timer, tears filled my eyes. It was exactly nine months to the day from that day in mid-December of 1987 when I had sung that song of conception with those who joined me for a day of song.

Something remarkable had indeed been born that day—just as I had scribbled with a green felt-tip marker nine months earlier. And the miracle continues to produce amazing fruit even to the present. Every country in Eastern Europe now has been impacted in profound ways through the ministry of Every Home for Christ since those young people prayed those prophetic prayers in the summer of 1988. Hundreds of new churches have been planted, and tens of thousands of people who lived behind the once infamous iron curtain have made decisions for Christ in the region. In fact, in just six months of the official removal of the Berlin wall in November of 1989, our Every Home for Christ office in West Germany already had received more than 120,000 requests for our Bible correspondence course as the result of evangelism in the former East Germany. These decisions and responses were from people who wanted to know more about how to know Jesus.

And what of those invisible seeds planted in the soil of Central Park in Sofia, Bulgaria? That following year, just two months after becoming the new international president of Every Home for Christ, I watched those seeds come to life in a most remarkable way.

It was mid-November 1989 when I arrived home late at night from our California office, collecting the *Los Angeles Times* just outside our door. With the paper in hand, I slumped into my easy chair to catch my breath after a busy day and to catch up on the news. The Berlin wall had fallen just four days earlier, and every day seemed to produce new and startling global developments. It was November 13, 1989. My eyes froze as I gazed at the front page of the *Los Angeles Times*. "Bulgarians Greet Change With Caution, Suspicion," the headline read. It was an above-the-fold front-page headline. I couldn't believe it.

My heart was pounding as I began reading the article. It spoke of how "revolution" had come to Bulgaria and how it had all begun in *a clearing in Sofia's large Central Park*. There demonstrators had set up a table, inviting fellow Bulgarians to sign a petition opposing actions of their Communist government in their plans to divert the river flowing through their capital. The demonstrations and petition signing were a ploy, the article explained, to allow people to vent their frustrations.

The initial group of signers was no more than the size of our original team of young intercessors who had prayed there the previous year.

But that number of demonstrators would soon grow into hundreds and then thousands. The Bulgarian Revolution had begun! Only days later, Bulgaria's Communist government would fall completely. And, as the article explained, it all started in a clearing in Sofia's Central Park. *I think some of our youthful intercessors might recognize that clearing.*

Before retiring for the night I phoned Wes Wilson and asked if he had seen that day's *Los Angeles Times*. He hadn't.

I said only, "Your prayer has been answered, Wes. It's on the front page of the *Times*. Get a copy as soon as you can," and I went to bed.

Chapter 28
PRAY THROUGH THE WINDOW

D URING SUBSEQUENT YEARS, MANY things happened involving the establishing of new prayer movements and the expansion of existing ones. Three years after the launching of the Prayer Corps ministry, I received an invitation from Vonette Bright, wife of the late Dr. Bill Bright and a cofounder with him of Campus Crusade for Christ. Vonette had a special passion for mobilizing prayer and in 1971 established The Great Commission Prayer Crusade, the prayer mobilization arm of Campus Crusade. Vonette invited several prayer leaders, including me, to Washington DC to the newly purchased residence of the Christian Embassy, a ministry Campus Crusade had helped establish. From this meeting it was learned that some seventy prayer movements and ministries existed in the nation at the time but often had little contact with each other. Vonette decided to mobilize another meeting the following year at the same location, and this time some fifty leaders participated. I still recall the circle of prayer leaders at this gathering as they shared their various visions with one another and the unique spirit of unity felt throughout the room.

Little could I have known that out of that second meeting in 1975 America's National Prayer Committee would be born. I had the joy of being a part of those early meetings of the committee, which formally took the name America's National Prayer Committee in 1981. Under the inspiration of Vonette Bright we began pursuing the establishing of a fixed National Day of Prayer. In 1952 a resolution by Congress, signed by President Harry Truman, declared a National Day of Prayer,[1] but without a fixed date little was done to promote it. With much prayer and many challenges, President Ronald Reagan would finally sign into law the bill establishing the first Thursday of each May as America's official National Day of Prayer.

It was clearly a miracle how the bill made its way through the Congress. I had the joy of being present with other committee members and several members of Congress in the East Room of the White House in early May 1988 when President Reagan signed the bill.

During those early years of the committee, there also was a burden to give leadership to an international prayer assembly. It was decided to conduct such a conference in Seoul, Korea, in June of 1984. I was asked by the committee to help serve as a co-coordinator of the event, along with a respected Chinese leader, Dr. Thomas Wang of Hong Kong. Some three thousand delegates from more than one hundred nations gathered in Seoul, Korea, where they were joined by an estimated one hundred thousand Korean intercessors. It was from these meetings that numerous national prayer movements were begun in the months and years to follow. But much more was yet to come.

A decade later, after Every Home for Christ had made the move from Southern California to Colorado Springs, we became significantly involved in the AD2000 and Beyond Movement, and specifically its prayer focus. A prayer track became central to the movement, and many diverse groups and strategies became involved. This included the development of a Spiritual Warfare Network, led by Dr. Peter Wagner, a former seminary professor at Fuller Seminary in Pasadena, California.

The AD2000 and Beyond Movement was largely the brainchild of Luis Bush, former president of Partners International, along with other mission strategists who had a special passion for seeing the literal fulfillment of the Great Commission in our generation.

At that time considerable emphasis was focused on seeing the world evangelized by the year 2000. Although this ambitious goal didn't materialize, the movement did mobilize thousands of leaders into different tracks, such as evangelism, discipleship, Scripture translation, and prayer, each related to discipling the nations and ultimately fulfilling the Great Commission. Two major Global Congresses on World Evangelism (GCOWE) were conducted with that goal in mind, the first in 1995 in Seoul, South Korea, and the second in 1997 in Johannesburg, South Africa.

It was during the early days of the AD2000 and Beyond Movement that one of the most significant prayer movements in our generation was born. Referred to as the Pray Through the Window campaign, the objective was to mobilize concentrated prayer focused on that geographic region so defined by its location: ten degrees above the equator to forty degrees, and stretching from the west coast of Africa all through the Middle East and into the Korean peninsula. The region represented one-third of the world's landmass but two-thirds of the earth's population. Further, 97 percent of the least-evangelized people groups in the world are inhabitants of the region. Additionally, it was in this very area that all the major religions of the world were born. Because the region represented a window, Luis Bush coined the now-familiar expression *the 10/40 Window.*

It was the spring of 1992 when Luis Bush phoned me at our home in Colorado Springs to ask if Every Home for Christ would consider hosting a small consultation regarding mobilizing intensive, focused prayer for this region. He also asked if I would be willing to serve as a co-chairman of the campaign along with Jane Hanson, founder and, at the time, president of Women's Aglow International.

So, on June 13, 1992, a Saturday, a small contingent of eight leaders met at the headquarters of Every Home for Christ in Colorado Springs to discuss what it would take to mobilize at least a million praying Christians for an entire month focusing specifically on the 10/40 Window. The month targeted was October 1993, some sixteen months later.

In addition to the eight of us in the conference room, an equal number of intercessors met in the prayer room adjacent to us. During our planning meeting we often heard the prayers of the intercessors through the walls. It was an encouraging sound.

That morning God gave us the name for the campaign—Pray Through the Window. The goal of mobilizing at least a million praying Christians in October 1993 was agreed upon as reasonable. Our ministry also agreed to design a reproducible thirty-one-day prayer guide listing the sixty-one nations of the region, along with related information to help intercessors pray more specifically. It was suggested that our various ministries also consider mobilizing churches and mission agencies to sponsor prayer journeys into the 10/40 Window.

Frankly, my faith was somewhat weak in the meeting, and I quietly wondered if a million intercessors could be mobilized to pray daily for an entire month. I also inwardly questioned how at least sixty-one prayer journeys might reasonably be organized.

I was obviously stunned and delighted the following year when all the documentation indicated that more than twenty million Christians had participated throughout the targeted month, and an amazing two hundred forty-nine prayer journeys had taken place. On average, this represented four journeys per 10/40 Window nation! It was to become an amazing miracle that would be repeated every two years, always in October, throughout the 1990s. The final campaign in 1999 involved more than fifty million praying Christians and several hundred prayer journeys into all parts of the region. By then, prayer journeys were being conducted almost every month, not merely in October.

Several years after the first campaign in 1993 I interviewed a leader involved with the Every Home for Christ strategy in the Middle East. The brother served in a rigidly Islamic nation. I asked him if he had seen any evidence of the impact of that first month of focused prayer. I remember his response vividly.

For two years prior to those concerted prayers of October 1993, this brother and his wife had visited many villages of their region attempting to share the gospel in as discreet a manner as possible. It was clearly a risky assignment. He explained that during those months not a single family invited them into their homes to hear more about Jesus, and they hadn't seen a single Muslim pray to accept Christ. The only thing that kept them going, the brother related, was that the Great Commission is the Great Commission even if no one responds. So they just kept going. I admired their fortitude.

Then the month of prayer occurred. The brother explained that he and his team were well aware of the monthly focus and had even given various mission and prayer groups, including ours, specific prayer requests for the month.

According to the brother, in the two years that followed that month of intensive prayer, he and his wife and other team members had been personally invited into the homes of hundreds of Muslims (in those same villages) and had led more than two thousand of them to a faith in Christ. Prayer had made the difference!

Then the brother shared something fresh in his mind.

"Just two weeks ago," he related, "a team of two of our workers were evangelizing in a village when an amazing thing happened." The brother smiled as he continued. "At three homes visited that day, when the various occupants opened the door, they were astonished. All three gasped, and one threw up her hands with joy."

He concluded, "All three told our workers they had had a dream the previous night, and in their dreams those very men, dressed in those same clothes, had visited their homes, offering a special gift. However, they had awakened before the gift could be given. 'So what is the gift?' they asked. The men then explained the gift of salvation in Christ to each of the three."

I believe these signs and wonders resulted from those focused prayers of October 1993. And they seem to be increasing as the global prayer movement expands and increases. Best-selling author Joel Rosenberg, in his powerful book *Epicenter*, devoted an entire chapter to such signs and wonders in recent years, particularly in rigidly Islamic areas of the world. In some of these regions, according to Rosenberg, scores if not hundreds of new believers have been meeting together and growing in Christ—none of whom had ever heard a preacher or attended a church. They had, in fact, never known another Christian before they had their dream or vision in which Jesus spoke directly to them. I am convinced that as prayers have dramatically increased targeting these regions, the signs and wonders also have increased. And in my opinion, far more in this regard is about to happen.

As we'll share in the remaining pages, emerging prayer movements throughout the globe are accelerating beyond anything one could ever have imagined even a decade ago. A new, radical generation of praying young people is in the womb of godly spiritual fathers and mothers, and the birth is about to take place.

Chapter 29
A DATE WITH DESTINY

I T WASN'T UNUSUAL FOR Cindy Jacobs to call early in the morning with
a message from the Lord that He had spoken to her for me in the
night. She has done it several times over the years. It was the first week
of August 2007.

Cindy explained that she had been up in the night feeling a strong
sense that God was speaking to her about a large unfinished, eight-thou-
sand-square-foot area we had in the lower level of the Jericho Center. As
mentioned earlier, the Jericho Center is our headquarters for global operations of Every Home for Christ. We had moved in and dedicated the facility
in August 2003. But two years earlier, when preparing the construction
project, the builder came to me holding the architectural drawings. He
pointed out that the way we were planning to construct the facility (on
a hill) minimized our capacity to use some extra space farther into the
mountain on the lower level. He showed me how once the building was
constructed, according to those initial plans, we could never recapture that
space again without tearing the entire building down. He pointed out that
to redo our present plans to utilize more space into the hill would, of
course, cost us more than our current budget—an additional half-million
dollars to be precise—but the builder stressed it would be worth it. We
would end up with eight thousand extra square feet for future use.

In consulting with our board and leadership team, it became clear we
needed to take that extra step. We proceeded with the building by going
farther into the hill. However, because of lack of additional funding once
the facility was completed, nothing had been done during the several
years following to finish out that space. It was just dirt, simply resting
dormant for future use. A staff member even suggested we rent it out to
a local church for storage purposes.

Cindy was calling because she was aware of that space and knew it
had sat unused for almost four years. In the night the Lord impressed her
to call me with the message that it was time to finish that space, because
God had a special purpose for it.

Cindy Jacobs is an unusual person. Her husband, Mike, a former airline executive, is a gifted manager of their ministry—Generals International. Cindy has spoken into the lives of Dee and me numerous times over many years. Of course, people who have gifts such as Cindy's are sometimes questioned and even criticized. But over the years I have come to recognize that Cindy really does discern the heart of God and has conveyed such to both Dee and me more than once.

A most memorable example of this happened several years earlier when I was dealing with some difficult changes in our ministry. It had to do with a transition in leadership and some painful decisions that had to be made. During a time of prayer the night prior to dealing with the situation, God gave me several steps for a smooth transition that I was to take in the next day's meeting. The impression was that if I would take these steps, harmony would result and relationships of all involved would remain healthy for the future. Further, those affected by these changes would be led into much greater dimensions of ministry in the future.

As I tried to get to sleep that night, a deep concern suddenly came over me. Had I really heard from the Lord, or was I heading for disaster in personal relationships? My stomach was in knots the rest of that very sleepless night.

About ten minutes before the scheduled meeting that following morning, my wife rushed from her office into mine with an urgent message.

Cindy Jacobs was on a pay phone at an airport in Texas. She wanted to speak to me immediately. She was in a terrible hurry and could miss her plane connection if I was unable to talk right then. Dee explained that Cindy told her God had spoken to her just as her flight was landing in Dallas about me and a meeting I was about to have that morning. Naturally this caught my immediate attention.

I picked up the phone and could tell Cindy was out of breath. She was hundreds of miles from our Colorado Springs office and calling because God had spoken to her very specifically about me. She explained that she had no idea all that I might have been facing during the previous twelve hours, but that as her plane was landing, God impressed her to call me with a very specific word. She was quick to add that she had no idea what it all meant. She then added, "The plan God gave you last night is His plan for the situation you are facing. The Lord is saying, 'Just stick to the plan!'"

I couldn't believe what I was hearing. How could she have possibly known? My wife, Dee, was the only person who knew anything of my plans for that morning's meeting, and she had only learned of them the night before. And Dee had not communicated any of this to anyone. I went into the meeting and followed the steps God had given the previous night exactly as they originally came during prayer. It was one of the most amicable transitions I recall in all my leadership experience. All involved that morning have remained dear friends to the present and are experiencing even greater fruit in the ministries to which God led them.

So, when Cindy phoned early that morning in August 2007, I was ready to listen.

"Are you awake?" Cindy asked.

"Yes," I responded.

Cindy then explained that God had awakened her in the night with the strong impression that she was to call me and tell me that God had something very special for the large empty area of the lower level of our Colorado facility. Cindy was bold as she added, "I believe you need to go to your board and ask them to help you bring about whatever God wants to do, and that you need to do it now."

Cindy expressed she was well aware I'd probably say we had no money for finishing out the space (which was true!), but she said she was certain that if we took this step of faith, God would let us finish the project debt free. She then explained that she heard something additional about this project.

Cindy added, "Whatever it is that will be built in this area will someday release rivers of healing that will flow out to all the nations on Earth. Dick, this is a part of God's destiny for your life."

I was especially stunned by her last statement. It confirmed to me that Cindy really had heard from the Lord. She was unaware that I had recently been conducting monthly Schools of Prayer at the Jericho Center, which had begun a year earlier. Two days later, a Saturday, our latest monthly seminar was scheduled. It was our August School of Prayer. I had already selected my theme and had prepared all my teaching notes and the student work sheets for the session. The title of the teaching was "Prophetic Rivers of Destiny."

Cindy also was unaware that during that teaching I had intended to share something profound that had happened at the groundbreaking for the Jericho Center eight years earlier in September 1999.

Prior to the groundbreaking, a friend involved in a ministry to Native Americans, Jean Steffenson, approached me about something that concerned her. Knowing that we were planning to build a facility on this particular plot of land in Colorado Springs, Jean wanted to remind me that this land once belonged to Native Americans of the region. It was land that generations ago had been stolen from them through broken treaties. She suggested that it would be very important, if not vital, to have a Christian Native American come and bless the land and, even spiritually, give it to us.

Jean further explained that another major church construction project concerning prayer had been undertaken several years earlier where this had not been done. The leadership involved in that project hadn't understood the significance of such a prophetic expression. Jean believed this cost them significantly, because as they began construction, a number of things went terribly wrong. One involved a major change order that necessitated rerouting water pipes required by the city. (A change order represents a change in the original plans of a construction project, which almost always increases the cost of the project, sometimes very significantly.) This one specific change order, I was told, cost $250,000 over the original construction budget. Jean believed we could avoid such a thing happening to us if we would honor our Native Americans by asking one of their representatives to sanctify the land at our groundbreaking.

As Jean was explaining all this to me, I recalled my participation in the October 4, 1997, Million Man Promise Keepers event in Washington DC. I led a portion of that program, and one of the brothers who participated with me in my time slot was Silas Correa, a full-blooded Otto-Missouri Native American. So the next day I called Silas and asked if he would be willing to come to the groundbreaking and lead us in just such a ceremony.

Silas graciously obliged and was a part of the groundbreaking. It was deeply moving. At one point Silas poured Communion wine on the soil, sanctifying it with the blood of Jesus. Then he picked up a handful of sand and poured it into my hands, presenting it to me as a gift from the Native Americans who once owned it. Before I knew what was happening, Silas was dancing before the Lord, chanting words of praise and worship in his native tongue.

Then Silas paused for a brief moment and told the gathering that God had just spoken to him. He explained tearfully, "God is showing me that rivers of His healing will be flowing from the top of this hill out to all the nations of the world."

Cindy had no idea when she phoned on Thursday that I already had intended to recount the experience of Silas at the groundbreaking when I taught two days later on Saturday. I wanted to point out to the class that in the years following the construction of the Jericho Center, we had seen extraordinary increases in the results of our ministry's home-to-home evangelism activities around the world. I believed what Silas had done had something to do with that. But there is even more to the story. Just after moving into our new facility in June of 2003, and a few weeks before the official dedication, our receptionist called my office to inform me that something quite unusual was happening outside the new building.

She said an old man whom she didn't recognize was dancing around the perimeter of the building. With uplifted hands he was weeping and praising God as he danced. She said it was quite a sight.

I rushed to the main entry to see what was happening. From the front windows I could see immediately who it was. It was my Native American friend Silas Correa. He had heard about the completion of the building and had driven from his home in Denver to dance around it, thanking God that it had become a reality.

I shared all this with our board, including Cindy's word to me as well as my recollections of Silas and his word at the groundbreaking. They already were well aware that our builder had informed us after the Jericho Center was completed that our project was the smoothest he had ever been involved in, which had been hundreds. And in so far as change orders were concerned, there had been only one—that of adding a door from my wife's office into mine, which wasn't in the original plans. It cost only two hundred dollars for this change, which was insignificant for a seven-million-dollar project.

As the board listened to what Cindy had felt and all the confirmations that accompanied her spiritual discernment, the board voted unanimously to move ahead with completing the unfinished area of our facility. In the interim days before the board met and made their decision, God had shown me and others of our staff that the newly developed area was to include a Watchman Training Center where people could come for both sustained worship and intercession as well as training in intercessory worship. Additionally, we were to construct a unique Wall of Prayer in the area, patterned after the Wailing Wall in Jerusalem. It would house numerous individual prayer grottos for those who would come for longer periods of personal intercession.

All this was to become a reality in the twelve months that followed. And even though the $2.4 million project would begin at the exact time the financial crash of 2008 occurred, within that same time frame God would provide 100 percent of the needed funds to complete the project, just as Cindy had said—debt free. The ministry had no capital campaign to raise funds for the project. In fact, we never sent out a typical appeal letter to our extended list of donors asking them to help finance the project. God did it all!

I saw the completion of this phase of the Jericho Center as the full-circle completion of the vision God had first given me four decades earlier to "call the world to prayer" with the launching of the 24/7 prayer ministry we called the Prayer Corps. And although the Prayer Corps as a specific ministry passed from the scene when I launched the Change the World Schools of Prayer through Every Home for Christ in the late 1970s and 1980s, the lessons learned from those Prayer Corps years ignited flames of 24/7 prayer in numerous other settings and movements throughout the world. But now, something greater is about to happen.

Never could I have imagined how much God was keeping those flames alive for what He was about to do with a new, far more radical genera-tion of youthful intercessors. Perhaps you are one of those passionate keepers of the flame He is about to use mightily! Indeed, the Prayer Corps vision never really died. It has just lain dormant for the next generation. What follows in the remaining pages of this book is how you can become involved.

Chapter 30
AN ACCELERATING HARVEST

LOOKING BACK AT THE fruit of those early days when Prayer Corps members prayed for every country on Earth, by name, every eight hours, I am overwhelmed at how God answered those prayers. I had no idea at the time that someday God would lead me into the international leadership of the Every Home for Christ ministry. As mentioned in chapter 24, "A Vision of Jericho," it was 1976 (four years after starting the Prayer Corps) that I became director of prayer mobilization for the EHC ministry. Then in 1988 I was appointed their international president. Over the ensuing years, as the prayer has increased, so has the harvest. It almost seems to be scientifically measurable.

In my book *Look What God Is Doing* (Chosen Books, 2009) I shared some of the fruit the Every Home for Christ ministry has witnessed as the prayer movements globally have expanded. Some specific examples were described in the previous chapter. Here I want to simply share how God marvelously answered those prayers prayed decades earlier by that small band of devoted young people.

Let me highlight specifically what has taken place in just a single decade, from 2000 to 2010. As stated, it was in this decade that so many remarkable prayer movements exploded on the scene. These included the Global Day of Prayer, the International House of Prayer (IHOP), Jericho Walls of Prayer in Africa (with nearly 8,000 different locations of day-and-night prayer), and the youth prayer movement simply called 24/7, born in the United Kingdom, which has now spread to some 60 nations. Additionally, there have been Walls of Prayer (168 hours per week covered) started by Every Home for Christ and YWAM. Recent reports indicate more than 2,000 functioning 24/7 walls have begun in a single year just in East Asia alone.

Every Home for Christ (EHC) focuses on mobilizing the church globally to personally take a presentation of the gospel, most often in the form of printed messages, one for adults and one for children, to every home in a nation. Every Home Campaigns have now been conducted in 205 of the world's 220 nations, though EHC has sent literature into every nation on Earth. To date 100 nations have had at least one full coverage, meaning every accessible home has been visited.

Born in 1946 in Canada, the ministry of Every Home for Christ has now planted more than 2.8 billion gospel messages home to home in these 205 nations. Because each message usually has some form of a response card, we are able to monitor how people respond to these messages and follow up with them appropriately. In the almost 65-year history of Every Home for Christ, more than 90 million such responses have been registered and more than 95 percent followed up with Bible lessons. These lessons usually consist of a four-part Bible correspondence course, with space to fill in answers to questions, which leads new believers (or inquirers) to a fuller understanding of what it means to be a follower of Jesus.

In places where there are no evangelical, Bible-believing church fellowships, EHC has historically (since the late 1960s) begun what we refer to as Christ Groups. These are New Testament church fellowships that most often meet in homes or available halls that can be rented inexpensively. Many of these have grown into sizeable congregations. To date, nearly 150,000 such groups have been planted globally.

One clear indication of the dramatically accelerating harvest in recent years has been the amazing increase in the establishing of these fellowships. This also, I believe, is a reflection of the impact of the dramatic increase of prayer movements globally, something I'm convinced is also a result of those early days of prayer by one hundred devoted young warriors in Sacramento who began day-and-night prayer for the nations. It was as if they released a tiny but significant spark that ignited a flame, birthing many movements of prayer throughout the world, many of which I'm sure had no idea where that spark originated.

How have these prayer movements impacted the harvest? Because I'm most familiar with has happened in the ministry of Every Home for Christ, let me use our statistics as one example. I'm certain other evangelism and discipleship ministries and denominations could testify to a similar impact.

Compare what happened in 2000 to our home-to-home campaigns a decade later in 2010. In 2000, the ministry followed up just over 756,000 decisions and responses. These individuals indicated on a response form that they either had prayed to receive Christ or wanted to know more about how to become a Christian. Of course, at the time we thought this number of responses was wonderful. Indeed, it represented a 69.5 percent increase from the 446,000 the previous year.

Then in 2000, as mentioned earlier, the first Global Day of Prayer was conducted in South Africa. The first full year of the International House of Prayer (IHOP) was also completed in Kansas City. That year also represented the culmination of a decade-long Pray Through the Window campaign, focusing millions of believers' prayers on the geographic region known as the 10/40 Window, as described in the previous chapter.

And what impact did all this praying have on ministries like Every Home for Christ? By year-end 2009, our decisions and responses skyrocketed to more than 12.4 million for that twelve-month period (or 33,972 average per day). That represented a remarkable 1,540 percent increase from the 756,000 a decade earlier. I believe the dramatic surge of prayer movements worldwide significantly contributed to this increase.

The planting of new church fellowships (Christ Groups) during that same time frame also exploded. In 2000 approximately four new fellowships were being established daily. Although we rejoiced over these results at the time, we never could have imagined what would happen just one decade later. By the beginning of 2010, the number of new fellowships of believers planted in a single year had grown to 18,322, or an increase of 1,122 percent in just a decade. The ministry had expanded from planting four Christ Groups daily to more than 50 per day. Funding for the work also dramatically increased. It seemed the more we worshiped and prayed (particularly on-site), the greater was the flow of resources. Income increased over 500 percent during those same years.

Consider also the number of new families being visited and given the gospel during that decade. In 2000, some 18 million homes were personally reached with the Good News of Jesus. By 2010, just a decade later, more than a million homes were being reached every week. In fact, in 2009 alone, 66 million homes were visited by a force of 4,000 supported Christian workers and an average of 27,000 volunteers monthly.

Based on an average of five persons living in each home, this means nearly a million new people were being exposed to the gospel on a daily basis.

Further, accompanying this dramatic increase in responses has been an increase of signs and wonders (as I also highlighted in chapter 28), especially in third world and least-evangelized nations. I recall an interview I did several years ago for a magazine article describing God's work globally. I had traveled to India for an Every Home for Christ conference, where several hundred leaders from every region of India had gathered. During the conference I spoke with a brother named Uhmahd Singh who coordinated our work in two states in India—Utter Pradesh and Bihar. I first asked Uhmahd how the ministry of planting Christ Groups was going in his two-state region.

Smiling brightly, Uhmahd responded, "Brother Dick, I'm pleased to say we have planted 457 new Christ Groups in just the past six months in my region." He added, "And two of these have already grown to more than 500 in size, which is a true miracle for our region of India."

I then asked Uhmahd if he had seen any signs and wonders that led to the forming of these Christ Groups in his area. He smiled even more brightly and added, "Oh, Brother Dick, that reminds me about one of our latest Christ Groups that has begun in a village called Balibaba in Bihar." To me, Balibaba, Bihar, sounded a bit like a title from an adventure movie.

Uhmahd then shared a most remarkable testimony. Two of our EHC workers had been evangelizing smaller villages in an area of Bihar state. They had visited numerous villages over a period of several days when they came to the last village on their map, that of Balibaba. As is typical of their mission, they visited every home in Balibaba, leaving a salvation message in the Hindi language for both adults and children. Most of the villagers politely accepted the messages but refused to allow the young men to enter their homes and tell them more about Jesus. They were Hindus and were not about to change their religion. They didn't want to offend their gods. Still, the two workers faithfully visited every home, leaving the gospel messages at each.

Then a miracle happened. They approached the last home in the village, where a young mother with a six-year-old daughter came to the door. As the workers began explaining why they had come, the woman broke into tears. She told them her name was Shanti, meaning "peace" in the Hindi language. But, she told the workers, she had no peace. She further explained that her husband had abandoned her and that now she was left alone to raise her six-year-old daughter. She didn't know how she could do it on her own. She wept as she spoke.

The workers quickly explained that God had one Son, Jesus Christ, who was called the Prince of Peace. He could surely give Shanti the peace she longed for. The more they shared, the more Shanti's interest grew.

Finally one of the workers asked, "Would you like to ask the Prince of Peace, Jesus Christ, to live in your heart?"

Shanti responded, "I would very much like that."

In moments, after repeating a simple prayer led by one of the young men, Shanti was gloriously saved. It was an instantaneous experience. Shanti became born again. The trip to that remote village had been worth it after all.

But the story doesn't end there. The workers gave Shanti several Bible lessons they were carrying with them for just such an occasion, plus a New Testament in the Hindi language. They told her they were working in other villages of the area, and in a few days they would try to return and tell her even more about Jesus. Shanti was grateful.

The workers departed, not knowing the challenge Shanti was about to face. Within a few days, Shanti's young daughter became seriously ill. The condition was life threatening. It appeared the daughter might not survive. None of the villagers were willing to help her, not even with traditional medicine. They accused her of bringing all this about because she had forsaken her Hindu gods.

Then Shanti did a most amazing thing. She went to all the homes in her small village, about one hundred in all, and asked if she could have the printed messages the young men had distributed throughout their village. Her neighbors questioned why she wanted them. Most, if not all, believed these messages offended their Hindu gods. Shanti simply said, "If you want to see what I want with them, you can come to my house and see for yourself."

Several neighbors responded and followed her to her front porch. What they saw was amazing. Shanti had placed her daughter on a small cot and had arranged the many messages, touching end to end, completely surrounding the child. Shanti's daughter was now circled by more than a hundred printed messages.

Then Shanti did something even more amazing. She took two steps back from her daughter, lifted her hands, and cried out to God in prayer. Here was someone who knew little if anything about prayer. Yet Shanti was desperate.

"Oh God of these pages," she pleaded, "if You are the one true God, and if Jesus Christ is truly Your one and only Son, I ask You to heal my daughter."

Villagers stood in a stunned silence as they heard Shanti cry out to the heavens with a faith none of them could understand. And then it happened. Shanti's six-year-old daughter, by now in a near-comatose state, coughed, stood on her feet, looked into the eyes of her mother, and said, "Mummy, I'm hungry. Give me something to eat."

The child had been healed in an instant. Several of the neighbors nearly fainted. One had the presence of mind to suggest that someone go find the two young men who had come to their village earlier and ask them to return and tell them more about this new God named Jesus.

With the help of the Holy Spirit, a villager did find the young men in a neighboring village and invited them back. They promptly returned and shared the message of salvation with the entire village. Most responded by receiving Christ as Savior that day. Others followed later. It was a remarkable miracle.

A year later my wife and I were back in India. We saw Brother Uhmahd at another EHC conference. I asked him how everything was going in Balibaba. He smiled brightly once again and pulled several photos from a folder he was carrying. Uhmahd said, "I knew you would ask me about this, so I brought you these photos."

Uhmahd showed me a group of perhaps eighty people standing in front of a thatched-roof hut. He explained it was the new church in Balibaba, Bihar. He proudly told me that the church now had a full-time pastor. I asked him who it was, and Uhmahd pointed to a lady standing in the middle of the group. Beside her was a small child that looked to be six or seven years old.

Uhmahd said, "That woman is the new pastor of the Balibaba Christ Group. She is Shanti. And the little girl beside her is her daughter who was healed."

I realized then that we were witnessing even more evidence of the impact of the 24/7 prayer movements exploding everywhere in recent years. The Book of Acts is indeed alive today. It didn't end with chapter 28, as we see in our Bibles. These are the days of Acts chapter 29. It's a chapter fueled by 24/7 prayer and will continue to be written until Christ returns.

Chapter 31
A MOUNT EVEREST MIRACLE

A S MIRACLES GO, THIS tops my list. And interestingly, this miracle comes from the actual top of the world—the Mount Everest region of Nepal, which boasts the highest mountain ranges on the earth.

Reflecting back four decades to my own miracle when my failing voice was restored at a Kathryn Kuhlman meeting (as told in chapter 8, "This Is the Year"), I think of a strange connection to the circumstances of that healing and what I describe here as my Mount Everest miracle.

You may recall from chapter 8 that for several months prior to my instantaneous healing, I had spent many long nights in prayer wondering if I would ever preach again. It was during one of those nights that I told the Lord that if I never preached again, I would still serve Him as a missionary in some faraway place. "Dee and I would go to Africa," I suggested, "and purchase a printing press. We would then preach the gospel via the printed page. And we would pray!" In fact, I saw prayer as the chief calling in my future, whether I was healed or not.

Little could I have known that God would not only heal me but also lead me and Dee into a ministry combining day-and-night global prayer with the sowing of the printed page into literally hundreds of millions of homes in more than two hundred countries—which brings me to a Mount Everest miracle.

Few nations on the earth qualify as Paul's description of "the regions beyond" (2 Cor. 10:16) as does Nepal. Some areas are so inaccessible that few would ever consider attempting to trek into them unless they were deeply motivated or unusually adventurous. Thankfully, Every Home for Christ workers clearly fall into the *deeply motivated* category and are willing to take whatever risks are necessary, because they don't want to miss a single home in their quest to reach every household and person with the Good News. The far eastern Dummana region of Nepal, just fifty miles south of Mount Everest, is certainly such a place.

Recently, our EHC office in Kathmandu received word of a large group of believers who have been worshiping regularly in this rugged

Himalayan region where an eight-man team of EHC workers trekked with the gospel sixteen years ago, searching out unreached villages of the area. Many such villages will never appear even on the best of government maps, so it takes a fierce determination to find them.

That first visit to Dummana by the eight-man team actually lasted less than a couple of hours because the village was deserted. But it was soon obvious to our workers that the village actually was inhabited because of small embers still burning in fire pits and a few chickens rushing about. They knew from experience that these villagers, along with their children, were somewhere in the nearby mountains tending their flocks or farming and that they probably wouldn't return for days.

Realizing they had other villages to reach, as well as facing a two-day trek back down the mountain, the team of EHC workers visited every home nonetheless, leaving a simple printed gospel message in their native language at each dwelling. They trusted God that at least a few of the village inhabitants would be literate and read the message of God's plan of salvation in Christ. Little could they have known that this single visit would result in the planting of a thriving church—one I have come to refer to as The Church of the Printed Page.

It all began with that two-day trek up the mountain back in 1993. And that might have been the end of the story, but for the rumors that began reaching EHC's Kathmandu office in recent months that a thriving congregation was growing atop that mountain and even planting other churches in the area. It was later learned that prior to 1993 no Christians had ever visited this area with the gospel. Hearing these rumors, our Nepal director decided to send a four-man team of EHC leaders to eastern Nepal to trek up the mountain and confirm, firsthand, if these reports were accurate.

What resulted from their journey is a wonderful account of the grace of God manifested through a simple gospel message in the language of these previously unreached people. It was, according to one of our veteran leaders making the trek, a long and arduous climb, with perspiration flowing freely. Unfortunately, they had chosen the monsoon season to make the journey. But it was worth it. The group would be amazed at what they would discover as they penetrated the jungle-covered foothills, climbing higher and deeper, and passing village after village of these once forgotten peoples.

As the survey team drove their Jeep toward the end of the last gravel road where they would begin their trek, they became increasingly concerned at the ferocity of the monsoon rainfall, believing that the numerous rivers they would encounter might be swollen to flood stage. They knew this might prevent their vehicle from making it through to the end of the road and the foot of the mountain, where their climb was to begin. Of even greater concern was the fact that flash floods can happen in an instant during this season, and their Jeep easily could be swept away, with them in it. In fact, as they neared the Dummana region, they faced a harrowing two-and-a-half-hour detour along a road that barely qualified as a road in order to get around a flooded area of the river. The leaders knew that not many months earlier an EHC worker was swept to his death in a similar area by a flash flood.

But it was along this rugged road that our research team came across an elderly woman whom one of the team recognized as being from the Dummana area—the very place to which they were traveling. The woman had trekked all the way down the mountain to obtain treatment for her ailing back and now was heading back home on foot. Our leaders were impressed greatly by the old woman's stamina. They, of course, made room in their Jeep for the woman and her lone companion, along with their luggage, and continued on their journey.

Having reached the end of the road, the team set off on foot. The first day would require a strenuous eight-hour hike before they reached the village where they would spend the night. Along the way, they passed through several small villages scattered about in the rugged terrain. In total, they crossed five swing bridges spanning deep gorges and raging rivers, cautious with each step when putting their weight on the some-times-rotted wood. Being the monsoon season made the experience of these crossings even more harrowing.

The team noticed how many *porters* (village people) were on the road carrying unbelievable loads on their heads and backs. That's how the old woman and her companion took their luggage up the mountain. Surprisingly, even young children braved the dangerous slopes.

It was a difficult journey to say the least. One of the team testified, "I was tired and dehydrated. We were forcing ourselves up jungle hillsides where we were warned repeatedly by villagers not to stop or lie down because wild animals might attack us! So we just had to keep going."

After trekking still higher and farther for eight hours on that first day, the four-man party reached the edge of the Dummana region, which covers a vast area requiring many hours to cross. Their actual destination was still five hours away, and it would have been far too exhausting to finish the climb in a single day.

That night they enjoyed cold baths and stayed in bamboo huts with thatched roofs. Before they knew it, they were awakened at 5:00 a.m. by their porter, who demanded that they leave immediately without any breakfast, tea, or even a bathroom break! He told them this was necessary to get to the village on time for their visit.

As the team trekked even higher into the Himalayas, they broke out in spontaneous songs of praise with shouts of joy as they reached each new summit, only to realize there was a further summit on the horizon yet to be climbed. During this portion of their journey, they stopped at a tea shop (something quite common in the region) for drinks and nourishment.

After the break it was time for their final ascent.

Upon entering Dummana Village, named for the same region, the trekkers were welcomed by EHC's very first convert sixteen years ago, Brinda Magar, who invited them to his home. (We later learned that *Brinda*, in the Nepali language, means "man of peace.")

Thus began a four-day stay that included much discussion to piece together the story of how this village had come to Christ thirteen years earlier. During this time of reflection, our research team came to a clearer understanding of the challenges EHC workers face in taking the gospel to such remote regions. Very often they are the only Christians to ever visit these areas.

First, the difficult terrain means field evangelists must limit any items they carry to gospel literature, Bibles, and follow-up materials. This often means they must leave much-needed personal items, including food supplies, behind. Further, they can't afford the luxury of hiring porters for the task, so they usually have to trust villagers to offer them food. It's an incredible step of faith. And even if they do carry small amounts of money to purchase food, they often must fast, as there are no shops to purchase the needed supplies.

Second, weather conditions frequently wreak havoc on those traveling into such regions where dangerous terrain can be life threatening. Nepal is known for having some of the most rugged terrain in the world.

Third, there is no guarantee that once workers arrive in a certain area they will be welcomed enthusiastically by villagers—they may be viewed as a threat. And finally, sleep is fleeting and very difficult in these extreme altitudes. As all the team confessed following this visit, their two-day trek reminded them of the profound dedication of those workers who do this as a lifestyle in order that everyone has an opportunity to hear about Jesus.

During their four-day visit with the villagers of Dummana, our EHC research team learned how it came to be that a church now numbering three hundred was born atop this remote mountain not far from Everest. When the original EHC workers first visited the village in 1993, as mentioned earlier, they found what appeared to be a deserted village. But when they realized the villagers were most likely tending their flocks in the nearby hills, the workers decided to visit every home anyway, placing gospel messages in each.

When Brinda, the Hindu priest of the village, returned to his modest home, he found one of the messages on his doorstep. It was simply titled "You Must Meet Him." (Interestingly, this was the very same message that was first printed at the launching of the EHC work in Nepal back in 1983, a full decade earlier. That first printing consisted of just ten thousand copies.)

Brinda was deeply moved by the message. He later told our research team that it was unlike anything he had ever read. He immediately prayed to receive Christ, just as the message instructed. In those moments, Brinda was gloriously converted as he read about how Christ could transform a person's life. He also was determined to send his completed request form to our Kathmandu office in order to receive the promised Bible correspondence course. For Brinda, this required a good deal of effort, because the nearest post office was a several-hour trek down the mountain. Before long, he was making that trek more than once—first to mail his initial decision response and then several additional times to see if the promised Bible correspondence course had arrived. It finally did, and Brinda studied it carefully.

The former Hindu priest's conversion was soon obvious to the locals, as God's Word took root in his life. Brinda soon found deliverance from Hindu practices as well as a severe drinking problem. All of this resulted just from studying the four-part Bible course from EHC. His wife and daughter also came to Christ and were delivered from years of demonic affliction. But Brinda's conversion did not spare him and his family from severe persecution and opposition from villagers. He and his family were told to move to the outskirts of the village. However, the Lord turned the persecution around when the village water supply was cut off, and the only person capable of fixing the problem was Brinda. The outcast soon became the hero by supplying the much-needed water to the entire area.

Soon Brinda's influence as a good Christian businessman grew. He established a flour mill and telephone system and opened a small shop. As his faith grew, so did his witness. A growing number of villagers came to faith in Jesus and wanted to know more about their new faith. They were even gathering in meetings and engaging in their own form of worship, including singing and praying together. One day a porter from another village farther down the mountain passed by and quipped, "You must be Christians!"

"What is a Christian?" Brinda asked.

The porter responded, "People like you who sing, pray, read the Bible, and call on the name of Yesu [Jesus]. In our village they are called *Christians*."

"We must be Christians then," Brinda affirmed. Until that time these new believers had never heard or used that expression.

One day Brinda and a fellow believer decided to make the two-day trek down the mountain to seek out more information about how they could better follow Jesus. God led them to a man in the town of Dharan who was a Christian and had, amazingly, served on the board of directors for EHC Nepal some years earlier! Most likely they had learned of this man through their correspondence with the Nepal EHC office. God truly had led them to this specific person, who soon trekked to the village to help them in further establishing a thriving church.

When our four-man team of researchers arrived in the summer of 2009, they were amazed to find an erected church building large enough to accommodate hundreds of worshipers at one time. They quickly learned that another church had been planted in a neighboring village, as well as seven smaller groups (similar to our Christ Groups) in nearby areas, all as the result of Brinda's conversion from reading a single gospel message. More than three hundred believers regularly worship in these churches and Christ Groups. Even during this trip, a young elder of the church was departing to plant yet another fellowship in a distant village seven hours away by foot!

Still, the surprises continued. Brinda's brother, Roshan, had just arrived home from Dehradun Bible College in Nepal, where he was soon to complete a degree in theology. Roshan was one who had come to Christ as the result of his brother's conversion sixteen years earlier. As Roshan grew in the Lord, he decided to go to this respected Bible college in Nepal to prepare to train others for ministry. Roshan was now convinced God was leading him back to Dummana to establish a Discipleship Training Center at the top of that mountain, just south of Mount Everest. What Roshan didn't realize, but now knows, is that EHC had already drafted plans to establish just such a Bible school for the region. Now we have a leader for this coming center.

And the fruit of that simple gospel message left at Brinda's doorstep in 1993 continues to grow. On June 27, 2009, when our EHC research team trekked up the mountain to Dummana Village to see if the miracle-church was true, they participated in yet another miracle—a miracle of multiplication. They had the joy or ordaining six new pastors, five additional elders, and thirteen deacons and deaconesses, totaling twenty-four persons—all of this happening at what I call "The Church of the Printed Page" in the shadows of Mount Everest.

When the team was ready to head back down the mountain, they had a final surprise. They met a ninety-year-old hunchbacked man who was smiling broadly, his wrinkled face beaming with joy. Like Brinda, he had been a Hindu priest for many years. Our team learned that just five months prior to their trek to the top of the mountain, the frail man had been led to Christ by one of the believers of Dummana Village.

Amazingly, all of this can be traced to that one printed message, not more than twenty pages in length, read by a Hindu priest in 1993 who was living a stone's throw from Mount Everest. What's especially exciting is that the booklet Brinda read was but one of 14,190,156 similar gospel messages that, as of this date, have been planted home to home throughout Nepal since EHC's first coverage began there in 1983. One can only imagine what has happened to all those other gospel seeds! We do know that more than 350,000 people of Nepal now have responded to our campaign there and requested our four-part Bible correspondence course. We also know that as of the publication of this book, at least 8,400 New Testament fellowships (our Christ Groups) have been formed as the result. The printed page—and prayer—had, indeed, become God's powerful means of gathering in the harvest He had promised me four decades earlier when I thought I'd never preach again. My Mount Everest miracle—the Church of the Printed Page—was all the proof I needed.

Chapter 32
THE PIG ON TOUR

W E WOULD LIKE TO do a Purple Pig Tour!"
I didn't know exactly what the young brother meant. Brian Kim, a twenty-seven-year-old leader from IHOP in Kansas City, sat across from me at a conference room table in the Jericho Center. It was the first weekend of May 2010.

"Why would anyone want to do a tour involving *The Purple Pig*?" I thought.

Brian had worked with IHOP's founder, Mike Bickle, since 2006. He had packed up everything that year and headed for Kansas City. It was, he explained, the result of a forty-day fast that he admitted transformed his life. During his prolonged fast, the Lord woke him up at 3:00 a.m. and spoke in an audible voice, "Are you willing to take your intercession to the center of the plague?" (See Numbers 16:47–48.)

Brian knew the Lord was talking about a new movement of young intercessors who would be willing to go into the darkest places on the earth and contend in fervent prayer for breakthrough in these troubled lands. As Brian shared, I couldn't help but recall my vision four decades earlier of an army of youthful intercessors sweeping across the planet like the wake of a wave on their way to transform peoples and nations.

Brian further explained that Lou Engle, an anointed leader with a powerful prophetic mantle for the younger generation, had launched a vision for empowering young people known as *TheCall*. Already Lou had conducted several large gatherings of thousands of young men and women who were being motivated to pursue much greater depths of discipleship and commitment. Some four hundred thousand had been at the first such event in Washington DC in 2000.

Brian then explained how my book *The Purple Pig and Other Miracles* first came into his hands not long after joining IHOP. I had given Lou Engle an original copy some years earlier that had touched his heart. One day Lou felt compelled that it held a special message for Brian regarding his life's destiny. Brian told me Lou had even written these words in the inside cover: "What Dick Eastman gave to me, I now give to you. Take this mantle. You are God's fire starter!"

Lou Engle's reference to Brian being a *fire starter* related to our early prayer centers, which we dubbed *fire houses*. He was challenging Brian to carry on this same vision. Of course, I knew nothing of what Lou had written to Brian in my book and was rather amazed as I listened to his story.

The more Brian shared, the more my heart was impacted. When he told me he was twenty-seven years old, I immediately recalled how the Holy Spirit prompted me back in 1964 when I was twenty years old that in my twenty-seventh year God would begin a ministry that would impact millions of souls through prayer (not that we would ever take credit for these souls coming to Christ, but that prayer movements would be instrumental in *praying in* this harvest).

I was fascinated to hear details of Brian's journey. It was September 2007, just after the TheCall touched tens of thousands of youth in Nashville, when Brian began reading a book titled *Spontaneous Expansion of the Church*. It was written in the 1920s by a missionary to China named Roland Allen, who described the beginnings of a church-planting movement in the Far East. The book had had a profound impact on John Wimber, founder of the Vineyard movement. Just before Wimber died, one of the Vineyard leaders met with him, and John handed him this book, saying, "Next to the Bible, this is the most important book I've ever read."

Brian Kim had heard this testimony and was determined to read the book. Soon Brian was sitting in the Global Prayer Room at IHOP in Kansas City struggling to get through the book. It was a tough read, Brain admitted. But suddenly he heard a voice cry out, "Give me ten thousand."

"Give me ten thousand what?"

He heard the words again: "Give me ten thousand!"

Brian immediately discerned that the Lord was asking him to set a goal of raising up ten thousand young pioneering leaders who would plant prayer furnaces in the hardest and darkest places on the earth.

Brian explained he soon discovered that his concept of *prayer furnaces* was nearly identical to what I had described in my vision several decades earlier of establishing *fire houses*.

According to Brian, it was in those solemn moments in September 2007 that a vision and mission for what he was to label the *Luke18 Project* was born. In the same way that a widow harassed an unjust judge "day and night" until she saw victory come (Luke 18:1–8), there would be a massive generation of young men and women who would cry out to the Lord day and night for the Good News of Jesus to impact all the world.

Soon God would link our vision at Every Home for Christ very directly with that of Brian's. It was January 2, 2008, at the very launch of the Luke18 Project in Kansas City, that Lou Engle would place in Brian's hand a 1974 first edition of *The Purple Pig and Other Miracles*. Brian was unfamiliar with the book. But as he began reading it, he saw how a 24/7 prayer ministry exactly as he was envisioning had actually begun way back in the early 1970s.

According to Brian, as he read each page, now broken from the original binding and held together with a rubber band, he saw it as an inspirational manual for young leaders who wanted to plant prayer furnaces or fire houses of prayer.

Of course, I had no idea all of this was happening. I only knew that it was at the exact time that Lou Engle gave Brian an original copy of *The Purple Pig* that we were finalizing the building of our Watchman Training Center at the Jericho Center (as you'll read about in my concluding chapter). Our intention in building this addition was to develop an IHOP model of intercessory worship. We wanted day-and-night intercessory worship to saturate our evangelism and discipleship strategies for all the nations of the world. We also recognized that God wanted to mobilize a movement of radical young intercessors who would spread a vision for such intercessory worship globally.

As Brian shared, I was hearing someone articulate my vision given four decades earlier. Of course, such a vision would not go unchallenged by the enemy. Brian explained how during the early months of his Luke18 vision, he released the leadership of the project to a colleague. At the time Brian felt that he was to give himself fully to other ministry. Although this didn't seem like a bad idea at the time, it clearly wasn't the best thing for Brian.

Some months after making this decision, his colleague returned to him with a word from the Lord. His friend said, "I keep hearing, 'Luke18 campus revivals!' God is telling me to tell you, 'It was not yours to give away!'"

Brian's friend was persistent, praying this same message over him four or five times during the course of a single evening. As this colleague continued sharing this word from the Lord with him, Brian received a message on his phone from yet another colleague. This friend told Brian that she felt the Lord had just spoken to her about the Luke18 Project. She said, "I just heard the Lord tell me to tell you, 'Luke18 campus revivals! It was not yours to give away!'" This was the same, exact message that Brian's other colleague had shared with him. Slowly Brian realized God had given him a vision that was to consume his life.

Within days, Brian went to Mike Bickle, founder of IHOP, to share with him all that was transpiring. Mike, discerning what the Holy Spirit was doing in Brian, told him, "I know how these things work. You don't have to force anything. You don't have to make it work! If God has given you the title deed to this vision, it will always boomerang back to you."

In less than twenty-four hours, Brian was asked by the colleague now heading the Luke18 Project to meet. His friend explained that the Lord had been speaking to him for several weeks about the vision. He felt he was not to lead the movement anymore, but he was to give the leadership back to Brian.

Soon after these events, the Lord spoke to Brian about the path he was to take for his future. Out of nowhere, as he was again reading that original copy of *The Purple Pig* given to him by Lou Engle, he heard an inner voice saying, "Now, fulfill the dreams of your fathers!" Brian believed the Lord was speaking to him about fulfilling the dreams of men like Lou Engle, Mike Bickle, and, surprisingly, myself.

Brian was now convinced the vision he had read in *The Purple Pig* was a word from the Lord directly for him. He was to participate in filling the Earth with worship and prayer. My original vision of fire houses spreading throughout the world was something he was to continue as his own vision. Brian was well aware that the vision God had given me so many years earlier had not yet reached its full potential.

True, there had been amazing prayer movements born out of the prayers of those young warriors at the Prayer Corps in the 1970s. Yet Brian knew instinctively there was far more God intended to do. With a humble spirit, the twenty-seven-year-old told me, "God has not fastened your soul to a dead-end dream!"

He committed himself to pick up the vision for global fire houses (or, as he described them, furnaces). Brian explained how he and his team already had planted more than four hundred day-and-night worship and interces-sion furnaces on college campuses throughout our nation. This included creating a database of some twelve thousand students who had committed themselves to the vision and mission of the Luke18 Project—to cry out to

God day and night for His justice to touch every part of our planet. Eventually, Brian believes, there will be prayer furnaces in every dark part of this planet as well as on all twenty-six hundred college campuses in America. That God had used the experiences in *The Purple Pig* to help inspire this amazed me. Could it be that the prayers of those radical young intercessors decades ago in our first Fire House were still powerfully active?

Out of all this, Brian believed (with Mike Bickle fully agreeing) there would rise up an End-Time student volunteer movement of passionate foreign missionaries, not unlike the movement that was born a hundred years ago through the ministry of John R. Mott. At that time, Mott chaired the historic World Missionary Conference in Edinburgh, Scotland, out of which many mission movements sprang up, impacting the world for generations. A vital aspect of all this, according to Brian, would be the commissioning of thousands of intercessory worshipers to the darkest and hardest places on Planet Earth to plant prayer furnaces. These furnaces (or, as I dubbed them, fire houses) would start fires of revival and awakening in these dark lands.

But how did a Purple Pig Tour fit into all of this? Lou Engle felt it was time to re-dig the wells of these earlier prayer encounters so that even greater rivers of healing might flow to the nations. (See Genesis 26:12–19.) Because Lou had scheduled TheCall for Sacramento, California, in early September 2010, it seemed fitting that a focus would be placed during that event on what had happened in Sacramento with the birthing of the Prayer Corps in the 1970s. Lou saw it as one of the first significant 24/7 youth prayer movements, one that birthed numerous other such movements. According to Lou, it was time to re-dig these wells, and there was no more fitting a place to do this than in Sacramento.

As Brian shared these details with me, he added something surprising and a bit baffling. Following TheCall in Sacramento, he and a team of his colleagues desired to conduct a twenty-one-day Purple Pig Tour. When I inquired what this might involve, he explained they wanted to visit as many college campuses as possible across California to share the message of this book and to spread the vision for establishing prayer furnaces on these campuses. According to Brian, there are ninety-nine accredited four-year colleges and universities in California alone, and their goal is to ultimately see 24/7 prayer furnaces functioning on all of them.

As I listened to Brian share his vision, I couldn't help but rejoice at how the Lord keeps His promises. Years ago I had heard a Bible teacher remind his students how the prophet Jeremiah prophesied certain things that didn't come to pass for decades, but when they did, they were history-making events. Some of those events even happened after Jeremiah's death. In 1971, God had promised me a massive youth movement of prayer with fire houses everywhere, but that really only began as a trickle at the time. Now, four decades later, I was seeing far more of the vision taking shape. I could only imagine what lay ahead.

As I arrived home later that evening after these inspiring moments with Brian, I quietly went to my prayer closet to sit alone in the presence of the Lord. I couldn't get out of my mind Brian's words: "God has not fastened your soul to a dead-end dream!"

"Yes," I thought, as I drifted to sleep later that night, "there are no dead-end dreams in Jesus!"

Chapter 33
A CALL TO THE WALL

THERE ARE FEW SIGHTS quite like it in the world. It was late at night, and I was seventeen stories high on the roof of my Hong Kong hotel, looking out over Victoria Harbor. An endless array of brilliant neon signs beamed brightly from towering skyscrapers across the harbor, reflecting off the mirror-like water, adding even more color to the scene.

I had been praying on the roof for some time. I was the only one there, because the doorway to the final staircase leading to the roof has a sign posted indicating no one is permitted beyond that point. However, several years earlier our ministry conducted a leadership conference at that same hotel, and we had been given special permission to go to the roof to view the sights. The hotel manager suggested we could go there any time we liked, so I took this to mean even on subsequent visits. However, I still felt like repenting every time I passed the sign.

This night was to become particularly meaningful and would provide significant guidance for the future of our ministry. As I prayed, the Lord reminded me of an experience I had had five years earlier in Hong Kong. Dee and I had been invited to lead a conference for intercessors by a long-time friend in Hong Kong—Agatha Chan. Agatha was a psychologist and university professor who had given up her practice and teaching position to establish a powerful prayer and deliverance ministry.

Several weeks prior to making the trip, I taught a prayer seminar at a church in North Carolina. It was a church with a full-time prayer pastor named Phil Bennett. Upon arriving for the seminar, Phil and I talked about the plans for the conference. He expressed excitement about the proposed teaching, because, as he told me, it would help fortify the churches' numerous Walls of Prayer. I wasn't familiar with that term, so I asked Phil to describe these walls. He explained that when all 168 hours in a week (24/7) are covered by individual intercessors who pray in agreement for similar daily focuses, a Wall of Prayer is established. Phil further explained that God had led him to go to other places, even England, to help start Walls of Prayer. I was amazed to hear that in Phil's

213

church alone, there already were five functioning Walls of Prayer.

On the final night of the conference, a Sunday, I spoke on Isaiah 62:6–7, which speaks of watchmen praying day and night on Jerusalem's walls. I was delighted that by the conclusion of the meeting, another 168 additional hours had been committed. The church now had six Walls of Prayer.

I emailed Agatha Chan about these Walls of Prayer prior to our visit, and she was excited about introducing the concept to Hong Kong believers. I also suggested I bring Phil Bennett with me to provide first-hand expertise, and Agatha agreed. Fortunately Phil's schedule was free, and he joined us for the conference.

On the flight to Hong Kong, Phil was to experience his own vision, which would soon deeply impact our ministry. In Phil's vision, he saw the Great Wall of China become a Great Wall of Prayer stretching across all of China. Every space on the wall was filled with intercessors. When Phil shared his vision with me, I became convinced that one day these Walls of Prayer would cover the landscape of China's mainland, which is what would eventually result following my Hong Kong rooftop encounter five years later.

But first, God wanted to make this happen in Hong Kong. It would begin with an unusual prophetic interruption at the conclusion of the conference. As the final session drew to a close, Agatha led the hundreds of participants in some concluding worship.

Suddenly, as the worship team continued leading, Agatha rushed toward me at the back of the platform. I had ended my teaching and had stepped aside to let her finish the session.

"Dick," Agatha whispered hastily, "come pray a prophetic prayer over Hong Kong." With that Agatha darted back to the lectern, leaving me standing without a clue as to what I should do. I had no opportunity to inform her that this wasn't my gifting. I can't just make up a sudden prophetic *anything*! I was numb.

Agatha then compounded the situation by informing the crowd that I was coming now to pray prophetically over the city.

I gulped. Sweat was beading on my face. I inwardly pleaded, "Lord, what shall I do?" In an instant that same still, small voice I had heard so many times returned.

"Pray Isaiah 62:1–7 over Hong Kong as if that passage had been written specifically for believers there."

"This will be interesting," I thought, as I walked tentatively to the lectern and opened my Bible to Isaiah.

I soon was praying Isaiah 62:1–7 from my New Living Translation as if this prophetic prayer of Isaiah had, indeed, been written specifically for the church in Hong Kong:

> I believe the Lord is saying, "Because I love My people in Hong Kong, because My heart yearns for the church of Hong Kong, I cannot remain silent. I will not stop praying for her until her righteousness shines like the dawn, and her salvation blazes like a burning torch."
>
> Lord, I believe You want to ignite fires of awakening in Hong Kong so that believers here will shine Your light of salvation "like a burning torch" to the nations.
>
> As Isaiah also prayed, "The nations will see your righteousness. Kings will be blinded by your glory. And the Lord will give you a new name. The Lord will hold you in his hands for all to see—a splendid crown in the hands of God. Never again will you be called the God-forsaken city or the desolate land. Your new name will be the city of God's delight and the bride of God, for the Lord delights in you and will claim you as his own."
>
> Lord, many have viewed Hong Kong as a city of sin for generations. But we declare that this "God-forsaken and desolate land" will be given a new name. We believe it is Your desire that Hong Kong becomes a "city of Your delight," and the people here "the bride of God" just as Isaiah declared over ancient Israel.
>
> Lord, Isaiah also declared prophetically, "O Jerusalem, I have posted watchmen on your walls; they will pray to the LORD day and night for the fulfillment of his promises. Take no rest all you who pray. Give the LORD no rest until he makes Jerusalem the object of praise throughout the earth."
>
> Lord, we claim an army of watchmen in Hong Kong who will declare Your promises day and night, not only over this city, but also over all the nations of the world. We believe that just as You declared that Jerusalem would become an object of praise throughout the earth, we pray that You will cause Hong Kong Christians to lift a canopy of praise and worship over all the nations of the world, creating an open heaven over those nations. Lord, we declare these things in Jesus's name.

I had no idea the impact these simple moments of praying God's Word prophetically would have on those present. One worship leader in attendance even wrote a song based on this prophetic prayer that is still being sung in Hong Kong. In the immediate weeks following the conference, six complete Walls of Prayer had been established. Soon 24/7 prayer ministries had begun in each of Hong Kong's sixteen districts.

All this came back to me as I stood alone on that Hong Kong hotel roof gazing across the harbor at a multitude of glowing neon signs. In those moments I too was fulfilling the role of a watchman, and, as God had shown me at that conference five years earlier with Agatha Chan, He was going to make Hong Kong a city of His delight. Further, Hong Kong believers were going to become profoundly significant in God's hands in transforming nations, especially mainland China. But I had mixed emotions as I prayed late into that night on the roof; just days prior to my arrival for this visit our cherished friend Agatha Chan had passed away.

Suddenly a strong impression came over me that I was to pray prophetically. I was to speak to each neon sign, declaring that the wealth of Hong Kong would be released for the healing of the nations. Because no one else was on the roof at the time, I realized I could speak boldly as I prayed. I spoke to such lighted signs as Phillips, Epson, Panasonic, Hitachi, China Mobile, Samsung, Olympus, and on and on. I lost count of the many signs as I prayed. My prayer continued until every sign I could see was prayed over.

As I concluded these unusual prayers, a picture came to me of what God wanted to do in our own ministry back in Colorado. It had been eight weeks since Cindy Jacobs had called about the unfinished space in the basement area of the Jericho Center. The board had just approved the finishing of the area, but we hadn't spelled out in detail all this might involve. I knew in that moment that God wanted us to build a literal Wall of Prayer that would be symbolic of an ancient wall in Israel. Our executive staff already determined that we needed some kind of a training facility in the space, and as I stood atop that hotel gazing across the harbor, I knew we should call it the Watchman Training Center.

Just before leaving for Hong Kong on this trip, one of our directors mentioned that what the Jericho Center presently lacked were individual places for people to pray. Standing on that roof I suddenly envisioned individual *prayer grottos* within this literal wall. Everything was coming together regarding the future of our ministry's prayer vision.

I rushed down the steps from the roof to catch an elevator from the sixteenth floor to my floor. I was excited about what I had just seen and heard. Once in my room, I immediately began sketching what I had just pictured in prayer—that of a wall in ancient Jerusalem with prayer grottos in it. When I later showed the sketch to our architect, Gary Larson, he immediately envisioned the Wailing Wall in Jerusalem. Within days we had a beautiful architectural rendering depicting this symbolism. Soon we had the plans for both the Watchman Wall and the Watchman Training Center.

One idea that came to our attention regarding the prayer wall itself was to build something similar to that of a typical rock-climbing wall at a sports facility. Of course, for us the finished product would look like the Wailing Wall in Jerusalem and not a rock-climbing wall.

We were about to sign a contract with a company that designs such walls when another miracle occurred. Just days before signing that contract, two owners of a company that imported Jerusalem stone showed up at the receptionist's desk of our architect. They had come from their new offices in Denver, Colorado, unannounced. Some months earlier their company had moved from New York to Denver to be more centrally located in our nation. They told the receptionist that they were randomly visiting architects in the city to see if they might be interested in using Jerusalem stone in any of their projects. This was, of course, amazing timing for our project at hand.

We soon discovered that for only slightly more than the funds needed to construct a fake wall, fifty tons of real Jerusalem stone could be imported from Israel to build a far more authentic symbol of a wall in Israel. We also learned that the stone would come from a quarry where stone originally was taken centuries ago to build the actual Western (or Wailing) Wall. And when our prayer wall was finally finished, it would even have cracks between the stones like the actual Wailing Wall in Jerusalem where people coming to our center could insert small written prayers, just as is traditionally done at the actual Wailing Wall in Jerusalem. Then, periodically, our staff here could collect these written prayers and send them to our EHC office in Israel, and they could be literally placed in the actual Wailing Wall. This further strengthened the symbolism of our identifying with Israel in the project. Particularly important concerning our Wall of Prayer was that it would represent potentially thousands of spiritual walls of 24/7 prayer begun throughout the world.

But to this point all this represented the visionary side of our prayer ministry at Every Home for Christ. I recognized that something more had to be done in a practical sense to help make all this happen. Most importantly, we needed the right leadership to direct this phase of the work. Further, because the harp-and-bowl model of intercessory worship was so vital to the carrying out of this phase of the vision, we needed leadership who understood this and had the gifts to make it happen.

Within weeks of beginning the construction of our Watchman Training Center and our Jerusalem Prayer Wall, we learned of a young couple, Deborah and Murray Hiebert, serving as worship leaders in a church in Idaho. They had met while working together during the formative years of establishing the International House of Prayer (IHOP) with Mike Bickle in Kansas City. In fact, Deborah had been involved with IHOP from the first day it was launched. Soon Murray also would join the IHOP ministry and become Mike's director of worship for several years.

Prayerfully we contacted Murray and Deborah, asking if they would consider joining us to direct this new prayer venture. It seemed to be exactly what God had prepared them for at IHOP. Even back in 2002 when Murray was preparing to leave a ministry position in Minneapolis to join the IHOP team in Kansas City, God's voice thundered in his spirit, "Worship and the nations…your move to Kansas City is all about worship and the nations!"

Murray soon would discover that IHOP was the perfect door to prepare him for his entry into that ministry and also would be the place where he would meet his bride, who had the same calling.

But it wasn't until Murray and Deborah were invited to Every Home for Christ that they would see how directly the vision God had given the both of them was soon to be fulfilled. By May of 2009, Murray and Deborah and their three young girls had moved to Colorado Springs, where Murray assumed his role as director of EHC's Watchman Training Center and related prayer activities of the ministry. Soon they would establish an internship program at EHC called TheWall. Through this program, now underway, mature youth and young adults are trained and equipped to serve as full-time singers, musicians, and intercessors in leading the intercessory worship at the Jericho Center.

TheWall also equips those who may be called as worship missionaries to take the vision of intercessory worship and houses of prayer to the nations. Each internship consists of a six-month program featuring five months of practical training in various aspects of prayer and worship, including how to build houses of prayer in the nations and how to model intercessory worship for those houses of prayer. All internships conclude with a two- to three-week short-term mission trip to a foreign field for on-site experience and opportunities to spread the vision of houses of prayer. Additionally, TheWall ministry seeks to enlist local intercessors of all ages and others from beyond the community who might come for a several-day worship mission to help sustain continuous intercessory worship at the Jericho Center.

Presently, the Watchman Training Center and Watchman Wall are functioning from 6:00 a.m. to 6:00 p.m., Monday through Friday. During these hours worship and intercession continue nonstop. Plans are underway to increase this to 24/7 on-site intercessory worship in the near future. EHC's unique Watchman Wall also serves as a visual symbol for mobilizing continual prayer throughout all the nations of the world, recruiting believers globally to find their place as part of a Wall of Prayer in their area. The ultimate goal of the Watchman Training Center vision is to fill every moment of every day in every geographic region of the world with focused intercession and worship for global evangelism and spiritual awakening.

Since the Watchman Training Center vision officially began in 2009, nearly three thousand different locations of 24/7 prayer already have been established in a single twelve-month period, many in East Asia. This number is expected to increase dramatically. In that same time frame, for example, the vision has been shared with more than twenty-five thousand pastors and other leaders in multi-hour training sessions specifically designed to challenge leaders of churches and networks to make Walls of Prayer a vital part of their overall prayer and evangelism strategies.

The thirteen prayer grottos in EHC's Watchman Wall also serve a unique function. Like the prayer grottos at Prayer Mountain in South Korea, these grottos exist for individual intercessors, couples, and Christian leaders to spend whole or half days in more focused, personal intercession. Each grotto comes equipped with a touch screen monitor to aid intercessors in prayer and worship and to help them focus their prayers on specific nations and needs. Twelve of these rooms are named after the tribes of Israel, and the remaining grotto is called the "Back to Jerusalem Room." The latter highlights the prophetic vision of the church in China to someday deploy tens of thousands of Christian missionaries who will evangelize unreached peoples along the old Silk Roads through South and Central Asia and the Middle East—all the way back to Jerusalem. In-depth training for this movement already has begun.

The reader is invited to visit Colorado Springs, Colorado, to participate in the worship and intercession, including setting aside a season of
prayer in one of the prayer grottos. Young people interested in pursuing
an internship at the Jericho Center are encouraged to contact our office.
(See contact information regarding this program and other general information about Every Home for Christ at the conclusion of this book.)

EPILOGUE

I CARRY IN MY WALLET a handwritten Bible passage (highlighted in hot pink) that I readily see every time I open my wallet. I intend to carry it with me the rest of my life. They are the words God spoke to King David through the prophet Nathan in 2 Samuel 7 when David desired to build God a temple. (David, of course, had the vision, but Solomon finished the task.) The how and why of my carrying that handwritten passage provides a fitting epilogue to the pages that have gone before! In fact, this brief epilogue is somewhat of a "bookend" to my prologue at the beginning—"Staying Small... Believing Big!"

Recently, following a Board of Directors meeting for Every Home for Christ, I came home rejoicing in the extraordinary things God had done through this ministry during the previous year. During those twelve months more than 12.4 million people (in 105 nations) had responded to our home-to-home evangelism contacts and were enrolled in EHC's Bible correspondence courses and other follow-up materials because they wanted to know what it means to be a true disciple of Jesus. This was the result of some 4,000 full-time staff and more than 25,000 monthly volunteers coordinating visits to at least a million homes (and often more) *every week* during those twelve months and sharing with them the Good News of Jesus.

We had never seen such results in our ministry's 64-year history. Our board meeting that day had ended with various directors praying over our senior leadership team. At one point one of the directors prayed rather boldly, and I was the focus of that prayer: "Dick can't begin to imagine or even dream in his wildest dreams what You, O Lord, are about to do in the global harvest. What has happened up to now, even as we hear these amazing reports, pales in comparison to what You are about to do!"

I, of course, wondered what more could possibly happen that "pales in comparison" to what we had seen in recent months, but I clearly agreed with one thing: these are extraordinary days of a great ingathering of lost souls globally, and this ingathering is certainly beyond what most of us are even capable of dreaming about.

Arriving home after that meeting, I went directly to my prayer room. I was overwhelmed with gratitude. Because I pray through my Bible each year, a few chapters a day, I opened to the assigned scriptures for that day's reading. I quietly asked God to speak to me about the meeting that day and especially about that director's prayer. What could there be that was beyond my "wildest dreams"?

That day's passage just happened to begin with 2 Samuel 7. I was reading in *The Message*. When I came to verse 18, it was as if David's experience had become mine:

> King David went in, took his place before GOD, and prayed: "Who am I, my Master GOD, and what is my family, that you have brought me to this place in life? But that's nothing compared to what's coming, for you've also spoken of my family far into the future, given me a glimpse into tomorrow, my Master GOD! What can I possibly say in the face of all this? You know me, Master GOD, just as I am. You've done all this not because of who I am but because of who you are—out of your very heart!—but you've let me in on it. This is what makes you so great, Master GOD! There is none like you, no God but you, nothing to compare with what we've heard with our ears."
>
> —2 SAMUEL 7:18–22, THE MESSAGE

This passage conveys the heart of what I have sought to share on the preceding pages. God does what He does in and through us not because of who we are but because of who He is. *He just lets us in on it.* Of course, the way to get in on what God is doing in His global harvest is through focused prayer and tangible involvement in helping gather in that harvest.

And that prompts a concluding question: Do you have a harvest to take with you to heaven? I've long believed that each of us, if we are true followers of Jesus, has our own God-appointed harvest to take with us into eternity—if we'll just pray faithfully, go confidently, and give sacrificially. If you cannot go, you can give. If you cannot give, you can pray. Indeed, many can do all three. But each of us can do something. I invite you in the days to come to sit quietly before God as King David did to let Him speak to you directly about your involvement in history's great End-Time harvest. If you're willing and available, I can promise you this—He'll let you in on it!

Appendix A
THE SPIRIT OF SACRIFICE

In chapters 10 through 13 I spoke of numerous incidents during the times of awakening in our early Prayer Corps years that involved unusual sacrifices. They resulted from God's dealings with young men and women, many who were teens. These were tangible sacrifices, not mere words of commitment. Having already shared many individual examples, let's consider what Scripture says concerning this subject.

Stirred by God's Message

A dramatic first-century revival is discussed by Luke in his narrative of the early church—the Book of Acts. Luke records:

> The story of what happened spread quickly all through Ephesus, to Jews and Greeks alike; and a solemn fear descended on the city, and the name of the Lord Jesus was greatly honored. Many of the believers who had been practicing black magic confessed their deeds and brought their incantation books and charms and burned them at a public bonfire. (Someone estimated the value of the books at $10,000.) This indicates how deeply the whole area was stirred by God's message.
>
> —Acts 19:17–20, tlb[1]

The revival described by Luke could certainly be termed *emotional* and even *radical*. It affected the people so intensely they acted in dramatic, tangible ways. Ten thousand dollars' worth of "incantation books" and "charms" were destroyed, according to commentators. In this account, three expressions in particular should be noted.

1. "The Lord Jesus was greatly honored." A true revival, that which affects people so deeply they lay aside idols of any sort, always brings glory to Christ.

2. It occurred "at a public bonfire." Some contend that such displays of commitment or sacrifice should be entirely

private. In this early church example it was public, for all could see.

3. "The whole area was stirred by God's message," or, as the New King James renders it, "...the word of the Lord grew mightily and prevailed." Any lasting revival or awakening, if fruit is to grow, must be centered in the Word of God.

Try It!

The above passage from Acts deals primarily with the sacrificing of those things that "take God's place in [our] hearts" (1 John 5:21, TLB). Scripture also speaks often concerning the believer's willingness to give freely of his finances. A study of God's Word reveals at least three types of giving.

First, there is *obedience giving*. As far back as Abraham in the Old Testament we see the biblical principle of the tithe set forth. (See Genesis 14:18–21). *Tithe*, of course, means "a tenth." It is giving a tenth of what we earn to the work of the Lord. This tithe ought to go into our store-house—that place where our spiritual food is obtained. In our context, this would be our local church. This guarantees those maintaining and keeping the storehouse a living so they can continue their ministry. The most familiar passage concerning the tithe is Malachi 3:10–12 (NLT):

> "Try it! Put me to the test! Your crops will be abundant, for I will guard them from insects and disease. Your grapes will not fall from the vine before they are ripe," says the LORD of Heaven's Armies. "Then all nations will call you blessed, for your land will be such a delight," says the LORD of Heaven's Armies.

Though Malachi 3 is an Old Testament passage, I believe it is New Testament in principle and scope. The principle of the tithe remains as important to Christians today as it was to Hebrew believers in Malachi's day. Tithing is "obedience giving." It teaches us that the firstfruits of all we receive belong to the Lord. (See Proverbs 3:9, NKJV.)

Second, there is *purpose giving*. Scripture describes this type of giving in Paul's writings to Corinthian believers:

> Whoever sows sparingly will also reap sparingly, and whoever sows generously will also reap generously. Each man should give what he has decided in his heart to give.
> —2 CORINTHIANS 9:6–7

The Living Bible renders verse 7, "Everyone must make up his own mind as to how much he should give." This kind of giving involves a thought process. We think it over, make it a part of our budget, and purpose in our mind what we can give.

Third, there is *sacrificial giving*. This final type of giving involves a true spirit of sacrifice. It is also the kind of giving that is open to criticism. Some Christians become upset when hearing of people giving car payment money or who empty their bank accounts during a church service where, for example, a missionary tells of some urgent need overseas. A particular New Testament passage describing this type of giving has deeply impacted my ministry and helped me put in perspective the waves of sacrifice I saw in the formative days of our prayer ministry.

Obsessed With Jesus

The account is recorded in Mark 14:3–8. Note six key verses in the narrative:

> And being in Bethany at the house of Simon the leper, as He [Jesus] sat at the table, a woman came having an alabaster flask of very costly oil of spikenard. Then she broke the flask and poured it on His head. But there were some who were indignant among themselves, and said, "Why was this fragrant oil wasted? For it might have been sold for more than three hundred denarii and given to the poor." And they criticized her sharply. But Jesus said, "Let her alone. Why do you trouble her? She has done a good work for Me. For you have the poor with you always, and whenever you wish you may do them good; but Me you do not have always. She has done what she could. She has come beforehand to anoint My body for burial."
>
> —Mark 14:3–8, nkjv

Here we discover an excellent example of sacrificial giving. The woman Mark describes was clearly obsessed with a love for Jesus. (You'll recall in the earlier chapter "The Minneapolis Miracle," my telling of a college student publicly bringing her wallet with all the money she possessed in response to hearing Jesus repeatedly ask her, "How much do you love Me?" Her deep love for Jesus initiated her sacrificial actions.)

As is usually the case (unfortunately), the critics were close at hand in Jesus's day—including Judas, who was the treasurer of the group of disciples. Naturally he would have liked to have seen the money stay in his possession, because we later learn he was pilfering these very funds (Mark 14:10; John 12:4–6).

Christ, however, knew the woman's true motives—and saw them as being far from waste. He even demanded that the critics leave her alone, because, in His words, "She has done a beautiful thing to me" (Mark 14:6).

The lesson here is clear. Sacrificial giving not only has its place in our Christian experience today, but it is also highly respected by our Lord. Note especially how Christ prophesied that this woman's experience would be remembered as a "memorial" throughout the world (v. 9, NKJV). Hundreds of millions of New Testaments—in many hundreds of languages—testify to the fulfillment of this prophecy and to the favor that God places on such sacrificial displays in our attitudes of devotion to Christ.

Moth-eaten Rags

During those days when I repeatedly witnessed this phenomenon of sacrificial giving, I came across an edition of *Time* magazine that devoted an entire page to the evangelical view of Christ's second coming. The article was titled "Is the End Near?" One thing was clear as I read the article: people everywhere are conscious of the age in which we live. In light of this fact, a depreciation of material ideals in the lives of Christians ought to be received as something healthy. But in sharing this reality, we must be careful to note that Jesus never truly condemned material things; He merely cautioned us regarding the worship of material possessions. He preached, "No one can serve two masters. For you will hate one and love the other; you will be devoted to one and despise the other. You cannot serve both God and money" (Matt. 6:24, NLT).

Concerning the last days, it was Zephaniah who declared, "Your silver and gold will be of no use to you in that day of the LORD's anger" (Zeph. 1:18, NLT). The Christian who listens closely to God's still, small voice in his or her heart in these exciting days of renewal will sooner or later hear this message: "Your wealth is rotting away, and your fine clothes are moth-eaten rags. Your gold and silver have become worthless" (James 5:2–3, NLT).

Christ clearly yearns for the releasing of our grip on any and all idols that may hinder our Christian walk. Only then can He bless His people as He truly desires.

Appendix B
GOD'S UNUSUAL POWER

E MOTIONAL RESPONSE IN CHRISTIAN revival and awakenings has been criticized as far back as the Upper Room incident when onlookers declared, "They have had too much wine" (Acts 2:13). And yet, down through the ages such emotional responses have cropped up in almost every revival. Why? Because man is an emotional being, and the new birth experience affects the whole man.

Revival history is filled with many examples. Peter Cartwright's biography includes this description of a meeting the evangelist conducted: "My voice was strong and clear... my text was 'The gates of hell shall not prevail.' In about thirty minutes the power of God fell on the congregation in such a manner as is seldom seen: the people fell in every direction, right and left and front and rear. It was supposed that not less than three hundred fell like dead men in mighty battle."[1]

One of the earliest biographies of D. L. Moody shares a similar demonstration of power, occurring in 1875. People had not only fallen in response to the manifest presence of God during the meeting, but some even began speaking in other languages spontaneously. (I understand this specific fact was removed from a later edition of the biography so as not to offend some Christians.)

Many noted evangelists witnessed similar reactions to God's presence. Whitefield, the Wesleys, Charles Finney, and Jonathan Edwards observed great emotion in their meetings. General William Booth, the founder of The Salvation Army, likewise witnessed unusual manifestations accompanied by deep conviction in his prayer meetings.

Booth's son relates one particular instance that occurred August 8, 1878: "Something of the same force which manifested itself on the Day of Pentecost manifested itself at these holiness meetings in London. Men and women would suddenly fall flat upon the ground, remain in a swoon or trance for many hours, and rise at last so transformed by joy that they could do nothing but shout and sing in an ecstasy of bliss."[2]

Indeed, the history of revival speaks repeatedly of unusual displays

of God's power affecting human emotions. But what does the Bible say
concerning the matter? In chapter 16 we shared several brief biblical
instances. Let's look more closely at these as well as several others.

Incident one: The arrest of Jesus in the Garden of Gethsemane (John
18:1–6). Here Jesus was betrayed by Judas Iscariot, who brought a
large company of soldiers to take Christ captive. When Jesus identified
Himself, something unusual transpired. Scripture relates, "As soon then
as he [Jesus] had said unto them, I am he, they went backward, and fell
to the ground" (v. 6, KJV). This happened (according to most commentators) to about six hundred unbelievers (soldiers) as they came in contact
with the power of Christ.

Incident two: The transfiguration of Jesus (Matt. 17:1–6). The word
transfigured in Matthew 17:2 comes from the Greek word *metamorphoo*,
which means "to change the form of." Here Jesus is changed in form
to His glorified body. Peter, James, and John witnessed the miracle of
Christ's changing form, accompanied by a supernatural voice. The reaction of these disciples is understandable. Scripture tells us, "And when the
disciples heard this, they fell facedown to the ground, terrified" (Matt.
11:6). We should note that this happened to followers of Christ, as each
was overcome by the awe of God's glory radiating from Jesus.

Incident three: The conversion of Saul of Tarsus (Acts 9:1–9). Alluded
to in chapter 16, this instance is familiar to most Christians. Luke's
narrative reads, "As he [Paul] neared Damascus on his journey, suddenly
a light from heaven flashed around him. He fell to the ground and heard
a voice say to him, 'Saul, Saul, why do you persecute me?'" (vv. 3–4).

According to verse 5, Saul saw and heard Christ Himself. Barnabas
later clarifies in this chapter that Saul indeed saw the Lord (v. 27). Saul of
Tarsus was, quite simply, overcome by the glory and presence of God.

Incident four: The trance of Peter (Acts 10:9–14). Peter was alone on
a housetop waiting for the noon meal when he decided to spend the time
in prayer. We read, "He became hungry and wanted something to eat,
and while the meal was being prepared, he fell into a trance" (v. 10). Of
the word *trance* one commentator explains, "It is a state in which one
seems to be insensible to his surroundings, except to the subject of a
vision." (The reader might wish to compare this account with Numbers
24:1–4, particularly noting verse 4.)

Incident five: The experience of Ezekiel (Ezek. 1:26–28). Ezekiel begins
his amazing prophetic dialogue with a single statement that sets the tone

of his narrative: "The heavens were opened and I saw visions of God" (v. 1). After the strange vision of the "wheel in the middle of a wheel" (vv. 15–19, NKJV), Ezekiel actually sees the glory of God. Ezekiel describes the extraordinary brightness of a man seated on a throne accompanied by brilliant colors of blue and amber. The prophet plainly describes what he saw and adds his reaction: "Like the appearance of a rainbow in a cloud on a rainy day, so was the appearance of the brightness all around it. This was the appearance of the likeness of the glory of the LORD. So when I saw it, I fell on my face…" (Ezek. 1:28–2:1, NKJV). (See also Ezekiel 3:23; 43:3; 44:4.)

Incident six: Daniel's vision of God's glory (Dan. 10:5–11). Daniel also witnessed the awe-inspiring glory of God. What was Daniel's reaction? He fell into a "deep sleep" or trance (v. 9, NKJV). Those with him at the time did not see the vision, though each was deeply affected by God's presence. Concerning this, Daniel relates, "But a great terror fell upon them, so that they fled to hide themselves" (v. 7, NKJV).

Incident seven: The encounter of John (Rev. 1:12–17). It is most interesting to compare the experiences of both Daniel and Ezekiel to the New Testament apostle John. The latter saw a man "like the Son of Man, clothed with a garment down to his feet and girded about the chest with a golden band" (v. 13, NKJV).

John's reaction was also predictable: "When I saw him, I fell at his feet as though dead" (v. 17).

Three Prostrations

It might be profitable to note there are actually three different types of prostration in Scripture. A brief consideration of these may increase our understanding of some of these emotional experiences some have witnessed in recent times.

First, there is prostration as the result of God's glory or presence. This is an involuntary experience. The seven instances cited above describe this type of prostration. Daniel, Ezekiel, and John did not decide they would fall when the glory of the Lord came upon them. It is also interesting to note that such prostration happened to both believers and unbelievers. (For a further study see Genesis 15:12–17; Leviticus 9:24; Deuteronomy 9:25.)

Second, there is prostration as a simple act of humility. This occurs when a believer chooses to prostrate himself or herself before the Lord. Though this is a voluntary experience, we sometimes find borderline cases where both types of prostration seem involved. The woman healed of a blood disease in Luke 8:43–47 may have fallen before Jesus purely as the result of His power or as an act of humility—or because of both. A careful review of this passage also reveals she was afraid. Thus the woman's prostration also included an emotional reaction of fear.

In Numbers 14:5 both Moses and Aaron fell on their faces in an act of humility, apparently because of desperation as well as attempting to set an example before the people. Later, in Numbers 16:22, we read, "But Moses and Aaron fell facedown and cried out, 'O God, God of the spirits of all mankind, will you be angry with the entire assembly when only one man sins?'" Again this prostration involved a voluntary act of humility. (For further references see Joshua 5:14; 7:6; 1 Kings 18:39.)

Third, there is prostration as an act of brokenness in prayer. This "prayer prostration" is common throughout Scripture and, like "humility prostration," involves a voluntary act of prostrating oneself before the Lord. We recall a desperate ruler of the synagogue, Jairus, whose daughter lay at the point of death. He came to Christ with an earnest petition. And just before his prayer he "fell at his [Jesus] feet" (Mark 5:22).

Christ Himself leaves us a powerful example of "prayer prostration." It happened in the Garden of Gethsemane, the night before Christ's trial. Matthew records, "Going a little farther, he fell with his face to the ground and prayed" (Matt. 26:39). (The reader also may wish to study Joshua 7:10; Mark 7:25; Luke 5:12; John 11:32.)

Deep Emotion in Scripture

It is in no way this author's desire to suggest some new *doctrine of emotion* in sharing these scriptural details. I simply share what the Bible says. We merely wish to establish that Scripture does contain numerous unusual emotional responses to God's presence and a humble reaction to the same. I disagree with those who say this is totally out of place in twenty-first-century worship. Likewise, I also emphatically disagree with those who contend a church is *dry* and *backslidden* if emotional manifestations are not witnessed in every service. Human responses, if there are to be any in our worship, should always result from coming near to God in worship rather than from attempting to work up emotional appetites in order to *outdo* some previous meeting.

To believers at opposite ends of the spectrum of religious experience, I would direct these final remarks. First, to those who wonder if emotion in our worship is Bible-based I offer a list of six deeply emotional responses in Scripture, with references the reader may wish to examine at his or her leisure.

1. Vocal praise and even shouting: 1 Samuel 4:5–6; 1 Kings 1:40; Isaiah 12:6; Luke 6:22–23.

2. Lifting hands and the clapping of hands: 1 Kings 8:22, 54; Nehemiah 8:6; Psalm 47:1; 1 Timothy 2:8.

3. Dancing or leaping: 2 Samuel 6:14–16; Psalm 149:3; 150:4; Luke 6:23.

4. Groaning in prayer: Romans 8:26; 1 Corinthians 14:14–15; Galatians 4:19; Ephesians 6:18.

5. Shaking or trembling: Ezekiel 12:18; Daniel 10:7; Matthew 28:4; Acts 16:29; Hebrews 12:21.

6. Intense weeping: Ezra 3:13; Job 3:24; Lamentations 1:16, 20; Romans 12:15; James 4:9.

To those who feel that emotion must be part of all worship, I offer a single passage, which deeply affected me during a treasured quiet time in prayer: "As you enter the Temple, keep your ears open and your mouth shut!" (Eccles. 5:1, TLB). The New International Version reads, "Guard your steps when you go to the house of God. Go near to listen.... Do not be quick with your mouth, do not be hasty in your heart to utter anything before God. God is in heaven and you are on earth, so let your words be few" (vv. 1–2).

There are many times we must sit back and let God do the speaking. Silence can be one of the highest forms of worship. Silence—in the final analysis—can be as deeply emotional as all other encounters put together. Silence is the laboratory of listening. Truly hearing God sets in motion what God wants to do in and through us. Never fear silence in God's presence.

Finally, Paul's scriptural exhortation on church order always bears repetition. He reminded the trouble-plagued Corinthian church: "For God is not a God of disorder but of peace" (1 Cor. 14:33).

Paul concludes his discussion of this sensitive subject of spiritual gifts with these words: "But everything should be done in a fitting and orderly way" (v. 40).

NOTES

Chapter 11
Call the World to Prayer

1. Andrew Murray, *With Christ in the School of Prayer* (New Kensington, PA: Whitaker House, 1981).

Chapter 12
The Minneapolis Miracle

1. See Appendix A, "The Spirit of Sacrifice," for scriptural instances of Christians becoming so obsessed with a love for Jesus Christ that they willingly sacrificed everything.

Chapter 18
Manifestations

1. See Appendix B, "God's Unusual Power," for a more detailed look at instances in Scripture where unusual emotional responses resulted when man came before God.

2. The reader may be interested to know Scripture contains several instances—in both Old and New Testaments—concerning the laying on of hands. In the Book of Acts alone, of the five reported instances of the coming of the Holy Spirit, three include the act of the laying on of hands (Acts 8:18; 9:12; 19:6). In Acts 6:6 the apostles "laid hands" on those selected to be deacons in the early church. Here, it was part of a commissioning ceremony. (See also Genesis 48:14; Numbers 27:18–20; Acts 13:1–4; 1 Timothy 4:14; 2 Timothy 1:6.) In the case of young Timothy, the laying on of hands concerned a stirring up of "the gift of God which is in you"— thereby focusing on spiritual gifts.

Chapter 21
The Victory Board

1. The victories of healing listed in this chapter appear as we received them from people by phone. Often we had no names or other detailed information on what happened, only that God had met a need.

Chapter 25
Agents of the Invisible

1. Some content in this chapter first appeared in my book *Beyond Imagination* (Chosen Books, 1997). That book has since been revised and re-released in 2009 under the title *Look What God Is Doing*. I share this information again here because

it is clearly one of the other miracles that have followed in the many years since the Prayer Corps was first established.

2. John Calvin, *Institutes of the Christian Religion*, Book 1 (Grand Rapids, MI: Eerdmans, 1972), 145.

3. Billy Graham, *Angels: God's Secret Agents* (Garden City, NY: Doubleday, 1975), 14–15.

4. Ed Silvoso, *That None Should Perish* (Ventura, CA: Regal, 1994), 181.

Chapter 28
Pray Through the Window

1. National Day of Prayer, "History of the National Day of Prayer," http://nationaldayofprayer.org/about/history/ (accessed July 16, 2010).

Appendix A
The Spirit of Sacrifice

1. History tells us that Savonarola, the noted evangelist of Florence, Italy, became so distressed at the sinful condition of his city that he lay prostrate before the church altar crying out to God for revival. His prayer brought similar results to those recorded by Luke in Acts 19. When revival settled in Florence, men and women came from everywhere bringing their idols. The men brought their magic books and playing cards and the women brought their dancing slippers. All of it was burned in a great bonfire for the whole city of Florence to see.

Appendix B
God's Unusual Power

1. Robert Bray, *Peter Cartwright, Legendary Frontier Preacher* (n.p.: University of Illinois Press, 2005), 42.

2. Adapted from *The Life of General William Booth*, chapter 25, 1877–1878, The Salvation Army, http://www.salvationarmysouth.org/booth/ch25.htm (accessed July 16, 2010).

HOW IS GOD
MOVING IN THE WORLD
TODAY?

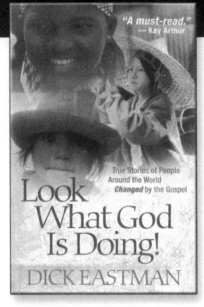

"A must-read."
— Kay Arthur

"I invite you to read *Look What God Is Doing!* As a matter of fact, I'll send you a free copy. These amazing true stories span the globe from the jungles of Brazil to the foothills of the Himalayas. My prayer is that you will be inspired to press into God, gain His compassion for those who don't know Him yet and long for a greater opportunity to help gather in history's greatest harvest."

True Stories of People Around the World *Changed* by the Gospel

Look What God Is Doing!
DICK EASTMAN

Dick Eastman
International President
Every Home for Christ

FREE
SPECIAL
OFFER!

HOW TO
GET YOUR
FREE COPY:

Call 1-800-322-4693, visit **www.ehc.org**
or write:
P.O. Box 64000, Colorado Springs, CO 80962
(U.S. Addresses Only, Limit One Per Individual)

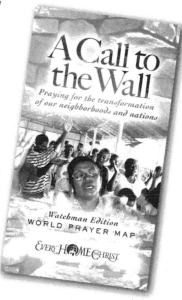

Every Home for Christ's Vision

Every Home for Christ exists to serve the Church
to reach every home on earth with the Gospel.

Every Home for Christ's
Three Unalterable Convictions

1. The Great Commission must be taken literally.
"All the world" and "every creature." *(Mark 16:15)*

2. Without unity, finishing the task of world evangelization
is impossible. *(John 17:21-23)*

3. Prayer, alone, will remove every obstacle that
stands in the way of fulfilling the
Great Commission. *(Mark 11:22-23)*

EHC's History at a Glance

The ministry of Every Home for Christ
began in Canada in 1946.

The first Every Home Campaign (EHC) involving systematic
home-by-home evangelism began in Japan in 1953.

There have been campaigns in 205 nations,
with complete coverage in 101 nations.

More than 2.8 billion gospel booklets and
face-to-face contacts have been made, resulting in over
82 million follow-up decision cards and responses.

Decisions/responses are followed-up with Bible
lessons. Where there are no churches, Christ Group
fellowships are planted. To date, more than 145,000
Christ Groups have been formed.

EHC workers visit an average of over 181,000
families every day, with an average of 30,000
decisions/responses received daily.

More than 29,000 workers worldwide are involved
with EHC in any given month, of which
80 percent are volunteers.

WANTED: The Next Generation

TheWall Internship Program: Where mature youth and young adults are trained and equipped to serve as full-time singers, musicians and intercessors in leading the intercessory worship in EHC's Watchman Training Center in Colorado Springs, Colorado.

TheWall also equips those who may be called as worship missionaries to take the vision of intercessory worship and Houses of Prayer to the nations. Each internship consists of a six-month program featuring five months of practical training in how to build Houses of Prayer in the nations as well as how to model intercessory worship for those Houses of Prayer.

All internships conclude with a two-to-three-week short-term mission trip to a foreign field for onsite experiences and opportunities to spread the vision of Houses of Prayer.

*For more information on
theWall internships, please contact:*

thewall@ehc.org | 1-800-423-5054
www.wallsofprayer.com
Every Home for Christ |640 Chapel Hills Dr.
Colorado Springs, CO | 80920

Untap the secrets of delightful new intimacy with God in prayer, every day.

Introducing

The Change the World School of Prayer

**on DVD
Newly-Revised**

Join the more than two million believers worldwide who have benefited by the inspiring instruction taught live by Dick Eastman on how to develop a daily prayer experience that not only draws us closer to God, but helps us change our world!

Topics include:

How to pray with spiritual authority that moves mountains!

How to pray with joy and meaning—no matter how you feel!

How to grow in delightful new intimacy with God, every day!

How to praise God in fresh biblical patterns!

Personal Kit Includes:

Seven-disc DVD set featuring seven Lecture Halls of Prayer;

The 353-page *Change the World School of Prayer* manual and Student Guide to assist in taking notes;

World Prayer Map.

(Group Kit is also available with enough materials for 25 students.)

Special Introductory Price:
$24.99 (Group Kits $150.00)
**Call 1-800-423-5054
or visit *www.ehc.org***

P.O. Box 64000 • Colorado Springs, CO 80962

About the

Author

Dick Eastman serves as International President of Every Home for Christ (EHC), a ministry committed to taking a printed presentation of the gospel of Jesus Christ to every home on earth, systematically. Dick is also the originator of the Change the World School of Prayer (a multi-hour training in prayer) that has equipped more than two million believers in 120 nations to pray more effectively.

Dick has authored more than 15 books on prayer, evangelism and Christian growth with more than three million copies in print. Since 1992 Dick has also served as president of America's National Prayer Committee, providing oversight to the planning of America's annual National Day of Prayer, the first Thursday in May. Dick's wife, Dee, is active in Dick's ministry, traveling with him more than four times around the world annually.